THE SECOND MOVEMENT

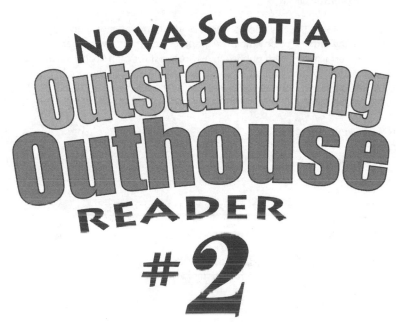

NOVA SCOTIA

Outstanding

Outhouse

READER

2

VERNON OICKLE

MacIntyre Purcell Publishing Inc.
194 Hospital Rd.
Lunenburg, Nova Scotia
B0J 2C0
(902) 640-3350

www.macintyrepurcell.com
info@macintyrepurcell.com

Printed and bound in Canada by Friesens

Cover design: Kevin O'Reilly
Book design: Denis Cunningham
Author photo (back cover): David Dobson

ISBN: 978-1-77276-146-7

Library and Archives Canada Cataloguing in Publication Title: Nova Scotia outstanding outhouse reader #2 : the second movement / Vernon Oickle. Other titles: Nova
Scotia outstanding outhouse reader number two : the second movement | Second
movement Names: Oickle, Vernon, 1961- author. Identifiers: Canadiana 20200227270
| ISBN 9781772761467 (softcover) Subjects: LCSH: Nova Scotia—Miscellanea. | LCSH:
Nova Scotia—Humor. | LCGFT: Trivia and miscellanea. Classification: LCC FC2311.6
.O33 2020 | DDC 971.6—dc23

MacIntyre Purcell Publishing Inc. would like to acknowledge the financial support of the
Government of Canada and the Nova Scotia Department of Tourism, Culture and Heritage.

Dedicated to my dear friends,
Debbie and Raymond.
Thank you for always being there!

5 FAST FACTS

1. Russian revolutionary Leon Trotsky was once incarcerated in Amherst for one month during the end of the First World War.

2. Jeopardy host Alex Trebek did a stint in Halifax as a CBC Radio host in 1965.

3. The first pulpwood mill in the province was the Nova Scotia Wood Pulp and Paper Company mill. It was built in 1880 at Salter's Falls near Charleston in Queens County and was destroyed by fire in June 1903.

4. The first recorded UFO sighting in North America occurred on October 12, 1796. Famous Liverpool diarist Simeon Perkins recorded in his diary that a young girl reported seeing an unusual glowing object in the sky over what today would be New Minas.

5. Before April 15, 1923, traffic moved on the left side of the road in the province of Nova Scotia.

Contents

From the Author 9

A Matter of Geography 11

A tale of two capes • Welcome to Christmas Island • The Drowned Forest of Cape Sable • A visit to Murder Island • Just add salt • Sable Island — Graveyard of the Atlantic • Gone to the animals • A famous resident • Explore The Hawk • The Principality of Outer Baldonia • Nova Scotia's Balancing Rock • Where is Devil's Island?

Built Heritage 21

Free Will Baptists • This important house has 'sole' • Province House is oldest in the country • Welcome to our country • The first yacht club in North America • Bridging the gap • Welcome to Bonavista Lodge • In a class of its own • The oldest of its kind • An historical place of worship • The 'San' • A forgotten piece of Nova Scotia history • Welcome to Sherbrooke Village • Bridgewater's historical Girl Guide cabin • The Fundy Dykelands • A fort named Anne and other forts • Reaching for the heavens • Grand Pré: a monument to a people • Halifax Town Clock • Jackson's Fort • Playing around at Keltic Lodge • A property of historical importance • Liverpool town hall • The churches of Lunenburg • Barrington's Old Meeting House • The oldest house in Halifax • The history of Port Royal • Ross Farm — the living museum • Uniacke Estate Museum Park • Riding the Shubenacadie Canal • The Lightfoot Tower • A church with history

Crime and Punishment...51

A Nova Scotia crime line • Canada's first trial for murder • Confessions of a killer • Mutiny and murder • The McDonald's murders • A dubious distinction • Guilty until proven innocent • The Butterbox Babies • Life with Billy • Random killings • Undercover spy and murderer • Leo Koretz — the gentleman swindler

Death and Destruction 65

Disasters • Hurricanes hit Nova Scotia • Wettest hurricanes on record • That's a mighty wind

Fascinating Facts 73

The Big Fiddle • What is your emergency? • The Sultan of Swat • Beep! Beep! • Turning on a dime • Sláinte! • Stamp of approval • A gift for Boston • Come and blow your horn • 'Farewell to Nova Scotia' • A future president comes to Oak Island • Harry Chapin and the Ovens Park • Life is a highway • Would you like one scoop or two? • To the moon and back • Hey mister, can you spare a dime or maybe $50? • Lovely lupines • Canada's first official tartan • A bird on the edge • The lonely road • This record bites • This one also bites • A small record • From the land to the sky • The dory story • That's one big fish • Flat-bottomed boats • Amelia Earhart lands in Nova Scotia • Hindenburg flies over Nova Scotia

Historically Speaking 93

All-Black hockey emerges in Halifax • Hitting the ice • Give it the old college try • In grand style • Historic Halifax • A history built of wood • Marvin the Mastodon • That's electric • On the rocks • Spanish flu ravaged province in 1918 • Who were the Acadians? • Remembering Africville • The two banks of Liverpool • A historic battle • Where was Beechville? • Canada's first all black battalion • Black milestones in Nova Scotia • A historic place • Rose's final resting place • The oldest marker in the land • Robert Ross rests here • Commemorating the Crimean War • Embracing Titanic victims • The German connection • You'll find Howe here • Oldest military burial ground in Canada • Nova Scotia man appears on D-Day coin • Port Mouton: the other Loyalist settlement • Shelburne race riots • Wreck of the SS *Atlantic* • The historic CSS *Acadia* • *Hector* delivers the Scots • The West Novies • VE Day riots in Halifax • A vote for women's rights • History and present collide

Important Landmarks 129

The Battle of Bloody Creek • Halifax Dockyard • King's College • Little Dutch (Deutsch) Church • Marconi National Historic Site • Marconi Wireless Station • Old Barrington Meeting House • St. Paul's Anglican Church • Thinkers' Lodge • Wolfe's Landing

Legends 131

Bridge over troubled waters • Who is Glooscap? • Are we alone? • What is the Runic Stone? • What really happened on Sacrifice Island? • How did that bloody handprint get on that rock? • Who pulled off the Red Ruse? • Is that The Young Teazer you see? • Is there treasure on Oak Island? • Who was Jerome and what happened to his legs? • The Mystery Walls of Bayers Lake • The Legend of Boxing Rock • Yo Ho Ho and a good pirate story • Did the Chinese settle in Cape Breton? • What's that under the street? • The Legend of the Lunenburg Werewolf • The legends of Seal Island • The ghost ship of Summerville Beach • The Great Amherst Mystery • At arm's length

Noteworthy People 163

First mayor of Halifax • Joseph Barss: the greatest of the privateers • Edward Jordan's skull • Nova Scotia's first female lawyer • From Sydney to Hollywood • An American war hero born in Yarmouth • A man of science • Breaking the gender barrier • Breaking the colour barrier • A Blue Man from Nova Scotia • A legendary trailblazer • Marking a milestone • It is written — on paper • A sad Nova Scotian link to the Vietnam War • Nova Scotia's first female doctor was a pioneer • The South Shore's lumber baron • George Price earns place in history • Kentville elects province's first woman mayor • The collector supreme • Battiste makes election history • A story carved in stone • This American hero has Nova Scotian roots • What's a Civil War hero doing in a Bridgewater cemetery? • His name was synonymous with true crime stories • The tallest man on record • The tallest Nova Scotian ever! • Knocking down the colour walls • The donut king • The Great Sam Gloade remembered for his bravery • Who was Sam Slick? • The mysterious Samuel Ball • A lifetime in services of others • Nova Scotia's man of science • Sophia's tragic tale • Bravery, valour and gallantry • A tale of true grit and lasting legacy • The father of street illumination • From Amherst to Nobel Prize winner • Innovator and businessman • Making hockey history • Remembering a fallen hero • A rock legend with Nova Scotian roots

Open for Business 211

Bluenose Ski Factory slides into history • Home of the handyperson • Chickenburger is the oldest diner in Canada • The oldest pub in Nova Scotia • The Frenchys story • The King of Pain Relief • A matter of convenience • A tasty tale

Glossary of Names 221

Index of Images 224

5 FAST FACTS

1. The Bay of Fundy has the highest recorded tides in the world. Twice a day, every day, 100 billion tons of water flow in and out of the bay which in some areas can rise to heights of 54 feet.

2. Eddie Martin, a black hockey player from Nova Scotia invented the slapshot in 1906, 11 years before the NHL was inaugurated.

3. Halifax is home to the only monument to the Crimean War in North America.

4. IKEA opened its first North American store in Halifax in 1977.

5. *The Casket* in Antigonish was first published in 1852, making it the oldest weekly newspaper in Canada.

From the Author

Nova Scotia, on Canada's Atlantic Coast, is also called Canada's Ocean Playground because the province is almost entirely surrounded by water.

The province is steeped in a rich and varied history. As its original Mi'kmaq people were joined by French (Acadian) settlers, British Loyalists, Scottish Highlanders, German and French Protestants, Irish peasants fleeing famine, and later by Italian and Polish miners, that history became diversified, influenced, and shaped by these settlers.

The province boasts many national and international firsts and historic records, including the first all-black hockey league in Canada, the tallest person ever on record, the first commissioned black officer in the British army, the first black Canadian soldier to receive the Victoria Cross, the first black hockey player to sign with the NHL, the first yacht club in North America and the smallest draw-bridge in the world.

Nova Scotia is also the birthplace of Freemasonry in Canada, the home of the first recorded instance of a black presence in Canada, home to Canada's oldest general store, the oldest diner in the nation, the oldest military burial ground in Canada and the first murder trial in Canada. It was also the place where paper was *actually* invented, as was Minard's liniment and the donair. It is also the birthplace of the man who is recognized as the last soldier of the British Empire to be killed in action during the First World War.

In addition to the rich heritage, Nova Scotia also boasts a pristine environment with a variety of ecosystems and unspoiled natural spaces with jaw-dropping vistas that rival any other place on earth.

Beyond all of this, the province has also produced some of the most talented and influential artists, politicians, entertainers, writers, and leaders who have not only impacted their generation, but future generations as well.

In the first volume of the *Nova Scotia Outstanding Outhouse Reader*, we learned what makes the province such a special place. Like its predecessor, *The Second Movement: Nova Scotia Outstanding Outhouse Reader #2*, collects intriguing information and captures some of the more interesting qualities that make it so unique.

— *Vernon Oickle*

A panoramic view of Nova Scotia's famed Cape Split

A Matter of Geography

A tale of two capes

The Battle of Cape Split happened during the American Revolution. Cape Split is a headland located in Kings County on the coast of the Bay of Fundy.

The Cape is a continuation of the North Mountain range, which is made of tholeiitic basalt. It separates the main part of the Bay of Fundy from the Minas Basin, a sub-basin to the east.

The cape itself is seven kilometres long and ranges between several kilometres to several dozen metres in width. Both sides of the headland end in high cliffs overlooking treacherous tidal currents in the Minas Channel.

The property was previously privately owned but is now a provincial reserve park of 427 hectares. A popular hiking trail has existed for decades on Cape Split, taking approximately two to two and half hours each way to the tip of the headland. Most of the Cape is heavily forested, but the tip of the peninsula is a meadow, providing excellent long-distance views in good weather.

The cliffs at Cape Split are actively eroding and potentially dangerous. The height of the cliffs is over 60 metres and a fall could be fatal. There are several features that appear to be trails, but are actually lines of erosion that lead to steep edges with loose soil and rocks.

That's one of Nova Scotia's famous capes. The second is Cape Blomidon and it too, is a headland located in Kings County at the northeast edge of the Blomidon Peninsula. And also like Cape Split, the Battle of Blomidon happened here during the American Revolution.

The geology of Cape Blomidon largely comprises sedimentary sandstone, which is unique since it is connected to the North Mountain range, made up of tholeiitic basalt.

Cape Blomidon features distinctive reddish-coloured cliffs that reach up to 100 metres in height above the Minas Basin, which stretches to the east. Cape Split is the geologic continuation of the North Mountain range and juts off the Blomidon Peninsula to the northwest.

According to Mi'kmaq legend, Cape Blomidon is the home of Glooscap First Nation. The cape and much of the coastal area of the Blomidon Peninsula are protected by Blomidon Provincial Park.

The name "Cape Blomidon" was officially approved on October 1, 1959, although the name had been in use many years beforehand. French explorer Samuel de Champlain called the cape "Cap Poutrincourt" and local Acadian settlers called it Cap Baptiste.

English speaking settlers called it Cape Porcupine. However, the common term used was Cape Blowmedown, from which "Blomidon" is derived.

Welcome to Christmas Island

Christmas Island in Cape Breton has a post office, a fire hall and a very small population. It also has a beach with access to the Bras d'Or Lakes, and a pond that runs into the lake.

Christmas Island got its name because of a native who lived there whose surname was Christmas. He died on Ghost Island, adjacent to the beach. The original inhabitants of the land, the Mi'kmaq people, called the area *Abadakwichéch*, which means "the small reserved portion."

The post office of Christmas Island literally gets thousands of postcards and packages a day — up to 2,000 on the busiest days — during the peak holiday season. These come from around the world during Christmas time so they can be sent on to their destinations with the unique Christmas Island postmark.

Greeting cards and packages come from as far as Hong Kong, Seoul, Paris, Mexico City, Sydney, Tahiti and various points across Canada and the United States from collectors and holiday enthusiasts to be franked with the official postmark of Christmas Island.

The original pictorial postmark design, dating from 1994, was a simple motif with three conifers. The current postmark is more ornate, including a wreath laden with decorations and a bow.

To make your holiday cards special with a postmark from Christmas Island, address and place the correct postage (or international reply coupon) on the actual greeting card, insert the card into a larger envelope and send to: Christmas Island Post Office, 8499 Grand Narrows Highway, Christmas Island, Nova Scotia, B1T 1A0.

The Drowned Forest of Cape Sable

The Drowned Forest of Cape Sable is described as a 1,500-year-old drowned forest, a broad area of petrified tree stumps still rooted in the original soil that are exposed at low tide.

The stumps are imbedded in a peaty soil, which has been dated to be 1,500 years old. When these trees were living there was a large lake in Barrington Bay; Cape Sable Island was linked to the mainland and the shoreline extended outwards almost a kilometre.

These centuries-old old tree stumps, submerged under 12 feet of seawater for half the day, can be seen at low tide. The Drowned Forest is in a protected, public beach area.

A visit to Murder Island

Just to the south of Yarmouth in Nova Scotia lies a series of islands, known as the Tusket Islands. Of the dozens of islands in the chain, one stands out as so notorious, so infamous, that it was actually named Murder Island. There are several stories regarding the name's provenance.

One story goes that during the middle of the 1700s, a French missionary was visiting villages and spreading Christianity to the native inhabitants. The missionary inexplicably told two coastal tribes about a buried pirate treasure on the island; when both tribes came into contact while looking for the alleged treasure, they soon attacked each other and a massive massacre ensued, which decimated each tribe.

The bodies of the tribe members who perished in the massacre were left to rot on the island. Later, French explorers landed on the island and finding piles of human remains, named the island Isle du Massacre, or Murder Island.

5 FAST FACTS

1. The oldest place name in Nova Scotia is Baccaro in Shelburne County. The name comes from the Basque word Baccoloas, meaning "for Codfish."

2. The oldest Acadian communities in the world are West Pubnico, Middle West Pubnico and Lower West Pubnico.

3. Nova Scotia produces an annual average of approximately 2.35 million bushels of apples and contributes more than $50 million to the provincial economy. Today, the Annapolis Valley is the centre of apple production on Canada's Eastern Seaboard. Records show the presence of apples in Port Royal in 1610 and at LaHave in 1635. It was reported that 1,584 apple trees were distributed among 54 families at Port Royal. It also shows an orchard of improved varieties planted in 1635 by Pierre Martin at Belleisle, Annapolis County.

4. The first export of apples in Nova Scotia is believed to have been made in 1849 by Benjamin Weir of Halifax and Ambrose Bent of Paradise, who exported them from Halifax to Liverpool, England.

5. The largest apple ever grown in the world was grown in Berwick in 1922. The Rome Beauty weighted a whopping three pounds.

A far more mysterious tale regarding the name of the island surrounds a ship named the *Baltimore*, which landed on the island's shore in the mid 1700s. The ship was covered in blood.

The entire crew but one was dead upon arrival. The sole survivor of the mysterious mass murder was a woman. She disembarked and disappeared into the mists of history.

Another explanation for the island's name has an epidemic of smallpox decimating a French fleet sent to capture Acadia in the 1700s. Hundreds of dead were supposedly unloaded on the tiny island. There had been numerous reports of bleached human bones emerging from the cobble beaches until this century, lending some credence to the story.

However, the mystery remains.

Just add salt

Pugwash, with an estimated population of roughly 700 people, is a village in Cumberland County on the Northumberland Strait at the mouth of the Pugwash River.

It sits atop a salt deposit measuring 457.2 metres thick and is home to the largest underground salt mine in Atlantic Canada. The Canadian Salt Mine Co. Ltd. is the only salt mine and only underground mine in Nova Scotia.

Open since 1959, the majority of the mine runs under the Pugwash River, some under solid ground, but none under the village.

The plant produces industrial grades of salt, salt blocks for farm use and refined salt for domestic consumption. The mine produces approximately 1,200,000 tonnes of salt per year. The salt is distributed by road or from the company owned ship-loading facility for which large ships can be seen in the harbour from early spring to late autumn.

Sable Island — Graveyard of the Atlantic

Sable Island is a long, narrow sandbar — 34 kilometres long and 1.5 kilometres wide — that is the highest point on the Continental Shelf running under the Atlantic Ocean off the east coast.

It's also called the Graveyard of the Atlantic because there have been hundreds of shipwrecks there with an estimated loss of 10,000 lives. The first reported wreck was in 1583 when the shoals surrounding the island claimed one of Sir Humphrey Gilbert's ships.

In the late 1700s, 60 horses were shipped to the island. Their descendants, now numbering about 250, still look like rugged horses of centuries ago. A solar-powered lighthouse now warns ships about the island.

The horses of Sable Island.

Gone to the animals

Shubenacadie Wildlife Park is a 40-hectare (99-acre) sanctuary for animals located off Highway 102, Exit 9 at Milford.

The park began in the late 1940s as a refuge for orphaned white-tailed deer and was run by Eldon Pace. By the early 1950s, there was so much interest from the public that the park officially opened in 1954. Pace was the superintendent of the park until 1988.

Throughout its history countless orphaned and injured animals, birds and reptiles have been cared for and rehabilitated. From the beginning, the park has been educating visitors about wildlife and environmental issues with thousands of school children participating in onsite education programming.

Between 2003 and 2008 the park was regulated as a game sanctuary under the Wildlife Act. In 2008, the regulations were changed to officially designate the park as a wildlife park under the act.

The park is home to about 90 species of mammals and birds including Dall sheep, Indian peafowl, Sable Island pony, moose, black bear, river otter, coyote, skunk, raccoon, marten, white-tailed deer, woodchuck, kestrel, beaver, turkey vulture, peregrine falcon, mink, Artic wolf, red-tailed hawk, gray wolf, bald eagle, porcupine, cougar, snowshoe hare, European magpie, three species of owl, three species of fox, and two species of lynx.

Nova Scotia's famous weather prognosticator, Shubenacadie Sam.

A famous resident

Shubenacadie Wildlife Park is home to Shubenacadie Sam, one of the first groundhogs in North America to predict the weather for the upcoming year.

Each February 2 at sunrise, Sam leaves his house and checks for his shadow. This fun event always attracts a large crowd eager to see what the spring holds in store for us.

Folklore says winter will last for six more weeks if the groundhog sees its shadow. No shadow is a sign of an early spring.

Explore 'The Hawk'

The Hawk on Cape Sable Island is the most southerly point in Nova Scotia, lined with a beautiful white sand beach and a unique drowned forest. The area is a bird lover's paradise, as a home to the endangered piping plover and a stopover for migrating shorebirds and other wildlife.

The Hawk is named after a schooner that was washed ashore there in the 1800s.

From the beach you can view Nova Scotia's tallest lighthouse, the Cape Sable Lighthouse, reaching skyward 101 feet. On foggy nights, the sound of the foghorn will lull you to sleep and in the mornings, the sound of the waves crashing on shore and the seagulls flying overhead are your alarm clock.

The people who live there are some of the friendliest people you will meet. The close knit community is always willing to lend a helping hand when needed, organizing welcoming, fun events such as Hawk Days, and a smile to greet you when you arrive.

From any point on The Hawk you will have an ocean view; it's part of the livelihood, culture and heritage of many of the residents here. Fishing is a way of life for many, from lobster fishing to tuna fishing.

The Principality of Outer Baldonia

Some small countries such as Andorra, Monaco and Luxembourg are well established on the world map. However, there are a variety of even smaller nations — known as "micronations" — scattered across the globe.

These mini-states, which are often as small as a single acre, are formed for a variety of reasons, ranging from artistic and political protest to good old-fashioned tax evasion. And although their more legitimate counterparts rarely recognize them as sovereign entities, some of them have even gone so far as to draft bizarre constitutions, coin money and hold elections. Most Canadians may not know it, but one of these "micronations" was actually located right here off the southern coast of Nova Scotia.

The Principality of Outer Baldonia was started in 1949 by a publicist for Pepsi and notorious eccentric named Russell Arundel. The nation was no larger than .00625 of a square mile in size, or about four acres.

In 1949, while fishing roughly 15 kilometres off the coast of Nova Scotia, Arudel stumbled across a small island near Yarmouth known as Outer Bald Tusket Island, located eight nautical miles off the southern tip of Wedgeport. The island is known to the locals in the Yarmouth area as Outer Baldy.

Declaring himself Chancellor of Outer Baldonia, Arudel bought the piece of real estate for $750, built a small fishing lodge there and began regularly going on weekend getaways with friends. They concocted a constitution during one drinking session—which mandated fishing and the consumption of rum as time-honoured state pastimes—and declared themselves an independent state known as The Principality of Outer Baldonia.

Government titles only necessitated catching a tuna and paying a small fee, upon which one became a "prince." They even developed a currency called the Tunar, released a state charter that banned taxes and women from the island, and declared that their main export was empty beer bottles.

Baldonia eventually became noticed when Arundel listed his office number in Washington D.C. as that of the Embassy for the Principality. Soon, he and his imaginary country were being invited to state functions, and Baldonia was even supposedly mistakenly asked to join the United Nations.

Arundel and his fake country even became famous enough to warrant criticism from a Soviet newspaper, which Baldonia responded to, naturally, with a declaration of war. The Baldonian navy, which was made up entirely of local fishing vessels, supposedly took to the sea in order to attack the Russians, but it can only be assumed that they got sidetracked and went drinking instead.

Endowed with a charter, flag and organized military, it was one of the more developed, and highly populated of the various historical micronations ever established. The Principality of Outer Baldonia is now defunct.

Nova Scotia's Balancing Rock

Balancing Rock, called Nature's Time Post, is part of the oldest, lowest, and most resistant basalt unit that erupted as more fluid lava and covered much of the Fundy area.

The nine-metre high column stands proudly on the cliffs overlooking St. Mary's Bay.

When the lava stopped flowing and cooled, it cracked to form column-like structures with five to seven sides. Later tectonic forces in the crust accentuated and added to these fractures. Balancing Rock is the most-photographed of Long Island's basalt formations.

No one knows for sure how long Balancing Rock has been hanging on for dear life, but scientists estimate it would be thousands of years.

The Balancing Rock overlooks St. Mary's Bay.

5 FAST FACTS

1. The smallest town in Nova Scotia is Annapolis Royal with 491 people.

2. The oldest town in Nova Scotia is Pictou, established in 1874.

3. The deGannes-Cosby house located at 477 St. George Street, Annapolis Royal, is the oldest documented wooden structure in Nova Scotia and has been continuously occupied since its construction in 1708.

4. Woozles, located on Birmingham Street in Halifax, is the oldest children's bookstore in Canada: the store opened in 1978.

5. Pictou Academy built in 1816 is the oldest school in Nova Scotia.

Where is Devil's Island?

Devil's Island located at the entrance to Halifax harbour was desolate and devoid of trees, but rich in Maritime folklore and music. It is located off the coast of the community of Eastern Passage. The name originated from an early French merchant and was first spelled Deville's Island.

The first permanent settlement on this 12-hectare island was established in 1830, and by 1850 there were three houses and a school. By 1901, the settlement had grown to 18 houses. A number of Devil's Island residents, notably Ben Henneberry, provided valuable folklore to pioneering Canadian folklorist Helen Creighton.

Most of the residents were moved to the mainland during the Second World War. The last permanent resident, a Norwegian artist, moved off in 2000. The island is currently privately owned.

The Devil's Island Lighthouse was built 1877 to replace an earlier tower that was built in 1852. Although no longer functional, the lighthouse is still standing.

The Free Will Baptists of Port Medway had this meeting house built by 1832.

Built Heritage

Free Will Baptists

The Free Will Baptists of Port Medway organized a congregation in 1825 and had a formal meeting house built by 1832.

Free Will Baptists evolved from the Congregational New Lights movement of the late 18th century in New England, brought to Nova Scotia by immigrants from New England. The Port Medway Meeting House was used by the local Free Will Baptist congregation until 1865 when it was sold to the Wesleyan Methodist Church, which became the United Church of Canada in 1925.

The Port Medway Meeting House is a simple wood framed building with a domestic exterior appearance, one of only a few unaltered meetinghouses in the province.

The interior arrangement of the pews which face the central aisle rather than the front of the building, is a unique feature of the Port Medway Meeting House.

This important house has 'sole'

Government House, the official residence of Nova Scotia's Lieutenant Governor, is the oldest vice regal residence in North America and the oldest consecutively occupied government residence.

In 2009, while extensive renovations were being undertaken on the historic mansion, workers made an unusual discovery.

Hidden inside the walls of the building were a number of boots and shoes.

Government House was built for Sir John Wentworth, the former Loyalist Governor of New Hampshire, and his wife, Lady Frances, between 1799 and 1805. At the time, the tradition of putting footwear inside walls during construction was common throughout the region.

Craftsmen apparently believed that placing shoes near doors and windows warded off evil spirits at entry points, acting as poltergeist scarecrows. Homebuilders often placed a shoe or boot in the wall next to the front door in order to kick out the Devil or evil spirits.

During the recent renovations and upgrades, in keeping with the old tradition, workers placed shoes in framed-in sections of the structure before putting up the new walls.

Throughout the month of March 2009, government officials collected used footwear. Eight shoes were put into the walls of Government House, while the remainder were donated to programs that support women in transition.

Meanwhile, the 181 original shoes found in the walls were removed, catalogued and eventually returned to Government House, where they are now on permanent display.

Government House is truly a Nova Scotian creation. Building materials from around the province were used extensively, including stone from Pictou, Antigonish, Cape Breton, Lunenburg, Lockeport, Bedford Basin and the North West Arm. Pine came from the Annapolis Valley, Tatamagouche and Cornwallis. Sand was brought in from Shelburne, Eastern Passage and McNamara's Island. The bricks were from Dartmouth.

Nova Scotia's historic Government House in Halifax.

Province House, home to the Nova Scotia Legislature, is the oldest symbol of democracy in Canada.

Province House is oldest in the country

Province House in Halifax is Canada's oldest legislative building. The cornerstone was laid in 1811 and the House was officially opened in February 1819.

The Nova Scotia House of Assembly met for the first time in the courthouse at the corner of Argyle and Buckingham streets in Halifax. After a succession of temporary accommodations, construction began on a permanent building in 1811 and the legislature met for the first time on February 11, 1819, in the building that continues to be used to today.

Province House played a major role in the constitutional evolution of Canada. Viewed as an important cultural asset for its rich history, unique architecture, and its continuity as the seat of government, great effort has been made in recent years to protect and maintain Province House as the symbolic home of all Nova Scotians.

Province House is one of the most historic buildings in Canada. During the 175th anniversary in 1994, Province House was commemorated as a National Historic Site when Queen Elizabeth II visited, and was cited for both its architectural and historical significance.

Welcome to our country

Canada has been profoundly shaped by immigration. The Canadian Museum of Immigration at Pier 21 aims to inspire and enable Canadians to explore their relationships with those migrations. Pier 21, a National Historic Site, was the gateway to Canada for one million immigrants between 1928 and 1971. It also served as the departure point for 368,000 Canadian Military personnel during the Second World War.

The Canadian Museum of Immigration at Pier 21 is Atlantic Canada's only national museum.

The first yacht club in North America

There is a long, international, historical tradition behind yacht clubs. According to the date of establishment, the Neva Yacht Club, founded in 1718 in Russia, is the oldest yacht club in the world.

However, since this Russian Yacht Club was established by a decree of Tsar Peter the Great, it does not fully qualify as a proper club in the modern sense, understood as a voluntary association of members who organize and run the club.

The Royal Cork Yacht Club in Ireland, founded in 1720, is also widely acknowledged as the oldest yacht club in the world, despite having gone through periods of dormancy and undergone name changes in its long history, much in the same manner as the Neva Yacht Club.

The first yacht club in Russia to adopt British-style Members Club regulations was established in 1846. Using this Western understanding of what constitutes a club or society, the Royal Swedish Yacht Club, KSSS, founded 1830, becomes the oldest European yacht club outside the British Isles, and the fifth oldest in the world.

A number of the world's most renowned yacht clubs are located in the United Kingdom, Australia, Germany, Canada, and the United States. The first yacht club in North America was the Royal Nova Scotia Yacht Squadron, located on the Northwest Arm in Halifax, established in July 1837.

Bridging the gap

The Sable River "swinging" bridge is a unique, one-of-a-kind piece of Nova Scotian history located in Shelburne County.

Founded in the 1700s and located where the Sable and Tom Tigney rivers converge, today the Village of Sable River is mostly a residential community with a few support services and a handful of businesses. In its formidable years of the early 1920s, however, the village boasted no less than three general stores, three post offices, a railroad, bus stop, a school, two service stations, a nursing home and 11 functioning mills.

Unique in Nova Scotia, the Sable River swinging bridge walking trail has been used for over 100 years and is known locally as the "footpath."

A wooden footbridge that was built around 1885 along with subsequent bridges in the ensuing years, not only connected both sides of the village physically but also became an important link in the community's social and economic wellbeing.

Unique in Nova Scotia, the swinging bridge and trail have been used by the Sable River community for over 100 years and is known locally as the "footpath." In the summer of 2015, the Mi'kmaq at Sable River interpretive panel was placed near the footbridge to highlight the importance of the site and Sable River in general to Mi'kmaq history.

The little bridge linked East Sable where there was a post office, to West Sable where there was a church, school and Daddy Lew's convenience store. It allowed people to easily go back and forth from one side to the other and it was used frequently.

As the original wooden structures were often washed out with the spring tides and run-off, the current steel and iron footbridge was built around 1905, making the 100-foot long bridge with a wooden planking deck a one-of-a-kind structure in Nova Scotia.

Remnants of Bonavista Lodge, built in the 1920s, can still be seen today.

Welcome to Bonavista Lodge

Located on the province's South Shore just past Exit 6 near Hubbards, there is an unusual stone structure that was once called Bonavista Lodge. It was built in the 1920s by an enterprising fellow named Guildford Harnish. He was in the fish business and did a lot of trade with Newfoundland. This was at a time well before Highway 103 was constructed and many believed Bonavista Lodge was built for its isolation.

In a class of its own

Big Tancook Elementary School is a unique school on an island and is one of Canada's last one-room schoolhouses. Built in 1949, the school is accessed by taking the ferry from Chester to Big Tancook Island (via Little Tancook Island).

Legend has it that there are 365 islands in Mahone Bay (the body of water, not the town). Big Tancook Island is the largest of those islands and is home to 100 year round residents.

The island measures approximately 4 kilometres (north to south) by 1.6 kilometres, roughly forming a "C" shape. The island is 550 acres (2.2 square kilometres) in size and has a rocky shoreline with open fields and softwood forest dotted by ponds, residential properties and fish stores.

Big Tancook Island is separated from nearby Little Tancook Island to the east by a 1 kilometre wide strait known as "The Chops." The nearest point of land on the mainland, Sandy Cove Point on the Aspotogan Peninsula, is approximately 4 kilometres away. Wildlife populations on the island are limited to deer, muskrats, snakes, pheasants, and a great variety of birds.

The only community located on Big Tancook Island is the settlement known as Big Tancook.

It has a population of about 200 residents in summer and roughly 120 in winter. Tancook is home to one of the last two remaining one-room schoolhouses in Canada — Big Tancook Island Elementary School, which also serves Little Tancook Island. High school students take the ferry every day to the mainland town of Chester.

The island has a long history and was once a summer fishing ground for First Nations peoples. It is no surprise that the word "Tancook" means "facing the open sea" in Mi'kmaq, the original inhabitants. When Europeans arrived in Nova Scotia, German immigrants located to Big Tancook where they established a settlement, eking out their existence from the land but mostly from the bounty of the sea.

Today, like their ancestors, those who call Tancook their home primarily make their living through the fishing and there was a time when the art of making sauerkraut was a mainstay of the local economy. As the traditional industries fall on tough times, however, many have turned to tourism to earn a dollar.

With no permanent link to the mainland, a scheduled ferry service operates daily year-round, running from Chester to Big Tancook Island and Little Tancook Island. The MV *William G. Ernst* is a passenger-only ferry operated by the provincial Department of Transportation and Infrastructure Renewal. Emergency response is provided by the Big Tancook Island Emergency Response Association, which is supported through volunteer efforts and community fundraising.

The oldest of its kind

The Sinclair Inn, located at 232 St. George Street Annapolis Royal, is the oldest surviving example of Acadian construction in Canada. Built in 1710, the structure is now a national historic site.

In 1738, the building was used by Erasmus Phillips as the first meeting hall of the Masonic Lodge in Canada. The site offers a fascinating insight into construction techniques spanning nearly three centuries, from the Acadian clay walls to modern wood paneling.

The Sinclair Inn, located at 230 St. George Street Annapolis Royal, is a designated national historic site.

The second floor includes the restored "Painted Room" created in c.1840.

A plaque commemorating the historical significance of this important structure reads:

The Sinclair Inn is an important document in the history of building in Atlantic Canada. In the 1780s, tavern-keeper Frederic Sinclair created this inn by combining two existing structures. Born were frame, and the walls of one were filled with wattle and daub, an insulation used in Acadia and New England in the 17th and early 18th centuries. Sinclair attempted to give his inn certain Georgian features of symmetry and classical detail. Restored to its present state in 1982, the building stands as a rich composite of materials, techniques and styles spanning three centuries.

An historical place of worship

The Northwest United Baptist Church on Big Lots Road in Fauxburg, Lunenburg County, built between 1818 and 1820, is the oldest documented Baptist house of worship in Nova Scotia.

The church sits on a small embankment and was built in the Transition Phase Meeting House style. The building, cemetery and property are a designated provincial site.

Northwest United Baptist Church is valued for its age, historical association with the spiritual history of Lunenburg County, and its Meeting House style construction. It is the oldest documented Baptist house of worship in Nova Scotia.

Northwest United Baptist Church is valued for its age, historical association with the spiritual history of Lunenburg County and its Meeting House style construction.

The congregation was formed in 1809 under the guidance of the New Light preacher Joseph Dimock, leader of the dissenting members of the Christian faith who followed more evangelical teachings such as those professed by Henry Alline, founder of the New Light movement.

Reverend Dimock led the Northwest congregation, while tending to his own parish in Chester until a permanent pastor was assigned to the congregation in 1817. Reverend Dimock continued throughout his life to be a leading religious figure in the province and was partly responsible for the conversion of many New Light churches to a more organized type of religion, which we now know as the Baptist faith. His evangelistic spirit remained with the small congregation and was highly influential in its continued existence.

Northwest United Baptist is an excellent example of the Meeting House style, featuring a plain symmetrical design which was common to buildings owned by dissenting religious groups in the eighteenth century. This church is particularly unique because it exhibits characteristics of the Transition Phase, which saw the slow adoption of more traditional church designs, including the addition of simple decorative elements.

According to the Provincial Heritage Program, the Northwest United Baptist church features several ornamentations such as corner boards styled as Greek Revival pilasters and an off centre doorway. These architectural features indicate the movement away from the traditional New England Meeting House style of basic design anchored in symmetry.

In addition, the layout of the church with the main entrance on the gabled end instead of along one of the longest faces, is indicative of a shift from the traditional Meeting House style. The pews in the church are situated with their backs to the main entrance as would be found in a traditional Meeting House layout. However, this means they are perpendicular rather than parallel to the longest face where the main entrance was traditionally located.

The later addition of a triple set of Gothic Revival arch windows on the rear elevation in the twentieth century also indicates a continuation of the movement toward more ornately styled buildings.

The Meeting House style is unique within Lunenburg County and the clear illustration of the Transition Phase in architectural design makes the Northwest United Baptist Church a unique example of architecture within the province.

The 'San'

The Nova Scotia Sanatorium was established in Kentville and operated between1904 and 1975 under medical superintendent Dr. Arthur Frederick Miller who retired in 1947.

The hospital began with 18 beds but over time grew to 20 buildings with 400 beds. Between 1910 and 1916, Dr. Miller was the only doctor on staff.

In the early 20th century, tuberculosis, an infectious lung disease, was killing about 1,000 Nova Scotians every year. The provincial government constructed the Nova Scotia Sanatorium, dubbed "the San," to treat these patients.

There was no major treatment center east of Montreal so Kentville was poised to introduce innovative cures to the Maritimes. The Sanatorium was downsized gradually, and then amalgamated with the memorial hospital in 1975.

A forgotten piece of Nova Scotia history

McNutts Island, located in Shelburne Harbour, was named after Col. Alexander McNutt, who lived here in the late 1760s.

During the Second World War, a battery of two guns was built on the island and became known as Fort McNutt. It was established by the Royal Canadian Army in 1941, and was armed with two ex-American, 10-inch M1888 guns on M1893 barbette carriages (Lend-Lease from Fort Worden, Puget Sound), garrisoned by the 104th Coast Artillery Battery until 1944.

Fort McNutt was officially abandoned in 1945 after the war ended, but the guns remain in place until today. Technically, the island wasn't abandoned in 1945 because there were a few families who lived there during and after the war.

Today, the ruins of the two gun emplacements can still be seen at what was Fort McNutt.

Welcome to Sherbrooke Village

The first European visitors to Sherbrooke were the French who were here as early as 1655. By 1815, the settlement which developed at the head St. Mary's River became known as Sherbrooke in honour of Sir John Coape Sherbrooke, Lieutenant Governor of Nova Scotia.

In the 1860s, timber for tall ships and gold ruled life along the St. Mary's River, turning the community of Sherbrooke into a prosperous boomtown. For years the community flourished, supported by farming, fishing and the timber trade. Busy mills produced planks, laths, spars, ships' knees and shingles for the British and West Indian markets.

Then in 1861, the cry of "gold!" was heard and the town became a lively and energetic mining camp. No fewer than 19 mining companies had flocked to participate in the discovery by 1869 and Sherbrooke boomed. The economic growth lasted approximately 20 years, a time that could be described as Sherbrooke's Golden Age.

Mining was reactivated in the early part of the 20th century but never reached the same success. Lumbering continued as a major industry. Until the Restoration Project was established, the chief visitors to this area were sportsmen fishing for salmon in the pools of the St. Mary's River.

The Sherbrooke Village Restoration area was established in 1969 to conserve a part of Sherbrooke as it was during the last half of the 1800s. Today, Sherbrooke Village is Nova Scotia's largest Provincial Museum with 25 heritage buildings brought to life by costumed interpreters from late May until early October.

Bridgewater's historical Girl Guide Cabin

A piece of property in the middle of the Town of Bridgewater has the distinction of being the location of the first Girl Guide Cabin ever built in Canada.

The land on which the Girl Guide Cabin sits, was deeded to the Town of Bridgewater in 1935, for the exclusive use of the Girl Guides Association of Bridgewater.

The original log cabin was built on the property in 1934, while the present structure, which is believed to be the third at the location, was constructed in 1974

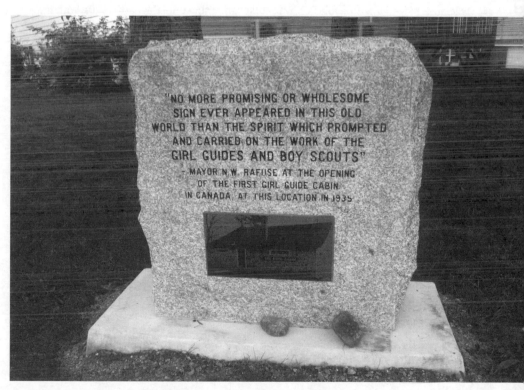

This monument marks the original location of the first Girl Guide Cabin ever built in Canada.

The Fundy Dykelands

Dykelands are agricultural lands developed from rich salt marshes found mainly in the upper Bay of Fundy of Nova Scotia and New Brunswick.

According to a Government of Nova Scotia website, dykelands occur in areas of high tidal range and owe their existence to dykes constructed to keep out the sea.

"Prior to dyking, extensive salt marshes occurred at the mouths of tidal rivers and in other low-lying coastal areas. Saltmarsh plants helped to trap nutrient-rich sediments from the tidal waters on vast level areas, which were ideal for development of agricultural lands."

The Acadians were drawn to the rich marshes of the Bay of Fundy over 300 years ago and designed and constructed many of the present-day dyke systems. They understood the high agricultural value of the marshes compared to the less fertile, forested uplands.

The dykeland farms of the Acadian settlers provided for their needs as well as supplying a surplus for export throughout the eastern seaboard.

"After the Acadians were expelled by the British in 1755, they were replaced by the New England Planters, Yorkshire farmers, and the United Empire Loyalists. Each new group of settlers claimed new areas of salt marshes, which they used primarily for pasture and hay production."

Dykelands played a central role in Nova Scotia agriculture until the early 1920s. With the increasing use of the internal combustion engine replacing the need for horses, the demand for hay was greatly reduced.

In subsequent years, low hay prices coupled with a loss of the labour force to wage the Second World War, reduced efforts in maintaining and rebuilding the dykes. By 1948, the dykes had deteriorated to such an extent that large tracts of dykeland had reverted once again to salt marsh.

In 1949, the Maritime Marshlands Rehabilitation Act was introduced by the Canadian government to prevent the loss of additional dykeland. From 1949 to 1970, over 30,000 hectares of dykeland were secured.

Prominent examples of dykelands include the Queen Anne's Marsh near Port Royal on the Annapolis Basin, the Grand Pré marsh in King's County, and the Minudie Marsh in Cumberland County.

Dykelands still play an important agricultural role and today are used largely for the production of hay and pasture, corn and cereal crops, and sod. As they hold water late in the spring and are not well suited for fall ploughing, dykelands have a shorter season for cropping and maintenance compared to many other agricultural lands.

However, they are naturally rich in nutrients, and are relatively flat and rock free. Research is ongoing to develop new techniques and crops for production on dykeland soils.

A fort named Anne and other forts

Fort Anne in Annapolis Royal became Canada's first National Historic Park in October 1917 and is the oldest National Historic site in Canada.

The star-shaped fortress was built to protect the harbour of Annapolis Royal. It was constructed to repel French attacks during the early stages of King George's War.

Fort Anne in Annapolis Royal is the oldest National Historic site in Canada.

Situated on 15-hectares of land in Annapolis Royal, Fort Anne was designed and built as a military fort with the first fort erected on the site by the Scots in 1629. Four forts were subsequently built by the French beginning in 1643.

The oldest English graveyard in Nova Scotia is also located on the Fort Anne site.

And here's an interesting note: the key to Fort Anne that had been taken to Boston in 1710 was finally returned to its original home in August 1922.

Citadel Hill, a national historic site, was one of four fortifications built on a hill overlooking the city of Halifax, which was founded by the English in 1749.

Even though all four were referred to as Fort George, only the third fort (built between 1794 and 1800) was officially named Fort George. According to General Orders of October 20, 1798, it was named after King George III.

The first two and the fourth and current fort were officially called the Halifax Citadel. The current concrete fort is constructed in the shape of a star. The Citadel is actually the fortified summit of Citadel Hill.

Halifax Citadel is the fourth fort built at the summit of Citadel Hill.

The hill was first fortified in 1749, the year that Edward Cornwallis oversaw the development of the town of Halifax. Those fortifications were successively rebuilt to defend the town from various enemies.

Construction and levelling have lowered the summit by 10 to 12 metres. While never attacked, the Citadel was long the keystone to defence of Halifax Harbour and the Royal Navy Dockyard. Today, it is a National Historic Site and is operated by Parks Canada.

Connaught Battery, located north of York Redoubt at Ferguson's Cove, is a harbour defence battery from the First World War. It took its name from the then Governor General of Canada, the Duke of Connaught, who was Queen Victoria's third son.

Cranberry Point Battery was a First World War era coastal defence battery, which defended the approaches to Sydney Harbour. It originally consisted of two, 4.7-inch quick firing guns, which were later removed and replaced with a concrete observation tower and two concrete searchlight emplacements.

Devils Battery or **Devils Point Battery, Hartlen Point** or **Hartlen Point Tunnels**, was a complex military installation at the mouth of Halifax Harbour in the community of Eastern Passage at Hartlen Point. It was built between 1940 and 1945 to protect the Halifax area against the German navy. It was operational until the 1950s. It is now a golf course; the original underground armaments remain buried. Devils Battery was named for Devils Island, which is adjacent to the embankment of Hartlen Point.

Fort Edward, a National Historic Site located in Windsor, was built during Father Le Lourtre's War, from 1749 to 1755. The British built the fort to help prevent the Acadian Exodus from the region. The Fort is most famous for the role it played both in the Expulsion of the Acadians in 1755 and in protecting Halifax from a land assault in the American Revolution.

While much of Fort Edward has been destroyed, including the officers quarters (which burned down in 1922) and barracks, the blockhouse that remains is the oldest extant in North America. A cairn was later added to the site.

Fort Sackville was a British fort located in present-day Bedford that was built during Father Le Lourtre's War. The British built the fort adjacent to present-day Scott Manor House, on a hill overlooking the Sackville River to help prevent French, Acadian and Mi'kmaq attacks

5 FAST FACTS

1. Yarmouth was the first town in the Maritimes to have its own electric streetcar service. It ran from Yarmouth South to Milton on a regular daily schedule from August 1892 until October 1928.

2. Built in 1810, Goat Island Baptist Church in Nova Scotia is the oldest Baptist church building in Canada.

3. The first school in Acadia (Nova Scotia) was a seminary at Port Royal that was opened in 1633 by pioneer schoolmasters who were members of the Capuchin Order of Missionaries. They came to Acadia with Governor Issac de Razillery to educate First Nations children and converts. It is also believed to be the first school in North America.

4. The first regular Roman Catholic priest at Port Royal was Rev. Jesse Flesche, who accompanied Poutrincourt from France in February 1610. He performed the first baptism in Canada on St. John's Day, June 24, 1610.

5. The first dyke in North America was built in 1710 in Annapolis.

on Halifax. The fort consisted of a blockhouse, a guardhouse, a barracks which housed 50 soldiers, and outbuildings, all encompassed by a palisade. Not far from the fort was a rifle range. The fort was named after George Germain, 1st Viscount Sackville.

Fort Vieux Logis (later named **Fort Montague**) was a small British frontier fort built at present-day Hortonville, (formerly part of Grant Pré) in 1749 during Father Le Lourtre's War. Ranger John Gorham moved a blockhouse he erected in Annapolis Royal in 1744 to the site of Vieux Logis. The fort was in use until 1754.

The British rebuilt the fort again during the French and Indian War and named it Fort Montague (1760). The site of the fort is near the field where the Acadian Cross and the New England Planters' monument are located. Despite archaeological efforts, the exact location of the fort is unknown.

Fort Clarence (formerly the **Eastern Battery**) was a British coastal fort built in 1754 at the beginning of the French and Indian War in Dartmouth. The battery was built on the grant of Capt. John Rous. Initially, it had eight guns mounted. In the spring of 1759, a Mi'kmaq attack on the Eastern Battery killed five soldiers.

On November 17, 1778, the King's Orange Rangers (KOR) arrived by sea at Halifax. The battalion of British Loyalists originated in what is now New York State; it is believed that the transfer stemmed desertions by relocating the men far from their homes. The KOR was assigned to protect the Eastern Battery on the shore of Halifax harbour at the south end Woodside, where the neighbourhood of Imperoyal now exists.

Eastern Battery was renamed Fort Clarence by Prince Edward on October 20, 1798, in honour of his brother, the Duke of Clarence and St. Andrews, later King William IV. In the late 1790s a Martello Tower replaced the blockhouse. The fort was rebuilt with stone in the 1860s.

In 1929, Imperial Oil purchased the site which became part of their Dartmouth Refinery and the remaining parts of the fort were buried in the 1940s. The refinery was converted to an oil storage depot in 2013 and archeologists are calling for the fort to be excavated.

Fort Ellis was a British fort or blockhouse built during the French and Indian War, located at the junction of Shubenacadie and Stewiacke Rivers, close to Stewiacke. (The location was labelled Ville Pierre Hebert by Charles Morris. The 14 Acadian families in the area vacated with the Acadian Exodus.)

Charles Morris recommended a fort on the Shubenacadie River in 1753. Governor Lawrence first considered the fort in 1754 as a means to protect Halifax from Mi'kmaq raids. Lawrence decided the fort would not be effective until after the Battle of Fort Beauséjour.

The fort was completed on October 18, 1761, shortly after the Halifax Treaties were signed. The fort was to guard the new road built to connect Truro and Halifax against Mi'kmaq raids.

The fort was called Fort Ellis after Governor Henry Ellis, who was appointed governor weeks after the fort's completion. The fort was never garrisoned and eventually abandoned in 1767.

Fort Belcher, named after Governor Jonathan Belcher, was built on Salmon River in Lower Onslow, (1761-67). Fort Franklin built at Tatamagouche in 1768 and named after Michael Francklin, lasted only a year.

Fort Sainte-Marie-de-Grace was the capital of Acadia (1632-1636) and its location is now a national historic site located in LaHave, currently known as the Fort Point Museum.

Following the signing of the Treaty of Saint-Germain-en-Laye between the English and French in 1632, Governor Isaac de Razilly returned to Acadia and decided to move the capital from Port Royal to LaHave and built the fort. The fort was abandoned in 1636 after the death of the governor and the fort was destroyed by fire in the 1650s.

This site in LaHave, Lunenburg County, was the capital of Acadia from 1632 to 1636.

The site of the fort was registered as an historic site on June 4, 1924. The land on which the fort was built has eroded, but a cairn commemorating the site is situated nearby.

Fort William Augustus (also known as Grassy Island Fort, Fort Phillips) was a British fort built on Grassy Island off of Canso, during the lead up to Father Rale's War. In the wake of The Squirrel Affair and the British attack on Fort St. Louis (at present-day Guysborough), Cyprian Southack urged Governor Richard Philipps to build the fort.

The Fort was named after Prince William, Duke of Cumberland, youngest son of King George II of Great Britain.

Georges Island (named after George II) is a glacial drumlin and the largest island entirely within the harbour limits of Halifax Harbour. The Island is the location of **Fort Charlotte** — named after Queen Charlotte, wife of King George III of Great Britain.

Fort Charlotte was built during Father Le Loutre's War, a year after Citadel Hill (Fort George). The island is now a national historic site.

Fort Lawrence was a British fort built during Father Le Loutre's War and located on the Isthmus of Chignecto (in the modern-day community of Fort Lawrence).

The Fortress of Louisbourg is a national historic site and the location of a one-quarter partial reconstruction of an 18th century French fortress at Louisbourg on Cape Breton Island. Its two sieges, especially that of 1758, were turning points in the Anglo-French struggle for what today is Canada.

The original settlement was made in 1713, and initially called Havre à l'Anglois. Subsequently, the fishing port grew to become a major commercial port and a strongly defended fortress.

The fortifications eventually surrounded the town. The walls were constructed mainly between 1720 and 1740. By the mid-1740s, Louisbourg, named for Louis XIV of France, was one of

The original settlement at Louisbourg was made in 1713.

the most extensive (and expensive) European fortifications constructed in North America. It was supported by two smaller garrisons on Île Royale located at present-day St. Peter's

5 FAST FACTS

1. Nova Scotia hockey phenom Sydney Crosby wears #87 on his jersey for good luck because August 7, 1987, is his birthdate — #87 represents the eighth month and the seventh day.

2. The first frozen food sold to the public was Ice Fillets frozen fish, which went on sale in Halifax in 1929.

3. The Snowbirds — Canada's flying acrobats also known as the air show flight demonstration team of the Royal Canadian Air Force — were named after Gene McLellan's song Snowbird. The song was the first international hit by Springhill, Nova Scotia, native Anne Murray. She was made Honourary Commander of the Snowbirds after her hit went Gold in the US.

4. The oldest student newspaper in North America is The Dalhousie Gazette of Dalhousie University. Its first issue came out in 1868.

5. The first female political party leader in Canada was Alexa McDonough. She was head of the Nova Scotia NDP party from 1980 to 1996.

and Englishtown. The Fortress of Louisbourg suffered key weaknesses, since it was erected on low-lying ground commanded by nearby hills and its design was directed mainly toward sea-based assaults, leaving the land-facing defences relatively weak.

A third weakness was that it was a long way from France or Quebec, from which reinforcements might be sent.

It was captured by British Colonists in 1745, and was a major bargaining chip in the negotiations leading to the 1748 treaty ending the War of the Austrian Succession. It was returned to the French in exchange for border towns in what is today Belgium.

It was captured again in 1758 by British forces in the Seven Years' War, after which its fortifications were systematically destroyed by British engineers. The British continued to have a garrison at Louisbourg until 1768.

The fortress and town were partially reconstructed in the 1960s and 1970s, using some of the original stonework, which provided jobs for unemployed coal miners. The head stonemason for this project was Ron Bovaird.

The site is operated by Parks Canada as a living history museum. It stands as the largest reconstruction project in North America.

Point Pleasant Park on the southern tip of the Halifax peninsula once hosted several artillery batteries, and still contains the Prince of Wales Tower, which is the oldest Martello tower North America (1796).

Point Pleasant Park is owned by the British government under the administration of the Minister of the Department of Canadian Heritage and is leased to Halifax Regional Municipality for a ceremonial one shilling per year. The original lease for the land was negotiated by Sir William Young in 1866.

Fort Ste. Anne was a former French military fort located at present-day Englishtown in Victoria County.

The fort was built by Captain Charles Daniel (1629) after he raided Balaine. The fort was occupied from 1639 to 1641. Two other military forts were eventually built adjacent to the fort: Simon Denys Fort (1650-1659) and Fort Daupine (1713-1758).

York Redoubt is a redoubt situation on a bluff overlooking the entrance to Halifax Harbour at Ferguson's Cove. It was originally constructed in 1793 and was designated a national historic site in 1962.

York Redoubt was a key element in the defence of Halifax Harbour in the 19th and 20th centuries, and saw many additions to its fortifications. It was a command centre for the local harbour defences in the Second World War, which included observation posts, a defensive minefield and a new gun battery below the fort at Sleepy Cove covering the anti-submarine net, which stretched across the harbour's entrance from Fort McNab on McNabs Island.

York Redoubt remained in military use until 1956. On 28 June 1985, Canada Post issued "York Redoubt, N.S.", one of the 20 stamps in the "Forts Across Canada Series" (1983 and 1985).

Reaching for the heavens

Église Sainte-Marie Catholic Church in Church Point is one of the tallest wooden buildings and the largest wooden church in North America.

Standing some 56.5 metres high, it took more than 1,500 parishioners to build the church between 1903 and 1905. It has long been a landmark along Clare's Acadian (French) Shore.

Built in the form of a cross, the church nave measures 58 metres in length, with transepts that are 41 metres across. The church spire rises 56 metres from floor to steeple with its cross adding another 1.67 metres.

Originally four and a half metres taller, the church steeple was struck by lightning in 1914, requiring part of the spire to be rebuilt.

The first church built in the Church Point area was at Grosses Coques. Built in 1774, it was a rough chapel to serve the needs of Acadians returning from Massachusetts and other areas, following the deportation of the Acadians known as the Great Upheaval.

A second chapel was built in 1786 on a point of land jutting into St. Mary's Bay, giving rise to the name Church Point.

A third church was built following the arrival of Jean-Mandé Sigogne, the first resident priest. This church was built along the main road in the community where the parish cemetery is now located, rather than on the point. It burned down in September 1820. It was rebuilt in a classical Georgian style, and served the community from 1829 to 1905, when the present church was opened.

Construction on the present church began in 1903. A pair of turrets, with four more turrets surrounding the spire, flank the central steeple.

Since the church is exposed to the strong winds from St. Mary's Bay, 40 tons of stone ballast was used to stabilize the steeple; canvas rather than plaster was used for the walls.

Église Sainte-Marie Catholic Church in Church Point is one of the tallest wooden buildings and the largest wooden church in North America.

The steeple holds three bronze bells imported from France, the largest weighing almost 800 kilograms. The bells were made in Arras, France. The largest one sounds the tone "fa", the middle sized one "so" and the smallest one "la." The combined weight of the three bells is 3,740 pounds.

The interior of Église Sainte-Marie features a high, vaulted ceiling lit by 41 stained glass windows, many depicting the life of the Virgin Mary, to whom the church is dedicated. They were shipped from France in crates of molasses for protection.

So renowned is the church that on February 3, 1969, it was featured in the popular *Ripley's Believe It or Not* column.

Due to dwindling attendance and rising maintenance and repair cost, the church held its last service on Christmas Eve of 2019. The church attracts thousands of tourists annually.

Since 2000, the church has been a registered museum with static and interactive displays located throughout and two exhibit rooms displaying religious artifacts and relics.

Grand Pré: a monument to a people

In 1680, Pierre Melanson dit La Verdue and his family settled in Grand Pré. Its French name translates to "Great/Large Meadow."

The Melansons were soon joined by other Acadians and they built dykes to create rich farmland and pasture. It became one of the biggest Acadian communities until the Nova Scotia government deported thousands of Acadians in 1755.

A Government of Nova Scotia tourism website describes Grand Pré as a powerful monument that unites the Acadian people as it marks the location of the Le Grand Dérangement: a tragic event in Acadian history that has shaped the vibrant culture of modern-day Acadians across the globe through its quiet but powerful renaissance.

The site commemorates the Grand Pré area as a centre of Acadian settlement from 1682 to 1755, and the Deportation of the Acadians, which began in 1755 and continued until 1762.

For many Acadians throughout the world, the site remains the heart of their ancestral homeland and the symbol of the ties that unite them to this day.

The statue of Evangeline, heroine of epic Longfellow poem, Evangeline, A Tale of Acadie.

Grand Pré was made famous by American poet Henry Wadsworth Longfellow's poem *Evangeline, A Tale of Acadie*. Set during the time of the Expulsion of the Acadians, the epic poem was written in English and published 1847. It follows an Acadian girl named Evangeline and her search for her lost love Gabriel.

The idea for the poem came from Longfellow's friend Nathaniel Hawthorne. Longfellow used a style known as dactylic hexameter, imitating Greek and Latin classics, to create the poem. Though the choice was criticized, it became Longfellow's most famous work in his lifetime and remains one of his most popular and enduring works.

Located in the heart of a UNESCO World Heritage Site, Grand-Pré National Historic Site is now the most significant memorial to the tragic story of the Acadians.

Halifax Town Clock

The Town Clock, also sometimes called the Old Town Clock or Citadel Clock Tower, is one of the most recognizable landmarks in the city of Halifax.

The idea of a clock for the British Army and Royal Navy garrison at Halifax is credited to Prince Edward, Duke of Kent, who arranged for a turret clock to be manufactured before his return to England in 1800. It is said that Prince Edward, who was the commander-in-chief of all military forces in British North America, wished to resolve the tardiness of the local garrison.

The clock tower is a three-tiered (three storey), irregular octagon tower built atop a one-storey white clapboard building of classic Palladian proportions. It was erected on the east slope of Citadel Hill facing Barrack (now Brunswick) Street. The clock face is four-sided displaying Roman numerals. As with most clocks the number four is shown as IIII for aesthetic symmetry and not as IV.

The clock mechanism was constructed by the House of Vulliamy, respected Royal Clockmakers based in London. It is driven by three weights, gears, and a 13-foot pendulum with the mechanism being housed in a cast iron frame located in the clock room, immediately below the belfry. Its bell strikes hourly and quarterly and the durability of the mechanism (which dates to the original installation) is attributed to its slow movement.

The Town Clock began keeping time for the garrison on October 20, 1803.

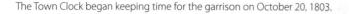

Jackson's Fort

The bridge that spans Hipson's Brook (also known as Hipson Creek, Larkin Creek, Caleb Creek and Trout Creek) has likely existed since 1785 and was originally made of wood. Because it required many repairs, people eventually questioned the safety of the old bridge.

This stone arch bridge was built in the summer and fall of 1900 by Irish immigrant stone mason David Jackson at a cost of $1,416.58. It is recognized as one of the best examples of preserved stonework in Nova Scotia.

The ornamental stones that top the railings are called soldier stones. The bridge is often referred to as Jackson's Fort, perhaps because of its fort-like appearance. It is also referred to as the bridge that Francois Xavier built — that is Xavier Muise from Quinan, an Acadian community in the region. The 1901 census indicates that 20 men from the community were stonemasons, so it's possible that more than one builder was involved in the construction.

This stone arch bridge was built in the summer and fall of 1900 by Irish immigrant stone mason David Jackson.

The tea-coloured fresh waters flowing underneath are produced by the many peat bogs in this area.

Playing around at Keltic Lodge

In 1936, the Government of Nova Scotia expropriated land from Henry and Julia Corson, an American couple from Akron, Ohio.

The Middlehead Peninsula on which the Corson's land was situated was highly desired after the federal government created the Cape Breton Highlands National Park. The Keltic Lodge opened in 1940 and was in operation for two seasons, but because of wartime shortages and overseas fighting, the government closed the hotel in 1942.

In 1943–44, with the abandoned luxury and nearby protected harbour, Keltic Lodge was a favourite shore leave destination for U-boat crews. In 1946, after the end of the war, the hotel reopened.

In November 1997, an electrical fire claimed the gift shop and coffee complex. The blaze erupted on a stormy evening and local firefighters had to battle high winds and snow to save the nearby structures from harm. In 1999, the Atlantic Restaurant and Birch Tree Shop opened on the site of the original complex.

Today, the Keltic Lodge continues to play a major role in the community of Ingonish as a source of employment and as a major attraction, drawing tourists to the area.

The mystique of the Keltic Lodge is enhanced by its prime location on the famous Cabot Trail, within Cape Breton Highlands National Park and by its proximity to Highlands Links, the number one golf course in Canada.

The course designer was none other than the legendary Stanley Thompson, a Canadian golf course architect, and a high-standard amateur golfer. He was a co-founder of the American Society of Golf Course Architects.

The community of Ingonish provided the land and labour for the creation of the course, which officially opened on July 1, 1941.

A property of historical importance

Killam Brothers Shipping Office in Yarmouth is Canada's oldest shipping office.

The property, located at 90 Water Street known as the Killam Building, was built in 1935 as part of the David and Wallace Flint shipping business. In 1956, it became part of the Killam Family Business, which extended to all parts of the world and was one of the largest dealers in hard and soft coal in Western Nova Scotia.

The Killam Family Business was the longest existing business in the Town of Yarmouth and as such, the building of 90 Water Street is recognized by the public as the Killam Building.

After the company closed in 1991, an agreement was reached between the Yarmouth Historical Society and the new owners, whereby the Killam Brothers offices would be maintained as a historical exhibit with a museum on site during tourism season.

The Killam Family Business was the longest existing business in the Town of Yarmouth.

The property is an example of Colonial Revival Style architecture. Three front gabled styled dormers and an octagonal cupola were removed from the building at some point in history and have since been restored.

Liverpool town hall

Liverpool Town Hall with a fountain in front and an opera house attached to the back was built in 1902 by George Boehner.

It is said to be one of only two wooden town hall structures left in Canada and was designated a national historic site In 1989. It is also home to the historic Astor Theatre, the oldest performing arts venue in the province and the oldest movie theatre in Canada.

Liverpool Town Hall was designated a national historic site in 1989.

The churches of Lunenburg

The building of the Dutch Reformed Church in Lunenburg took place in 1769. It would eventually go on to become St. Andrew's Presbyterian Church, the oldest Presbyterian congregation in Canada.

From the left: St. Andrew's Presbyterian Church, Zion Lutheran Church, and St. John's Anglican Church.

The St. Andrew's Presbyterian Church was then built around 1830 with an extensive enlargement in 1879. The presence of a Presbyterian Church in Lunenburg dates back to the town's founding in 1753.

Zion Lutheran Church was built in 1841 and then dismantled in 1890. An interesting note about this church is that the bell in this tower, as well as the original 1772 church, was taken from the Fortress of Louisbourg when it was captured by the British in 1758. It is currently on display in the present church.

St. John's Anglican Church was built in1754. Following St. Paul's Anglican in Halifax, St John's is the second oldest Church of England in Canada. The original timbers were brought from Boston in 1754, with several expansions and additions over the centuries.

Barrington's Old Meeting House

Among the oldest in North America, Barrington's meeting house was a building-in-progress for its first 100 years. Built by Cape Cod Congregationalist fishermen and farmers called Planters, the windows, doors, box pews and a pulpit were added by the mid-1800s.

Barrington's Old Meeting House is among the oldest in North America.

People have gathered in this building for both township business and religious worship for two centuries. Inside, see period "graffiti" and listen to the resounding acoustics as you read a historic sermon. Outside, on gravestones in the cemetery, discover the stories of some early settlers.

The structure, which was originally located at 1273 Hollis Street, is the oldest house in Halifax.

The oldest house in Halifax

Morris House — also known as the Morris Office — is the oldest wooden residence in Halifax (circa 1764) and the former office of Charles Morris, who was the surveyor general of Nova Scotia.

The house was originally located at 1273 Hollis Street, and since January 2013 has been located at 2500 Creighton Street. Due to the efforts of the Heritage Trust of Nova Scotia along with others, the house was salvaged from demolition in 2009.

The Morris family — a dynasty of surveyor generals of Nova Scotia — used the house as their office for 80 years. There were four generations of the Morris family who used the building as their workplace.

The original property was owned by Dennis Heffernan who sold it Charles Morris Jr. in 1777, who likely had his father stay with him.

The history of Port Royal

Port Royal, predominantly a farming community in Annapolis County, is situated on the north bank of the Annapolis Basin approximately eight kilometres from the town of Annapolis Royal.

Port Royal is also a significant tourist destination in Nova Scotia as the location of a historic French colonial settlement, commemorated by Port-Royal National Historic Site, which was established in 1925. A replica of the original settlement was constructed in 1939-41 by the federal government.

Name of the village of Lower Granville was officially changed to the original French name of Port Royal in 1949.

The Geographical Names Board of Canada officially established the name Port Royal for the community on March 2, 1950.

The original French settlement and capital of the colony of Acadia was named Port Royal.

It was located in the present-day community of Port Royal from 1605 until its destruction by a company of Englishmen from the Jamestown settlement in Virginia led by Samuel Argall in 1613.

After 1613, France moved the settlement/capital of Port Royal approximately eight kilometres upstream to the south bank of the Annapolis River at present-day Annapolis Royal. This second settlement was seized by British military forces in 1710 in the Siege of Port Royal and was renamed Annapolis Royal in honour of Anne, Queen of Great Britain.

Ross Farm — the living museum

Ross Farm Museum on the South Shore is a window into the province's rich agricultural history.

Established in 1969, The Ross Farm Museum is located in New Ross. The museum is a living, working farm depicting 150 years of agriculture in Nova Scotia. The property is a single-family upland farm on land originally granted to Captain William Ross.

The Ross Farm Museum is a living, working farm depicting 150 years of agriculture in Nova Scotia.

Today, Ross Farm Museum is still being farmed with oxen, the way it was in the late 1800s. In Rosebank Cottage, the original home of the Ross family built in 1817, food is still being prepared over an open fire, straw hats are still being woven, wool or flax is still being spun and butter is still being churned.

There is also a working blacksmith shop on the property where hardware is produced for the farm and approximately 30 teams of oxen are shoed each year. There is also a working stave mill and cooperage producing barrels, the original workshop where products such as butter churns, spoons, buckets and even snow shoes are made.

Uniacke Estate Museum Park

Turn along the treed roadway at Uniacke Estate Museum Park and feel like you're traveling a direct route to the 1800s. Arrive at an elegant home overlooking Lake Martha, once known as a prominent place on one of only two "great roads" in Nova Scotia.

Here, Richard John Uniacke, a prosperous Irish politician, built his country mansion in 1816. One of the grandest houses in Nova Scotia, it became a favourite home for seven generations of his large family.

Inside, find a rare survival of one family's treasured possessions including fine, labelled London furniture and exquisite portraits, at home in this house for hundreds of years. Outside, explore the English country landscape, do some bird watching and stroll or hike along seven modern walking trails.

Riding the Shubenacadie Canal

The Shubenacadie Canal is a 114 kilometre long, man-made waterway in central Nova Scotia that links Halifax Harbour with the Cobequid Bay by way of the Subenacadie River and Shubenacadie Grand Lake.

The canal, which was started in 1826, was not completed until 1861 and was subsequently closed in 1871. Currently, small craft use the river and lakes but only one lock is operational. Three of the nine locks have been restored to preserve their unique fusion of British and North American construction techniques.

The Shubenacadie Canal was originally surveyed by William Owen in 1767, which lead to the proposal of the canal 30 years later. The Government of Nova Scotia commissioned Owen to follow the Shubenacadie waterway from the Atlantic Ocean to Cobequid Bay.

The Shubenacadie Canal was planned to facilitate transportation between Halifax and the agricultural, timber and coal producing areas of northern Nova Scotia and the Annapolis Valley.

Construction was started in 1826 by the Shubenacadie Canal Co., which went bankrupt in 1831. Several Scottish and Irish stonemasons had immigrated to Nova Scotia to work on the project but were left stranded in the colony with few resources after the project had halted.

Construction then started again in 1854 under the Inland Navigation Company. The new company altered the original British stonework lock designs to use more inexpensive North American stone and wooden construction.

Steamboats and barges started using the canal in 1856 and the entire system was completed by 1861. The canal enjoyed a few years of healthy traffic, especially during the Waverley gold rushes of the 1860s.

However, the canal company showed little profit and experienced many problems relating to frigid winters, which damaged the locks linking the freshwater lakes.

The canal's ongoing construction delays were partly responsible for the 1851 decision by Nova Scotia's colonial government to build the Nova Scotia Railway, which built lines from Halifax to Windsor and Truro by 1858.

Railway construction created a short-term surge in canal traffic. In 1870, the Intercolonial Railway decided to replace the Waverley draw bridge over the canal with a fixed bridge which blocked canal steamships and severely limited canal traffic, a conflict related to the frog wars, which plagued rival railways crossings.

A final blow was a takeover by the Town of Dartmouth of the Dartmouth Lakes for the city's water supply, which ended canal operations in 1871.

5 FAST FACTS

1. Canada's first permanent covered skating rink opened in Halifax on January 3, 1863, as a private club — the Halifax Skating Rink.

2. The first license plate issued in Nova Scotia went to William Black of Wolfville on May 8, 1907, for an Oldsmobile Touring Car. The second was issued to Mr. W.L. Kane of Halifax. The plates had large black numbers on a white background along with the letters NS. In total, 62 license plates were issued that year. However, number 13 was not issued.

3. A staple in homes today, the frozen fish fillet was invented in Halifax in 1926 by Walter H. Boutilier and Frank W. Bryce. Sometime around 1940 they patented a process that allowed them to impregnate raw fish with a flavouring substance before freezing it.

4. In 1959, Charles Coll of Truro invented the mosquito repellent Muskol. Its magical ingredient is the chemical DEET.

5. What came to be known as "long johns" were invented in Truro in 1915 and were originally called "underwear combinations." Essentially, they were long underwear in two pieces that could be adjusted to fit different body lengths. Frank Stanfield came up with the idea in 1898. He and his brother John had developed "Stanfield's Unshrinkable Underwear" and they caught on.

The Lightfoot Tower

The Lightfoot Tower is a three-storey, octagonal observation tower with an open rail covered deck on the
grounds of the Zoé Vallé Memorial Library in Chester.
It was built around 1904 by American attorney Alfred
Ross Lightfoot to get a better view of sailing activity
in Mahone Bay.

According to information on the Zoé Vallé Memorial
Library website, Lightfoot was born in Pass Christian, Mississippi, in 1852. His father, William Bernard
Lightfoot, was Recorder (mayor) of Pass Christian and
owned a large cotton plantation on a fine estate prior
to the Civil War.

Alfred's mother was Sarah Bee Ross of Mobile,
Alabama, the daughter of Jack Ross, the first State
treasurer. An antebellum seaside community, Pass
Christian was in Alfred's day an internationally known
resort and the Gulf Coast was called the American
Riviera. The family had a home on the Gulf Coast next
to the Pass Christian Hotel.

Vernon Oickle photo
The Lightfoot Tower was built around
1904.

It's easy to understand why Lightfoot would have
wanted to build the tower to view sailing in Mahone Bay, as he grew up next to the Pass
Christian Hotel, which was known as the "birthplace of yachting in the south."

The Southern Yacht Club started at the hotel and was just three years old when Lightfoot
was born in 1852. Living right beside the hotel, he would have seen sailing activity and
regattas throughout his youth.

A church with history

St. George's Anglican Church is located in downtown Sydney at the corner of Charlotte and
Nepean Streets. The stone, Gothic Revival style church was built between 1785 and 1791. The
building and the graveyard are included in the provincial designation.

St. George's Anglican Church is the oldest Anglican Church in Cape Breton and the oldest
building in Sydney. Many of Sydney's early and prominent citizens are buried in its cemetery.

Building St. George's Church began in 1785 by engineers of the British 33rd Regiment of
Foot, concurrently with the founding of Sydney and its designation as the capital of the new
Colony of Cape Breton. However, it was not completed and designated as a parish until 1791.

According to the website Canada's Historic Places, part of the heritage value of St. George's
Church relates to its many changes since its construction.

The original building was a simple stone structure, approximately 18 by 12 meters with three

St. George's Anglican Church is located in downtown Sydney at the corner of Charlotte and Nepean Streets was built between 1785 and 1791.

circular windows on the north and south walls. In 1853, a chancel and vestry were added.

Starting in 1859, and continuing into the early 1860s, the church was rebuilt from its foundations in the Gothic Revival style, with an open roof and pointed windows, which were slightly ornamented with stained glass. In 1888, a stone tower and spire replaced a wooden tower, which had been destroyed by a gale in 1873.

With the exception of a crypt constructed in 1974, St. Georges is much the same as it appeared in 1873 after its last major renovation. The church's stone Gothic Revival styling is valued as a visible expression of the missionary ideals of its period and of an expansive period in the history of English Christianity. Examples of this style executed in stone are rare in Nova Scotia.

St. George's Graveyard is important for its early sandstone and limestone grave markers. These markers are good examples of a large concentration of early grave markers that have a design and folk-art significance; unusual styles (a high concentration of large tomb-style markers); and locally-significant markers that were produced by local monument makers.

For almost 220 years, St. George's Church has been a place of worship, serving the people of Sydney. Originally, the Parish included the whole of Cape Breton Island, and St. George's served as the British garrison chapel.

As a garrison chapel until 1854, it was granted a Royal Pew and became the official place of worship for members of the Royal Family, if they should ever visit, a role that it still retains.

St. George's Church also played an integral part in Cape Breton's history as an independent colony. During the Island's Colonial Period (1784-1820), the colony's House of Assembly was never called to sit.

As a result, the vestry and warden positions at St. George's were the only elected positions in Cape Breton Island during its Colonial Period. Many prominent local figures made their bid for the vestry in the hopes that it would further their political interests.

Many of Sydney's prominent citizens from the Colonial Period onwards are buried in St. George's Graveyard. Memorials, such as a memorial tablet to Judge A. C. Dodd, the first Chief Magistrate of the Island of Cape Breton, are situated inside the church.

The church chancel contains a memorial window to Bishop Hibbert Binney, who was born in Sydney and was the fourth Church of England Bishop of Nova Scotia. The nave contains a memorial window to the Honourable John Bourinot, father of Sir John Bourinot, who wrote the rules of order for the Parliament of Canada.

Crime and Punishment

A Nova Scotia crime line

The following are 14 noteworthy dates on the Nova Scotia crime line.

1. *1749:* First murder in Halifax, followed by Canada's first ever trial under British law.

2. *1754:* The Nova Scotia Supreme Court is established.

3. *1835:* Joseph Howe publishes his famous letter and is charged with libel. After defending himself, Howe is acquitted.

4. *1923:* J.B. McLachlan is charged with sedition and sentenced to two years.

5. *1937:* In Nova Scotia's last execution, Everett Farmer is hanged for murder.

6. *1971:* Donald Marshall Jr. is wrongly accused of murder.

7. *1987:* Crime Stoppers program is launched in the province.

8. *1989:* 19-year-old Kimberly McAndrew is seen leaving her workplace at Canadian Tire and is never heard from again.

9. *1990:* The province officially apologizes to Donald Marshall Jr.

10. *2002:* Clayton Johnson, wrongfully convicted for the 1993 murder of his wife, has his conviction overturned and is freed.

11. *2004:* Theresa McEvoy is killed when a stolen car driven by a delinquent teen runs a stop sign and crashes into her car. The death sparks a major wake-up call to the government in relation to troubled teens and youth crime.

12. *2007:* On New Year's Eve, police make the shocking discovery of 20-year-old Jennifer Horne's lifeless body in a closet, wrapped in a carpet. She had been assaulted, tortured, and then brutally murdered. Desmond Maguire, 37, and Ashley Haley, 20, are charged with her murder.

13. *2013:* On April 27th, 2013, Rehtaeh Parsons was taken off life support after a suicide attempt. Rehtaeh Parsons had been a victim of sexual abuse and cyberbullying at her high school. In response, Nova Scotia introduced legislation to "create a new criminal offence prohibiting the non-consensual distribution of intimate images." The *Cyber-Safety Act* came into effect in 2013.

14. *2020:* On April 18-19, — in what is Canada's worse mass murder — a killing spree by one man in the central region of the province resulted in the death of 22 victims.

5 FAST FACTS

1. North America's first Boy Scout troop was organized in Port Morien, Nova Scotia, in 1908, just a year after Lord Baden Powell began England's scouting movement. William Glover, an official at one of the coal mines officially organized a troop of 10 boys.

2. The famous logo of a girl wearing a white bonnet on the Old Dutch Cleanser cans was designed by Maude E. Sutherland, daughter of a Pictou doctor. In 1907, the company ran a continent-wide logo contest and young Maude was the winner.

3. Each time you snap close a carry case or buckle up your seatbelt, you can thank inventor Arthur Davy of New Glasgow that releasing the belt will only require a flick of your thumb. Seatbelts weren't what Davy had in mind when he invented the quick-release buckle in 1911. His idea was to simplify attaching and detaching the reins from a horse.

4. A rare breed of snake is found only on two small islands in Halifax Harbour. Wildlife experts have determined that the unusual looking black snakes are actually ordinary garter snakes and that their black pigmentation is a genetic aberration caused in part by inbreeding.

5. John B. Porter of Yarmouth patented the portable ironing board in 1875. Today, it is the standard design of all ironing boards.

Canada's first trial for murder

Peter Cartcel has the dubious distinction of being the first Halifax murderer charged and tried for his crime. On August 26, 1749, Cartcel fatally stabbed Abraham Goodsides as the two fought on the streets of the infant city.

Because Nova Scotia had no court system at the time, the murder required Gov. Edward Cornwallis to take immediate action. Empowered to establish courts for the fledging city, Cornwallis named himself and six councillors to the city's first court.

On August 31, five days after he committed the crime, Cartcel appeared without a lawyer before the hastily established court for Canada's first ever trial under British law. After hearing four witnesses, the court deliberated for just half an hour before they found the defendant guilty.

Cartcel was hanged two days later.

Confessions of a killer

"I've done a terrible thing. I shot four people."

This was the chilling confession that Aubrey Lutz made to officers at the RCMP detachment at Kentville, Nova Scotia, on February 12, 1964.

Lutz had recently married 18-year-old Rosalie Pudsey. But not long after the nuptials, Rosalie and Aubrey's marriage began to sour, and fearing for her safety, Rosalie took the couple's newborn baby, Kimberly, to live with her parents and two sisters. Rosalie's move enraged Aubrey, and on that fateful day he loaded his gun and went to confront his wife and her family. At the house, Aubrey met and killed Rosalie's mother first.

When Rosalie's younger sister, Audrey, sought refuge in the bathroom, Aubrey fired through the door, instantly killing the 15-year-old.

On hearing the commotion, Rosalie Lutz climbed the stairs from the basement and placed baby Kimberly on the living room couch. When she confronted her husband, he fired, striking her in the shoulder. Just as Aubrey was about to make his escape, Arthur Pudsey returned home to the awful scene. For the fourth time, Aubrey fired his gun, this time killing his father-in-law.

Aubrey grabbed his unharmed baby and travelled to Kentville where he confessed to police. Rosalie Lutz and her nine-year-old sister, who had been at school, were the sole surviving members of their family.

Deemed unfit to stand trial, Lutz was sent to the Nova Scotia Hospital. For almost 15 years he remained a volatile, dangerous man who was heavily medicated and received almost 500 shock treatments.

In the late 1970s and 1980s, however, Lutz's demeanour improved and he was classified a voluntary patient, free to check himself out. On December 27, 1990, the murderer of three left the Nova Scotia Hospital a free man and returned to his Annapolis Valley home.

Horrified, Rosalie called police. Lutz was again arrested, charged with three counts of murder and prepared for trial. In March 1991, the courts made a familiar ruling — Lutz was deemed unfit for trial, and remanded into the custody of the Nova Scotia Hospital.

Amazingly, Rosalie has forgiven Aubrey: "I believe everyone should leave him alone. I have forgiven my husband for what he has done."

Mutiny and murder

In May of 1844, the ship Saladin ran aground on Nova Scotia's eastern shore. Claims made from the small crew of six were that the captain and other crew members had died at sea, which raised immediate suspicions.

The crew was placed under arrest, and charged with killing their captain and five crewmates. As confessions were elicited, a grizzly story of mutiny and murder took shape.

The ringleader, George Fielding (this former captain had been in prison prior to the journey, but made a deal with authorities to work the trip for free passage for himself and his 14-year old son), had convinced four crewmen to help him carry out his dastardly deed

On April 14, 1844, they used axes and other tools on board to kill the captain and five mates. When his compatriots learned of Fielding's plans to sweeten his own share of the loot through further killings, they turned on him, throwing him and his son overboard.

After only 15 minutes of deliberation, the jury returned guilty verdicts in three cases. Two of the men, tried separately, were acquitted. The convicted pirates were hanged on July 30, 1844. Hundreds of Haligonians brought their families to witness the event on the South Common, the site today of the Victoria General Hospital.

The McDonald's murders

In the early pre-dawn morning of May 7, 1992, three young Sydney-area men arrived at the city's McDonald's restaurant intending to commit robbery. Derek Wood, Darren Muise and Freeman MacNeil were sure that the restaurant's safe contained as much as $200,000.

The robbery turned deadly when the three encountered the four staff members on the midnight shift. Armed with knives, a .22 caliber pistol and a shovel, the three robbers brutally murdered Donna Warren, Neil Borroughs and Jimmy Fagan, and left Arlene MacNeil badly wounded and near death.

The horrific crime stunned and outraged the small city, and indeed the whole nation, as national media descended on Sydney. The perpetrators denied their involvement but evidence against them mounted, and by the middle of May all had confessed their crime.

They were variously charged with murder, robbery and the unlawful confinement of Donna Warren, who had been forced to open the safe before she, like the others, was shot in the head.

Harsh punishment was meted out to the murderers. Darren Muise was sentenced to life in prison without parole for twenty years and Freeman MacNeil got life in prison with no parole for twenty-five years. Derek Wood was sentenced to two life terms in jail, and ten years for robbery and unlawful confinement.

In 2012, Darren Muise was granted full parole and in 2015, Derek Wood was denied day parole for his part in the murders.

A dubious distinction

Everett Farmer, a Nova Scotian labourer charged with murdering his brother-in-law, has the distinction of being the last person to be hanged in the province.

As a poor, black, Shelburne County man, Farmer had access to legal counsel of dubious quality. Farmer insisted that his crime had been one of self-defense, but without adequate representation it was hard for him to make his case.

A lawyer was not assigned to his defense until just one week before the opening of his September 1937 trial. As the first capital case to be heard in Shelburne County for a century, the Farmer trial became a media circus.

Juried by 12 white men, the trial lasted just two days and ended in a murder conviction. Everett Farmer was sentenced to die. According to a newspaper account, at five a.m. on December 15, 1937, Farmer climbed the stairs of the hanging scaffold "with the same coolness that [had] characterized him since he [had] been in jail."

As the hood was placed over his head, and as his spiritual advisor recited scripture, Farmer uttered his last words before the trap was sprung: "Good-bye, boys."

5 FAST FACTS

1. In 1909, James Rooney invented a tea and coffee pot whose design is still in use today. It's a perforated receptacle with a plunger, which fits inside a tea or coffee pot, allowing leaves or grounds to be easily removed after infusion.

2. Nova Scotia was home to Canada's first decorated Christmas tree in 1846. The first time an evergreen was used as a Christmas tree was in Sorel, Quebec, in 1781 where German Baroness Riedsel made her three children happy and made history by erecting the first Christmas tree on the continent.

3. Charles L. Grant of Grand Pré invented the gum rubber shoe in 1920. His innovation was a rubber-coated tongue fastened to the shoe, making it waterproof. His invention is now standard practice in shoe manufacturing.

4. John Forbes of Dartmouth invented the clip-on skate in 1867. Instead of screws and plates to attach the blade to the boots of the wearer, Forbes' invention required only a single lever. Forbes came up with the idea while he was foreman at the Starr Manufacturing Company. More than 30 different kinds of skates were patented by Nova Scotia and New Brunswick inventors between 1867 and 1933.

5. Do you enjoy your Raisin Bran or Apple Crisp flakes? If you do, you can thank George F. Humphrey of Bridgetown who in 1924 and 1927 patented hot and cold breakfast foods infused with real fruit.

Guilty until proven innocent

On May 28, 1971, 16-year-old Donald Marshall Jr. was walking through a Sydney park when he met up with Sandy Seale, another youth from Sydney. The two teenagers then encountered Roy Ebsary, described as an "eccentric old man with a fetish for knives."

Without warning, Ebsary brutally and fatally stabbed Seale.

Marshall, a Mi'kmaw from Membertou, was arrested and charged with Seale's death, and in November 1971 was sentenced to life in prison. For 11 years Marshall was incarcerated; for 11 years he maintained his innocence.

In 1982, Marshall was released on bail as then Justice Minister Jean Chrétien referred the case to the Nova Scotia Supreme Court for rehearing.

In 1983, Donald Marshall Jr. was acquitted of all charges, but in a strange outcome the police who had wrongly charged him were absolved of all wrongdoing. In a now infamous statement, Chrétien reasoned that any miscarriage of justice was "more apparent than real."

Roy Ebsary was eventually convicted of manslaughter in the death of Seale. For 11 lost years of his life, Donald Marshall accepted a lump sum payment of $270,000 from the Nova Scotia government, but was required to pay his own legal bills.

Marshall died in 2009.

The Butterbox Babies

This is one of the darkest chapters in Canada's history. William and Lila Young operated the Ideal Maternity Home in East Chester from the late 1920s through the late 1940s.

In 1928, Lila, a 29-year-old recent graduate of the National School of Obstetrics and Midwifery, and her husband, a 30-year-old, un-ordained Seventh Day Adventist minister, missionary and licensed chiropractor, opened the Life and Health Sanitarium, which by the 1940s became known as the Ideal Maternity Home.

The Home promised maternity care for married couples, and discreet birthing and placement for the children of unwed mothers. In truth, it was a source of babies for an illegal trade in infants between Canada and the United States. At this time, U.S. laws prohibited adoption across religious backgrounds, which led to an acute shortage of babies available for Jewish couples to adopt. The home in East Chester would provide these desperate people with black market adoptions, charging up to $10,000 for a baby.

In the 1940s, many of the babies ended up in Jewish homes in New Jersey. The Youngs also charged the new mothers $500 for the services they received in the home, which were often performed in unsanitary, deplorable conditions. Since many of the mothers could not afford this amount, which in those days was a large sum, they were often forced to work at the home for up to 18 months to pay their bills.

Years later, it was discovered that the Youngs had purposely starved "unmarketable" babies to death by feeding them only molasses and water. On this diet, the infants would usually last only two weeks. Any deformity, serious illness, or "dark" coloration would seal a baby's fate.

In some cases, married couples that had come to the home solely for birthing services were told that their baby had died shortly after birth. In truth, these babies were also sold to adoptive parents. The Youngs would also separate or create siblings to meet the desires of their customers by pretending unrelated babies were siblings. It is estimated that between 400 and 600 babies died at the home, while at least another 1000 survived and were adopted.

Babies who died were disposed of in small wooden grocery boxes typically used for dairy products. That is how the term "Butterbox Babies" originated. The bodies were buried on the Youngs' property, at sea, or adjacent to a nearby cemetery. Some were burned in the Home's furnace.

By 1933, the Youngs' lucrative business had attracted the attention of the Nova Scotia child welfare director as well as the health minister. Health officials finally intervened in 1945, and won convictions against the couple for violating new adoption licensing laws.

New regulations were slowly introduced. A new amendment to the Maternity Boarding House Act of 1940 had broadened licensing requirements to apply to incorporated companies and the Youngs' licence application was swiftly rejected. The Ideal Maternity Home was ordered shut down in November 1945, but the Youngs' legal woes were mounting amid stories of illegal baby smuggling and medical malpractice.

On June 5, 1946, the Youngs were convicted of illegally selling babies to four American couples and were fined $428.90. William was later convicted of perjury based on his testimony at the June trial, but babies were still being born at the Ideal Maternity Home in early 1947. The Youngs, bankrupt and debt-ridden by the end of 1947, sold off their property in East Chester and moved to Quebec. The Home, which was scheduled for conversion into a resort hotel, burned to the ground on September 23, 1962. William died of cancer before Christmas that year, and Lila died of leukemia in 1967.

Following their deaths, the truth about the Ideal Maternity Home remained buried for many years. The full scope of this heinous story was not known until decades later, when a caretaker admitted to Canadian journalist Bette Cahill that he was paid to bury the babies in open graves and in butter boxes from the local LaHave Dairy.

Cahill's 1992 book, *Butterbox Babies*, became an international bestseller, and was subsequently made into a movie under the same title.

5 FAST FACTS

1. The highest tide ever recorded in the Bay of Fundy occurred during a storm in 1869 when tides rose to 70.9 metres.

2. The highest point of land in Nova Scotia is White Hill in Cape Breton Island.

3. The most northern point in the province is Saint Paul Island.

4. On the other end of the compass, the most southern point in Nova Scotia is Cape Sable Island.

5. Cape Sable Island near Barrington Passage is the home of the famous Cape Island boat first built by Ephraim Atkinson at Clark's Harbour in 1907. A typical Cape Islander is 11.5 metres long with a 3.5-metre beam. It draws little water, sitting on top of the water and is used mostly in the lobster fishery.

Life with Billy

On March 11, 1982, Jane (Hurshman) Stafford killed her abusive common-law husband, Billy Stafford, as he slept drunkenly slumped behind the steering wheel of his pickup truck near their home in Bangs Falls, Queens County. She had no idea of the impact her actions would have on the Canadian legal system and the issue of domestic violence.

Hurshman's first degree murder trial at the historic Liverpool Court House, and the publicity that surrounded the sensational case, eventually helped to broaden the legal definition of self-defence in Canadian law.

Hurshman was famously acquitted in the first trial. But, concerned with the legal precedent, the Crown later appealed, and in turn, Hurshman pled guilty to manslaughter. She received a six-month sentence and was released after two months. Following her release, she became an advocate for women's rights, conducted one-on-one counselling with other victims, and led the charge against spousal abuse.

The Stafford case spawned several books, including *Life With Billy* by Brian Vallee and a television movie of the same title; and it exposed the issues of wife battering and domestic violence for the crimes that they truly are.

On February 23, 1992, Jane Hurshman's body was found in a car on the Halifax waterfront, dead from a single gunshot wound. Autopsy results showed that she died from a bullet that hit her heart and right lung. The autopsy report said the bullet wound was consistent with suicide.

Random killings

On the evening of August 8, 1964, 11-year-old Gordon Hartling had accompanied his sister to the corner store on Halifax's Tower Road located on Halifax's south end. She went into the store to buy Popsicles. Gordon was waiting outside on the sidewalk when a teenager on a bicycle rode up and shot him in the head with a pistol.

Gordon Hartling was one of three boys shot in the span of 40 minutes that day. He died, as did 12-year-old James Squires. Michael Smith, also 12 years of age, miraculously recovered.

It has never been determined what made Edward Thomas Boutilier shoot a boy standing on a sidewalk, another picking blueberries with his mother, and another on his way home from the Waegwoltic Club. But for two days, until Boutilier gave himself up, Halifax lived behind locked doors, in fear.

That night, 20 minutes before Gordon was gunned down, Michael Smith was walking home along the railway shortcut near Jubilee Road after sailing at the Waeg. He stepped out of the way of a cyclist and then, just after someone yelled a warning, felt what he thought must have been a boulder slam into the side of his head. In fact, he'd been shot just below the ear.

"The next thing, everything was reddish liquid. I had a funny taste in my mouth," Smith, who has since died, told The Chronicle Herald in 1999. "I heard them scream, then just a bunch of confusion and then the ambulance came. The last thing I remember is going up in the elevator in what must have been the old Victoria General Hospital."

Jimmy Squires was also near the railway tracks when he was shot at the Maplewood crossing. He had asked his mother that afternoon to take him blueberry picking. The two had just moved from one patch to another when Jimmy's mother saw Boutilier approaching on a bicycle. At first, she thought he was another blueberry picker.

"He … let Jimmy walk about three steps ahead of him," Verna Squires told a reporter from the Mail-Star at the time of the shootings. "There was a terrible bang and, just then, Jimmy fell in a heap. I had to walk over to him to convince myself he had been shot and I saw blood gushing from his head."

As the streets emptied, 200 police officers, some carrying machine-guns, began to comb the city for a suspect for which they had just a vague description.

Two days later, Boutilier turned himself in to police near Halifax Stanfield International Airport. By a pre-arranged signal, a police officer fired three shots into the air and Boutilier walked out of the woods and surrendered.

Psychiatrists quickly diagnosed Boutilier, aged 18, as "grossly mentally disturbed" and "definitely certifiable." He was committed to the Nova Scotia Hospital for an indefinite period, where he spent 10 years before killing himself.

Undercover spy and murderer

Notorious 19th century criminal Alexander "Sandy" Keith, Jr. was born in 1827 in Caithness, Scotland, immigrating to Halifax when he was a small boy. The nephew of Alexander Keith, founder of the Alexander Keith's Brewery, the younger Keith worked for a time as a clerk in his uncle's brewery.

Keith became a secret agent for the Confederate States of America during the American Civil War, acting mostly as a blockade-runner and courier. Keith assisted in helping Confederate sympathizers escape justice in the Chesapeake Affair. He was also involved with Luke Blackburn in an infamous plot to send clothes infected with yellow fever to northern cities in the United States.

In 1865, he swindled his associates-in-crime and fled to St. Louis, Missouri, finally settling on the prairie. There, he married Cecelia Paris, a milliner's daughter from St. Louis.

Hunted down by one of his victims, Keith fled again with Cecelia to Germany, where they lived the high life hobnobbing with wealthy socialites and Saxon generals under the assumed name of "William King Thomas."

When the couple began to run out of money, Keith concocted a plot to blow up passenger ships and collect the insurance money. This led to a major catastrophe in Bremerhaven, on December 11, 1875, when a time bomb he had placed in a shipping barrel accidentally went off on the dock, killing 80 people, most of them aboard the steamship Mosel, a German emigrant ship. She was under the command of Captain Leist, replacement for the ailing captain Hermann Neynaber for a crossing to New York.

The explosion happened when the passengers were on board and the final baggage was being loaded. With only a few large shipping crates on the pier, one of Keith's barrels slipped out of the stevedores' hands while being loaded and struck the ground, exploding in a huge column of fire whose blast caused two ships at the quay to overturn. At the time, the deed was called the "crime of the century."

Keith was aware of the premature detonation of his time bomb, and the massive carnage that ensued. At the time of the explosion, he was aboard another ship in Bremerhaven. He went to his suite and shot himself, and died a week later.

After the tragedy was revealed as a murder/insurance scam on a large scale, the disappearance of other ships were looked into to see if Keith and his possible associates were involved. One was the disappearance of the SS *City of Boston*, which vanished in January 1870.

Leo Koretz — the gentleman swindler

Leopold "Leo" Koretz was an American lawyer and stockbroker who ran an elaborate Ponzi scheme in Chicago called the "Bayano oil fraud," which garnered an estimated $30 million (about $400 million today) from dozens of investors in Chicago.

The scheme worked by using fraudulent claims of oil interests in Panama in a criminal career that predated his contemporary, Charles Ponzi. Koretz was so trusted and admired that after Ponzi's fraud was exposed in 1920, his investors nicknamed him "Our Ponzi," never suspecting they were being duped as well.

Koretz was born to German Jewish parents on July 30, 1879, in Rokycany, Bohemia, the seventh of nine children. He arrived in the United States in 1887 at age eight and the Koretz family settled in Chicago.

Koretz was a star debater at Lakeview High School. He studied at night and graduated from the Chicago-Kent College of Law in June 1901. One of Koretz's associates when he began to practice law was Robert E. Crowe, who as the Cook County state's attorney, would later investigate Koretz and arrange for his arrest.

Koretz's swindling career began in 1905, when he forged and sold a series of mortgages on non-existent properties, using the proceeds to cover interest payments and finance an opulent lifestyle. He soon graduated to land speculation in Arkansas, flogging more fake mortgages and bogus stock in Arkansas rice farms.

In 1911, Koretz began selling stock in the Bayano River Syndicate, which he claimed controlled millions of acres of prime timberland in a remote region of Panama. His announcement of the "discovery" of oil on the property in 1921 — and a promise of 60-percent annual returns — sparked a stock-buying frenzy in which many investors begged Koretz for a chance to invest.

The scheme was exposed in November 1923 when a group of Koretz's wealthy investors traveled to Panama to see the purported oil operations and discovered the fraud.

Koretz fled to New York City and then to Nova Scotia where he posed as Lou Keyte, a wealthy retiree and literary figure. He purchased and renovated a secluded lodge in South Brookfield, Queens County, where the unassuming "gentleman" was quickly welcomed into the community.

Soon, he was lavishly entertaining a new circle of friends that included the American famed western novelist Zane Grey, who regularly came to Nova Scotia to engage in the tuna fishery, and future Canadian author Thomas H. Raddall.

Koretz was identified and arrested in Halifax on November 23, 1924, through a suit he had brought to a tailor for repair. A label sewn into the lining displayed his real name as well as the name of the Chicago clothier from whom the garment had been purchased.

He was extradited to Chicago and pleaded guilty.

Shortly after he was sent to the state prison in Joliet, the 45-year-old Koretz who had been diabetic since 1919, died on January 8, 1925, of an apparent suicide. He deliberately ate an entire box of chocolates that had been smuggled into the prison; the high blood sugar levels triggered a fatal diabetic coma.

Koretz was buried the following afternoon in a graveside service at Waldheim Cemetery in Forest Park, Illinois.

5 FAST FACTS

1. St. Paul's Church, built in 1750, is the oldest Protestant church in Canada still standing. It is basically a simple wooden box with a peaked roof and steeple at one end. The church miraculously survived the Halifax Explosion on December 6, 1917, but the story goes that its force blew a man through the Argyle Street window of the church. The silhouette was etched into the glass and no matter how many times the window is replaced, the man's silhouette reappears.

2. The first zoo in North America was opened near Halifax in 1847 by Andrew Downs, a world-famous naturalist and taxidermist. His five-acre zoo had been in operation for 12 years before the first American zoo was founded in Philadelphia. Downs expanded his zoo to 100 acres and its inhabitants became a favourite attraction for Halifax area residents who arrived by steamboat.

3. James William Black from Berwick invented the icecream soda in 1886 when he created and bottled syrup made from whipped egg whites, sugar, water, lime juice or citric acid, flavouring extract and bicarbonate of soda. When ice water was stirred into a small ladle of the mixture it produced a delicious, foam-topped drink.

4. An innovation that has become invaluable to modern machine design was invented in 1879 at Bear River, Nova Scotia. George Welton Thomas wanted to eliminate or reduce the friction of moving parts against stationary ones such as a wheel revolving on an axle. Thomas achieved this with rollers in a cage, a design that continues to be used today in milling and factory machinery and just about everything that runs on wheels.

5. John Alexander Douglas McCurdy (1886-1961) was the first person to fly an airplane in the British Empire when he piloted the Silver Dart at Baddeck in 1909. In 1910, he was the first Canadian issued a pilot's license and in 1911, he made the first flight from Florida to Cuba. He was the 19th Lieutenant Governor of Nova Scotia from 1947-52, and established the first aviation school in Canada.

The Halifax Explosion occurred on December 6, 1917. Up to that point, it was the largest man-made explosion in history.

Death and Destruction

Disasters

The impact of a catastrophe is the same, whether caused by nature or humans. Over the course of its history, Nova Scotia has had its fair share of disasters, including:

The Halifax Explosion: A massive explosion on December 6, 1917, which was the result of the SS *Imo*, a Belgian relief ship travelling in ballast, colliding with the French ship *Mont-Blanc*, laden with more than 2,500 tonnes of high explosives, in the narrowest part of Halifax Harbour. It remains the largest man made, non-nuclear blast in history. There are 1,950 recorded names of people who died as a result of the explosion but it is believed the total could be as high as 2,500.

Great Nova Scotia Cyclone: A hurricane that was reduced to Category 2 by the time it paralleled the province's coastline on August 24, 1873. It never made landfall here; most of those killed were sailors at sea. It is estimated that this storm killed 500 in Nova Scotia plus another 100 in Newfoundland and Labrador.

Swissair Flight 111: A scheduled international passenger flight from New York City to Geneva, Switzerland, in which the airplane, a McDonnell Douglas MD-11, experienced a total loss of power due to a fire and plunged into the Atlantic Ocean eight kilometres from Peggy's Cove on September 2, 1998. With the death of all 229 passengers and crew on board the plane, it remains the second largest loss of life of any air disaster in the country, while its investigation became the largest and most expensive transport accident investigation in Canadian history.

The aftermath of the crash of Swissair Flight 111.

Great August Gale of 1927: A Category 3 hurricane that made landfall on August 24, 1927, near Yarmouth and then travelled across the province. With the death toll ranging from 173 to 192, it was not only the deadliest Canadian hurricane since at least 1900, but also the strongest tropical storm ever to strike the country.

1891 Springhill mining explosion: Springhill's first mining disaster — and its worst — occurred in No. 1 and No. 2 Collieries, which were joined by a connecting tunnel 400 metres below the surface on February 21, 1891. In addition to those killed, dozens were injured, with many of the 125 victims being boys between the ages of 10 and 13.

1958 Springhill mining "bump": The most severe underground earthquake, or "bump," in North American mining history not only hit Number 2 Colliery (one of the deepest in the world) on October 23, 1958, but also injured town residents and destroyed its economy, as the mines were never reopened. A total of 75 people were lost in this tragedy. Rescue operations continued for a week, ending with 99 trapped miners being saved.

Drummond Mine Explosion: Actually, a series of explosions that were likely caused by a fire in Canada's leading colliery at the time, Westville, Pictou County, May 13, 1873. This explosion resulted in the loss of 70 lives.

Great August Gale of 1926: A Category 1 hurricane whose remnants hit Cape Breton Island on August 8, 1926, after having sunk several ships and boats offshore, including two Lunenburg fishing schooners that crashed onto Sable Island, killing 49 fishermen. In total, 55 to 58 people died in the storm.

1956 Springhill mining explosion: Several cars from a mine train hauling a load of fine coal dust to the surface of Number 4 Colliery broke loose on November 1, 1956, derailed, hit a power line and caused an arc that ignited the dust at 1,700 metres below the surface. Heroic rescue operations resulted in 88 miners being saved but 39 died in the accident.

Westray Mine explosion: A total of 26 miners died on May 9, 1992, when underground explosions ripped through mines at Plymouth, Pictou County. Initially, the explosions were caused by methane gas and subsequently coal dust, which were the result of unsafe working practices.

Hurricanes hit Nova Scotia

Canada is usually only hit with weak storms, due to the generally cool waters immediately offshore. However, some hurricanes can strike the area full force as the warm Gulf Stream extends fairly close to Atlantic Canada.

According to the Canadian Hurricane Centre, Hurricane Ella in 1978 is the strongest tropical cyclone on record to pass through Canadian waters, passing approximately 540 kilometres south of Halifax as a Category 4 hurricane. Despite this, however, Ella did not make landfall.

The strongest hurricane to make landfall in Canada was Hurricane Ginny in 1963. The storm had winds of 175 kilometres per hour, making it a strong Category 2 hurricane at the time of its landfall near Yarmouth.

These cyclones have either made a direct landfall in Nova Scotia or made a notable close approach as a tropical cyclone:

- August 23, 1863: A Category 1 hurricane hit Nova Scotia just before losing tropical characteristics.

5 FAST FACTS

1. Oxford claims to be the Blueberry Capital of the World. It also boasts the world's largest blueberry, which is located at a gas station. The incredible giant is 2.4 metres (7.5 feet) tall.

2. The replaceable pool cue tip was patented in 1920 by George W. Leadbetter of Springhill. His metal sleeve has now been replaced by plastic and the tip is glued on, but Leadbetter's invention is credited with forever changing the construction of pool and billiard cues.

3. The W.D. Lawrence, the largest square-rigger ever built in Nova Scotia and the largest wooden ship ever built in Canada, was launched at Maitland in 1874 by W.D. Lawrence.

4. In 1985, the largest fossil find ever in North America was unearthed on the north shore of the Minas Basin near Parrsboro. More than 100,000 fossil specimens were found, some more than 200 million years old, including penny-sized footprints. In 1984, collector Eldon George found the world's smallest dinosaur tracks at Wasson's Bluff.

5. The fishing village of Port Mouton in Queens County was named "sheep port" by French explorer Du Gua de Monts in 1604 after a sheep jumped overboard and nearly drowned. Luckily for the sheep, the crew saved it, but they subsequently ate the waterlogged animal.

- October 5, 1869: The 1869 Saxby Gale struck the Bay of Fundy region damaging parts of Nova Scotia and New Brunswick, killing 37 people offshore.

- October 13, 1871: Unnamed hurricane hit Nova Scotia.

- August 26, 1873: The Nova Scotia Hurricane of 1873 drifted south of Nova Scotia as a Category 3 hurricane. It weakened to a Category 1 before slowly making landfall in Newfoundland. It was a devastating hurricane that killed over 600. Damage in Nova Scotia was severe. It destroyed over 1,200 boats and over 900 homes and businesses. This is one of Nova Scotia's worst cyclones on record.

- September 8, 1891: A hurricane struck both Nova Scotia and Newfoundland as a Category 1 hurricane.

- September 12-14, 1900: After leaving behind a trail of devastation in the United States, the 1900 Galveston hurricane affected six Canadian provinces as a powerful extratropical cyclone, killing 52 to 232 people, mainly due to shipwrecks.

- August 8, 1926: The 1926 Nova Scotia hurricane made landfall in Nova Scotia as an extra tropical storm, killing 55 to 58 people.

- August 24, 1927: The 1927 Nova Scotia hurricane made landfall in Nova Scotia as a Category 2 hurricane with winds of 165 kilometres per hour, causing immense damage reaching $1.6 million and killed 172 to 193 people.

- September 26, 1937: The extratropical remnant of a hurricane caused damage in Nova Scotia. The storm was moving swiftly, so most of the damage was strictly wind related.

- September 17, 1940: The 1940 Nova Scotia hurricane struck Nova Scotia as a Category 1 hurricane before weakening.

- August 21, 1950: Hurricane Able struck Nova Scotia as a strong tropical storm, causing only minor damage.

- October 5, 1950: Hurricane George passed a few miles south as a tropical/extratropical storm.

- September 7, 1953: Hurricane Carol struck the New Brunswick and Nova Scotia border. It caused about $1 million in damage, mainly to boats and fish craft.

- June 19, 1959: The 1959 Escuminac Hurricane was a devastating hurricane that hit Nova Scotia. In total, 22 boats were lost during the storm and the hurricane killed 35 people. The hurricane was so devastating that a monument was erected on Escuminac Harbour in memory of those lost.

- July 12, 1959: Tropical Storm Cindy struck north of Nova Scotia as an extratropical cyclone.

- October 8, 1962: Hurricane Daisy struck Nova Scotia as a hurricane, near the same area as Frances a year earlier, which struck the area while extratropical.

- October 29, 1963: Hurricane Ginny struck Nova Scotia as a strong Category 2 hurricane, the strongest to ever make landfall in Canada. Ginny was unusual in the fact that the hurricane produced snow.

- August 16, 1971: Hurricane Beth struck Nova Scotia as a minimal hurricane, bringing over 275 millimetres of rainfall.

- July 28, 1975: Hurricane Blanche struck Nova Scotia as a tropical storm, dropping over 75 millimetres of rainfall.

- August 7–8, 1988: Tropical Storm Alberto, the furthest north forming tropical storm ever recorded in the Atlantic, struck the Maritimes and became extratropical over Newfoundland. Alberto was the first storm with a masculine name to directly strike Canada.

- November 2, 1991: The 1991 unnamed hurricane, although staying mostly out to sea, made landfall in Nova Scotia as a tropical storm.

- July 9, 1995: Tropical Storm Barry hit Nova Scotia while tropical with no known damage.

- September 15, 1996: Hurricane Hortense, the first hurricane to directly strike Nova Scotia while at hurricane strength since Blanche in 1975, struck the Nova Scotian coast as a Category 1 hurricane with strong winds, heavy rain, and power outages causing $3 million worth of damage.

- September 18, 1999: Hurricane Floyd struck the Maritimes after losing tropical characteristics. Despite high interest in Floyd by the CHC, little damage was inflicted in Canada. Floyd did, however, bring winds of 82 kilometres per hour and high seas.

- October 15, 2001: Hurricane Karen brought heavy rain after striking Liverpool. Winds there only gusted to about 102 kilometres per hour, and little damage was reported.

- September 12, 2002: Hurricane Gustav struck Nova Scotia and Newfoundland, both as a Category 1 hurricane. Gustav brought hurricane-force winds to Nova Scotia and dropped at least 50 millimetres of rain across all Nova Scotian sites. The highest rainfall amount was 100 millimetres in Ashdale.

- September 29, 2003: Hurricane Juan is sometimes considered Atlantic Canada's most widely destructive hurricane in over a century. Juan killed eight and caused over $200 million in damage. Power outages in Nova Scotia and Prince Edward Island left over 300,000 Canadians without power for two weeks. Many marinas were destroyed and many small fish craft were damaged or sank. Hurricane-force gusts were reported as far out as 160 kilometres on either side of Juan at landfall with an astounding peak gust of 229 kilometres per hour (equivalent to a Category 4 hurricane) recorded in Halifax Harbour, although it was a Category 2 at landfall with sustained winds of 160 kilometres per hour.

In 2003, Hurricane Juan killed eight and caused over $200 million in damage.

- September 17, 2005: Hurricane Ophelia, after stalling for several days off the coast of the southeastern states, raced up the Atlantic coast. On September 17, Ophelia became extra tropical and moved parallel to the Nova Scotian coast, never making landfall. Ophelia later struck Newfoundland. Although strong winds were forecast, they did not occur and over all damage was less than expected. One indirect death was reported from Ophelia.

- November 6–7, 2007: After gaining hurricane force north of The Bahamas, Noel moved north toward the Cape Cod region of the Massachusetts coast. After swiping southeast of Massachusetts with hurricane-force winds, the offshore center transitioned to a sub-tropical and then extratropical stage. The storm slightly intensified and moved north-northeast to the Nova Scotia coast near Yarmouth. Full hurricane-force conditions occurred over much of southeastern and eastern areas of Nova Scotia from Yarmouth north and eastward to Halifax where 135.16 kilometre per hour winds were recorded at McNabs.

This same area reported large-scale power and utility line damage as well as widespread tree damage. In areas south of Halifax, the tree damage was more severe than destruction caused by Hurricane Juan in 2003, due to the longer transition of Noel over the southern peninsula of Nova Scotia. Though at Category 1 status, Noel in its extratropical stage was responsible for coastal damage to some structures from waves and tides, and wind damage to roofing and windows. Western areas of the province, even well inland received strong gales, the strongest of which occurred in relation to a tropical system since Hurricanes Gerda 1969 and Ginny of 1963.

- September 28, 2008: Hurricane Kyle, after forming as a tropical storm just east of the Bahamas, headed north, making landfall in Nova Scotia as a Category 1 hurricane, causing power outages to 40,000 and $9 million in damage.

- August 23, 2009: Hurricane Bill, a Cape Verde hurricane, brushed by Cape Breton Island causing up to 58.42 millimetres in of rain. An estimated 32,000 residences were reported to have lost power in addition to winds recorded up to 80.47 kilometres per hour. Bill then made landfall at Point Rosie in Newfoundland.

- September 3, 2010: Hurricane Earl made landfall at Western Head, as a minimal hurricane. Earl produced sustained winds of 80 to 120 kilometres per hour throughout Nova Scotia, which resulted in widespread power outages, fallen trees, and minor coastal flooding. After crossing Nova Scotia, Earl sped across Prince Edward Island before emerging into the Gulf of Saint Lawrence. As the storm tracked through the Gulf, western and northern Newfoundland experienced sustained tropical storm conditions. Earl finally transitioned into a non-tropical low approximately 120 kilometres northeast of Anticosti Island.

- October 29-30, 2012: Hurricane Sandy crossed into Canada on October 29 through to early October 30, bringing heavy rain, high winds, and in some places, snow to Ontario, Quebec and the Maritimes, including Nova Scotia.

- July 5, 2014: Hurricane Arthur made landfall in southwestern Nova Scotia on July 5, 2014. The storm at the time was downgraded to a tropical storm. Arthur brought heavy rain, winds and pounding surf to parts of the Atlantic Coast of the province. The strong storm resulted in the loss of power to one-third of the households in Nova Scotia and an estimated 65 per cent of households in New Brunswick.

- October 10, 2016: Hurricane Matthew's remnants affected Nova Scotia and Newfoundland causing heavy rain and strong winds. In Nova Scotia, rain amounts were recorded from east to west as 224.8 millimetres in Sydney and 129.2 millimetres in Port Hawkesbury. More than 100,000 Nova Scotia Power customers lost power. Damage was estimated to be at $7.6 million.

• September 7-8, 2019: The post-tropical system that was once Hurricane Dorian made landfall in Nova Scotia with hurricane-force winds and in Newfoundland with tropical storm-force winds causing millions of dollars worth of damage.

Wettest hurricanes on record

Five of the 10 wettest hurricanes in Canadian history were recorded to have hit Nova Scotia starting with storms holding down the first and second place positions. Two storms tied for the 10th place position.

1st - Harvey (1999), Oxford, 302.0 mm
2nd - Beth (1971), Halifax, 249.9 mm
4th – Matthew (2016), Sydney, 224.8 mm
7th – Bertha (1990), Hunter's Mountain, 191.0 mm
10th – Cristobal (2008), Baccaro Point, 165.0 mm
10th – Leslie (2012), Shubenacadie, 165.0 mm

That's a mighty wind

Nova Scotia has only seen five confirmed tornadoes in all of Nova Scotia's weather record-keeping history and none of them were very strong.

The first known tornado actually touched down on January 30, 1954, in White Point during a rare mid-winter thunderstorm.

On July 22, 1980, an F0 tornado touched down in Roseway. On August 16, 1980, (same year!) an F0 tornado was confirmed in Northport.

On June 24, 1997, an F0 tornado touched down in a ball field in Lantz, Nova Scotia. Golf ball sized hail and intense lightning were also reported in this storm.

On August 18, 1999, a small F0 tornado touched down in Pugwash.

There hasn't been a confirmed tornado touchdown in Nova Scotia since, but as climate change continues, scientists say it's certainly possible for them to become more frequent.

The largest fiddle in the world is located in Sydney, Cape Breton.

Fascinating Facts

The big fiddle

In 2005, Sydney unveiled an eight-ton tribute to the folk music and traditions of the province's Celtic community.

Designed and constructed by Cyril Hearn, the fiddle and the bow reach a height of 17 metres and can be seen by the incoming cruise ships in the harbour.

Made of solid steel, the giant fiddle was dubbed *FIDHEAL MHOR A' CEILIDH* or the "Big Fiddle of the Ceilidh." *Ceilidh* is a Gaelic word which translates into "visit."

The Big Fiddle celebrates the important role fiddlers and their music have played in the cultural heritage of Cape Breton. Fiddle music was first brought to Cape Breton by Scottish immigrants. Today's music also features Acadian, Irish and Mi'kmaq influences.

It took eight months to build this monument which today holds the record for being the largest fiddle in the world.

What is your emergency?

On July 7, 1997, Nova Scotia launched the first province-wide 911 services in Canada.

The state-of-the art 911 system links callers to fire, police, ambulance and poison information within seconds, helping to protect Nova Scotians and their property. The 911 services have 170 dispatchers at four locations that answer about 220,000 calls each year.

Interpretation services are available in more than 170 languages, and texting and TTY services are in place for people with hearing or speech impairments.

The Sultan of Swat

George Herman "Babe" Ruth was born on February 26, 1895, and went on to become one of the best major league baseball players of all time. During two seasons — 1920 and 1927— he hit more home runs (114) than any entire team in the American league, a feat never repeated again by any other player.

While his exploits on the baseball diamond are the stuff of legend, "The Sultan of Swat" made many hunting and fishing trips to Nova Scotia during the early part of the previous century.

Ruth, guided by famed Acadian-French outdoorsmen, Peter and Louis Vacon, was said to have made Tusket one of his favourite destinations, and stories were told about his exploits throughout the province. He could often be seen throughout Southwestern Nova Scotia during his many excursions.

One of those excursions brought the famed New York Yankee to Liverpool in 1937.

This picture shows Babe Ruth at Fort Point in Liverpool during a hunting trip to Nova Scotia in 1937. In this photo, he is holding toddler Hugh Byrne.

Beep! Beep!

If you grew up in Nova Scotia in the mid to late 1960s, then you will know that the word "beep" doesn't necessarily mean move over or get out of the way.

Instead, you will know that "Beep" was a fruit-and-juice-based drink that was made in Nova Scotia during that era and widely distributed across the country.

Originally made by Farmers Cooperative Dairy in the 1960s, Beep was discontinued in March 2010. It was temporarily revived in 2012 as a seasonal summertime drink and was discontinued a second time in 2015.

The ingredients listed on the carton indicated the drink contained water, sugar, fruit juices (orange, apple, apricot, prune and pineapple), citric acid, orange pulp, natural flavours, sodium citrate, canola oil, modified corn starch, sodium benzoate, caramel colour, annatto and ascorbic acid.

Turning on a dime

The original *Bluenose* was built in Lunenburg's legendary Smith and Rhuland Shipyard to compete for the International Fishermen's Trophy. In October 1921, *Bluenose* won her first race and for the next 17 years, she defeated all contenders.

Bluenose as featured on the back of the Canadian dime.

In 1928, *Bluenose* defeated *Thebaud* in the final race series and was named Queen of the North Atlantic fishing fleet. *Bluenose* had become the pride of Nova Scotians and in 1937 the Canadian dime was changed to include an image of the mighty ship.

In 1942, despite the efforts of *Bluenose* Master, Captain Angus J. Walters and others to keep the ship in Nova Scotia, the vessel was sold to the West Indian Trading Company. Four years later, *Bluenose* struck a Haitian reef and sank.

In 1963, *Bluenose II* was built from identical plans as *Bluenose*. She was built in the same shipyard of Smith and Rhuland by some of the same men who had constructed her mother before her.

Bluenose II was sold to the government of Nova Scotia for $1 in 1971 by the Oland family of Halifax and has served as Nova Scotia's tall ship sailing ambassador ever since. The original *Bluenose* and her captain, Angus J. Walters, were inducted into the Canadian Sports Hall of Fame in 1955.

Sláinte! (That's pronounced "slawn-tcha")

When the Scottish arrived on Cape Breton Island in the early 1800s, they brought with them many of traditions and customs of their homeland. One of those secrets was the making of a spirited whisky.

It is that tradition on which Glenora Distillers, based in Glenville located between Mabou and Inverness, has built its business and reputation.

Today, Glenora has the distinction of being Canada's first single-malt distillery. However, because it is not distilled in Scotland, the whisky cannot be called "Scotch."

Glenora's most prominent product is Glen Breton Rare whisky, made in the Scottish-style in that it is a single malt whisky, not a rye, as is the tradition in Canada.

The distillery also makes several specialty whiskies and rum, and operates the Glenora Inn & Distillery as a tourist attraction and bed and breakfast.

Bluenose was launched on March 26, 1921, and won her race in October 1921. Bluenose would remain undefeated in every International Fishermen's Race from 1921 to 1938, giving her the title of the Queen of the North Atlantic Fishing Fleet.

Stamp of approval

Created by the Canadian Bank Note Company, the 50-cent Bluenose stamp from 1929 is considered to be the finest stamp ever produced in Canada. It touts the design of the racing schooner *Bluenose*, sailing around Halifax Harbour. *Bluenose* won the International Fishing Trophy in 1921, 1922, 1923, 1931 and 1938.

The stamp's design is based on pictures of *Bluenose* taken by W.R. MacAskill in 1922-23. The engraver took two of the best pictures of the ship and put both of them into the stamp.

About one million copies of this stamp were printed. Today a mint, never hinged copy of a *Bluenose* stamp in sound collectible condition can command many hundreds of dollars, a testament to the high esteem in which this stamp is held by collectors worldwide. Its estimated value is $700.

A gift for Boston

A year after the Halifax Explosion, the province of Nova Scotia donated a large Christmas tree to the city of Boston to thank the Boston Red Cross and the Massachusetts Public Safety Committee for the assistance they provided during the catastrophe.

The tradition was revived in 1971 and has continued every year since.

The province has very specific guidelines for the selection of the tree that goes to Boston. It must be an attractive balsam fir, white spruce or red spruce, 12 to 16 metres tall, healthy with good colour, of medium to heavy density, be uniform and symmetrical and easy to access.

This monument is dedicated to the unidentified victims of the Halifax Explosion.

The trees usually come from open land, where they can grow tall and full, rather than from tree farms.

Before a tree is cut, each branch is individually tied to the trunk. It takes two men a day and a half to prepare the tree to be cut down. A crane holds the tree at the top while it is cut at the base by a chainsaw.

The tree travels over 1,200 kilometres to Boston, with a stop at the Grand Parade in Halifax for a public send-off. It then travels by truck across Nova Scotia, crosses the Bay of Fundy by ferry and continues by truck to Boston.

The tree arrives in Boston under police escort. In the same way schoolchildren see the tree off in Nova Scotia, schoolchildren from Boston are on hand to welcome it to the Boston Common. Officials placed the tree at the Prudential Center from 1971 until 2002, when they moved it to the Boston Common because of a planned development.

The official tree lighting ceremony usually takes place in November. Traditionally, the Nova Scotia tree is always the first tree lit on the Common. The event is broadcast live and attracts about 20,000 people.

The tree normally requires more than 3,200 hours to decorate, as well as seven kilometres of wire and 7,000 multi-coloured lights.

Come and blow your horn

Founded in 1873 and incorporated in 1906, the Chester Brass Band is a British-style brass ensemble based in Chester. A non-profit volunteer organization funded by its membership, concert series and local patrons, it is the oldest brass band in Nova Scotia.

The band's repertoire includes classical works, marches, hymns, popular melodies and original works written and arranged specifically for them.

The band has performed around the province and across the world. On five occasions, Chester Brass was a top-three finisher at the International Brass Band Championships.

'Farewell to Nova Scotia'

The official song of Nova Scotia, *Farewell to Nova Scotia*, which has also become known as *The Nova Scotia Song*, is a favourite folk song of unknown authorship.

It is believed to have been written shortly before or during the First World War. The song invokes images of a time when Nova Scotia was famed for wooden ships and iron men.

Derived from the 1791 Scottish folk song *The Soldier's Adieu* based on a poem by Scottish poet Robert Tannahill and printed in 1803 in a Glasgow newspaper, the song was changed to reflect a soldier's sorrow at leaving the hills behind as he heads out to sea.

In 1928, famed Nova Scotian folklorist Helen Creighton met with Dr. Henry Munro, the Superintendent of Education for the Province of Nova Scotia, as she began her search for localized literary material. He showed her a copy of *Sea Songs and Ballads from Nova Scotia* by W. Roy MacKenzie and suggested Creighton attempt to find more songs.

Creighton took his advice and throughout the 1930s, she travelled around Nova Scotia, collecting songs, tales and customs of Gaelic, English, German, Mi'kmaq, African and Acadian origin. Frequently, she had to walk or sail to remote regions to satisfy her interest, all the while pushing a metre-long melodeon (an accordion or organ) in a wheelbarrow.

Among Creighton's many contributions to Nova Scotia culture and folklore was the discovery of the traditional *Nova Scotia Song*, first collected in 1933 from Ann Greenough in Petpeswick on the Eastern Shore.

Farewell to Nova Scotia gained its greatest popularity when it was recorded in 1964 by Catherine McKinnon to be used as the theme song of the Halifax CBC television show *Singalong Jubilee*.

Today, the song is used by many to reflect the sentiments of mass migrations of young people from Nova Scotia westward to Ontario and Alberta.

5 FAST FACTS

1. The longest stretch of fog ever recorded in Nova Scotia was 85 days in the summer of 1967 in Yarmouth. There were only seven days that summer when Yarmouth was fog-free.

2. The Prince of Wales Tower was built between 1796 and 1797 and was the first of its kind in North America. Edward, Duke of Kent, ordered the tower built on high ground behind Point Pleasant to defend batteries on Pleasant Point in Halifax, located to prevent enemy ships from entering the harbour. The Martello tower, named for Edward's older brother, is round, built of stone and is almost three times as wide as it is tall. There were six mounted guns on the roof and four on the second story. Today it is national historic site.

3. In 1854, when Samuel McKeen of Mabou, Cape Breton, arranged a series of cogged gears to record the distance travelled by a wheel, which in those days was a carriage wheel, he was actually inventing the odometer. He took it a step further by adding a hammer and bell so the carriage passenger could hear as each mile marker was passed.

4. The first reported quintuplets in Canada were born in Little Egypt, Pictou County, in 1880. The three girls and two boys all died within two days.

5. James A. Ross of Halifax is responsible for the backup lights on your automobile. In 1919, Ross realized the importance of such a device and connected the light to a switch on the gearshift lever. By doing so, he lit the way for all future drivers.

A future president comes to Oak Island

In 1909, at the age of 27, future U.S. president Franklin Delano Roosevelt joined the ranks of the Old Gold Salvage and Wrecking Company seeking treasure believed to be hidden on Oak Island.

The affluent, Harvard-educated Roosevelt spent that summer off the shores of Nova Scotia, as hopeful to find the treasure as any who had preceded him. According to written correspondence, Roosevelt nurtured an interest in the Oak Island mystery well into his presidency.

In a letter to a friend, the president intimated his intentions to return to the island on Mahone Bay, but was prevented from doing so by the outbreak of war in Europe. However, Roosevelt was not the only historically prominent treasure hunter with dreams of finding the Oak Island treasure.

Famed Hollywood actors Errol Flynn and John Wayne also sought to solve the buried mystery in the 1940s. And today, despite decades of searching and hundreds of millions of dollars, the Oak Island Mystery remains intact.

Harry Chapin and the Ovens Park

The Ovens Natural Park is located near Feltzen South in Lunenburg County on the province's South Shore, a busy summer campground that boarders on the Atlantic Ocean.

It was once the gold mining property of Samuel Cunard, a Halifax businessman who had much greater success in developing his shipping and mail-delivery business between Halifax, Boston and England than in mining gold for profit.

The Ovens refers, in fact, to the sea caves excavated by Cunard's miners during the gold-rush days of the 1850s. They are deep enough to kayak into on calm summer days. Appropriately, the park's restaurant is called the Ol' Miners Diner.

The Ovens Park is owned by Steve and Angel Chapin and has been in their hands for more than 30 years. Steve is Harry Chapin's younger brother and was his musical director during Harry's busy touring days in the 1970s.

Highway 103, also known as Fishermens' Memorial Highway, runs from Yarmouth to Halifax.

Life is a highway

All the major highways crisscrossing Nova Scotia have a number attached starting with 100. Of those, some also have alternate names:

Highway 101: Harvest Highway; 310 kilometres from Bedford to Yarmouth through the Annapolis Valley.

Highway 102: Veterans' Memorial Highway; 100 kilometres from Halifax to Truro.

Highway 103: Fishermens' Memorial Highway; 294 kilometres from Halifax to Yarmouth through the South Shore.

Highway 104: Miners' Memorial Highway (Trans-Canada Highway); 322 kilometres from the New Brunswick border across the Canso Causeway to St. Peters in Cape Breton.

Highway 105: Mabel & Alexander Graham Bell Way (Trans-Canada Highway); 294 kilometres from Port Hawkesbury through Baddeck to the Newfoundland ferry terminal in North Sydney.

Highway 106: Jubilee Highway (Trans-Canada Highway); 19 kilometres from Westveille at the Pictou Causeway to the PEI ferry terminal in Caribou.

Highway 107: 38 kilometres from Burnside through Lake Echo and Porters Lake to Musquodoboit Harbour.

Highway 111: 38 kilometres from Eastern Passage to Dartmouth.

Highway 113: 9.9 kilometres from Highway 102 to Highway 103.

Highway 118: Lakeview Drive, 15.5 kilometres from Dartmouth Crossing through Waverley to Fall River.

Highway 125: Peacekeepers' Way, 18 kilometres from North Sydney to Sydney.

Highway 142: 6 kilometres from Highway 104 to Springhill.

Highway 162: 4.3 kilometres from Highway 105 in Bras D'Or to Point Aconi.

Would you like one scoop or two?

For all the various and weird ice cream flavours available on the market today, one of the most popular continues to be one that was first created over a century ago right here in Nova Scotia.

Chef Hannah Young in Wolfville is credited with creating grapenut ice cream in 1919 when she ran out of fresh fruit to add to ice cream, and decided to throw in several handfuls of the popular Grape-Nuts cereal.

One version of the origin story says Hannah worked at The Palms restaurant when the recipe was created.

Another version explains that Hannah and her son, Cecil, ran an ice cream parlour in Wolfville in which they sold various items including chocolate treats, biscuits, and sauces. However, one of their most popular products was homemade ice cream.

The Youngs sold a variety of flavours including those infused with corn syrup, maple walnut, and pieces of ribbon candy at Christmas, as well as a variety of fruit and nuts. The grapenut flavour became an instant success and, to this day, continues to be one of the best-selling flavours of ice cream amid the myriad of strange and exotic choices available to consumers.

In 1920, the Young's ice cream parlour moved across the street and became renamed as the The Palms restaurant.

To the moon and back

Another popular ice cream flavour with Nova Scotian roots is one with the unusual name, Moon Mist, an eye-catching, mouthwatering blend of three distinct flavours — grape, banana and bubblegum. It's a curious combo, to say the least.

One origin theory says that a flavour company shopped the combination around in the early 1980s, as Nova Scotian dairies started churning out the tricoloured variety at roughly the same time. The result was a hit in Canada's Atlantic provinces, where it's the most popular flavour on the market.

Opinions vary on the reason for its rating. There's the nostalgia factor, and its status as a regional specialty makes it a rare treat for Nova Scotians far from home —dairies outside of the province sometimes offer it, too. But much of the appeal may lie in its vibrant colours — the purple, yellow, and blue of Moon Mist ice cream are as vivid as a summer day by the water.

One of the most popular ice cream flavours in Canada — Moon Mist — was invented here in Nova Scotia.

An image of Crescent Beach as seen on the Canadian $50 bill.

Hey mister, can you spare a dime or maybe $50?

Three pieces of Canadian currency depict images synonymous to the South Shore:

Bluenose first appeared on the dime in 1937.

Lunenburg waterfront was featured on the old Canadian $100 bill.

And Crescent Beach, 1.5 kilometres of sand in Lockeport, was once featured on the Canadian $50 bill.

Lovely lupines

In summertime, we see lupines everywhere in Nova Scotia.

For roughly two to three weeks, the tall stalks of pretty pink, white or purple flowers appear in the ditches, along the roadside, at the water's edge, in open fields and even in our backyards. They are so common that we assume they are native to the habitat, but we assume incorrectly.

It is believed that all of the lupines blooming every summer in Nova Scotia actually came from a single planting in Yarmouth in the 1970s when they were sold as garden plants.

According to the Facebook group Maritime Monsters, a Dutch woman, Miss Phoebe Robbins brought the seeds from Holland and planted them in the Chebogue region early last century. From there they spread throughout the countryside and across the province.

Despite their abundance in Nova Scotia every summer, lupines are not a native plant.

Canada's first official tartan

In 1953, one of Nova Scotia's talented home weavers, Mrs. Bessie Murray, designed a tartan in response to a province-wide request from the Nova Scotia Sheep Association for examples of the many ways local wool could be used.

Originally intended only for display at the agricultural exhibition in Truro, Mrs. Murray's design so captured the imagination of Nova Scotians that it was adopted as the Provincial Tartan by an Order in Council in 1955, making it the first provincial tartan in Canada.

The following year, the Tartan was submitted to the Court of the Lord Lyon King of Arms, and was registered with Her Majesty's Register Office in Edinburgh, Scotland.

As a note of interest, the Lord Lyon King of Arms is the Scottish official empowered to regulate heraldry in that country, to oversee state ceremony in Scotland, to grant new arms to persons or organizations, and to confirm or deny pedigrees and claims to existing arms. That officer is the judge of the oldest functioning Heraldic court in the world.

In 1964, the House of Assembly passed the Tartan Act, which describes the design and outlines how it is to be manufactured and used. The Nova Scotia Tartan does not represent a clan; it can be worn by anyone.

In the design, blue denotes the ever-present sea; white is the colour of the foaming waves and granite shore. Green recalls "the forest primeval" of Acadia. The Province's historic Royal Charter is represented by twin bands of gold enclosing a red line honouring the royal lion rampant found on the Nova Scotia Coat of Arms.

A bird on the edge

Shelburne County has the highest concentration of plover beaches in the entire province.

The piping plover is a small bird with a large rounded head, a short, thick neck and a stubby bill. It is a sand-coloured, dull gray/khaki, sparrow-sized shorebird. The adult has yellow-orange legs, a black band across the forehead from eye to eye, and a black ring around the neck during the breeding season.

During the non-breeding season, the black bands become less pronounced. Its bill is orange with a black tip and it ranges in size from 15 to 19 centimetres in length. They only have a wingspan of 35 to 41 centimetres and a mass of 42 to 64 grams.

The piping plover lives the majority of its life on open sandy beaches or rocky shores, often in high, dry sections away from water. They can be found on the Atlantic Coast of North America on the ocean or bay beaches and on the shores of the Great Lakes. It builds its nests higher on the shore, often near beach grass.

The piping plover is threatened and endangered globally and in Eastern Canada, is found only on coastal beaches. In 1985, the Committee declared it an endangered species on the Status of Endangered Wildlife in Canada.

The endangered piping plover.

A large population in Ontario has disappeared entirely largely because of human incursion on their natural habitat.

Many of the region's beaches take precaution during breeding season, posting warning signs and closing off specific areas. In partnership with the Canadian Wildlife Service and Department of Natural Resources, Bird Studies Canada runs the piping plover Conservation Program in Nova Scotia.

Staff and volunteers monitor plover beaches and aside from outreach activities, use signs and sometimes signs and rope (symbolic fencing) to alert beachgoers to the presence of plovers and their nests.

The lonely road

Route 203 is a collector road located in Shelburne and Yarmouth Counties.

The road runs through a sparsely populated area including Argyle Municipality from Shelburne at Trunk 3 along the boarder of the Tobeatic Wilderness Area through Kemptville and connects to Route 340 at Carleton.

The village of East Kemptville is the only part of a municipality in Nova Scotia disconnected from the rest of the district by roads, and accessible only from other districts via Highway 203.

At 83 kilometres in length, Route 203 is considered the loneliest road in the province because it has the longest uninhabited stretch of any paved highway in Nova Scotia.

A stretch of Route 203, the loneliest road in Nova Scotia.

This record bites

In August 2004, while a local man was participating in the annual shark derby in the waters off the coast of Yarmouth, he ended up making a catch that was one for the record books.

Fishing with a rod and reel, using a 200-pound test line and a hook baited with mackerel, and chumming 48 miles out of Yarmouth, it wasn't long until Jamie Doucette felt the bite.

He knew right away it was a big one. He worked it for 30 minutes before he saw the fin, rising a good foot from the water about 150 yards out. It was a shortfin mako shark. A regular visitor to Maritime waters, the sharks are often reported chasing mackerel with the Gulf Stream into the Bay of Fundy.

When they finally got it on the official scale, lifted into place by a forklift to keep the scale from tipping, the shark weighed in at an astonishing 1,082 pounds — a Canadian record and one of the largest ever caught. The female mako shark measured 10 feet, 11 inches in length and was estimated to be about 25 years old.

In August 2016, the second largest shark ever caught near Nova Scotia was landed in waters off the coast of Lockeport. It weighed in at 1,076 pounds and was only three pounds lighter than the shark caught in Yarmouth.

Marshall Bower, captain of the *High Interest* out of Lockeport, along with his crew caught the 11-foot, 10–inch shark. It only took him 45 minutes to reel in.

A local company provided a backhoe to help get the shark off of the boat.

When Department of Fisheries and Oceans officials cut open the shark's belly, they found a full-sized harbour porpoise inside.

This one also bites

While shark attacks in Nova Scotia waters are rare, two have been recorded.

The first shark attack was reported to have occurred August 30, 1891, in Halifax. The victim, John Roult, died from his injuries.

The second attack occurred on July 9, 1953 at Fourchu on Cape Breton Island. The male victim survived his injuries.

A small record

Sandford, a popular fishing spot for the last hundred years near Yarmouth, is home to the world's smallest operating drawbridge.

Located at the Sandford Wharf (500 Ross Durkee Road) the drawbridge was built in 1915 so that fishermen and visitors could cross from one side of the Sandford wharf system to the other without having to travel back on the road.

The smallest drawbridge in the world is located in Sandford, Yarmouth County.

From the land to the sky

The Mill Village Teleglobe Earth Satellite Station located in Charleston was the first ground station for satellite communication in Canada.

Built in 1963 at a cost of $9 million, the vast complex was part of an extensive satellite program for the transmission of telephone and television signals between North America and Europe.

Built just after the Russians launched the Sputnik satellite, the Charleston station was one of only five in the world at the time — and one of only two in North America.

Mill Village, Nova Scotia, was chosen because of its remote location — with very little radio interference — and was also close to railways and roads to bring the large equipment necessary to build the station. It was dedicated to beaming telephone and television signals from a fixed satellite, and drew in other major events such as Muhammad Ali's Rumble in the Jungle.

During its heyday, there were probably up to 60 people working there.

As the technology became obsolete, the station was eventually phased out and permanently shuttered in 1986.

The first ground station for satellite communication in Canada was located in Charleston, Queens County.

The dory story

The Grand Banks dory is an old design originally developed to fish the Grand Banks off the coast of Nova Scotia.

The dories filled the need for a lightweight boat able to cover many miles by oar or sail to survive the sudden gales that frequent that area. They were originally built in boatyards in Nova Scotia; one of the most famous is the J. C. Williams Dory Shop in Shelburne.

When John Williams' shop was established in 1880, it was part of a booming dory-building industry, which at its peak, included at least seven shops along the Shelburne waterfront.

During the early part of the century, Williams' business produced 350 dories per year. Most of these dories were sold to Nova Scotian and American fishing captains who called at Shelburne to outfit their schooners before sailing to the offshore fishing grounds.

That's one big fish

The Town of Wedgeport was once known as the Sport Tuna Fishing Capital of the World and attracted such historical figures as President Franklin D. Roosevelt, Amelia Earhart, Michael and Helen Lerner, Zane Grey and Ernest Hemingway.

Grey, the famed American writer of western novels, was known to have come to the province's South Shore on many occasions during the first half of the previous century in pursuit of his favourite sport, tuna fishing. He would hire Capt. Laurie Mitchell of Liverpool as his guide for his fishing excursions. In his book *Tales of Swordfish and Tuna* (1927), Grey says, "We left the boats and motored back to Liverpool where we purchased rubber boots, coats, pants, and hats called southwesters. Now let it rain!"

Renowned novelist Zane Grey with his world record tuna, weighing 758 lbs., caught off the coast of East Jordan, Shelburne County, on August 22, 1924.

The world's biggest Atlantic Bluefin Tuna ever recorded was caught by Ken Fraser in Aulds Cove on October 26, 1979. He landed the 1,496-pound (679 kilograms) fish in an impressive 45 minutes. It measured 13 feet in length.

On average, Bluefins typically weigh more than 750 pounds.

The Atlantic Bluefin Tuna is one of the largest, fastest and most gorgeously coloured of all the world's fishes. Their torpedo-shaped, streamlined bodies are built for speed and endurance.

Their colouring — metallic blue on top and shimmering silver-white on the bottom — helps camouflage them from above and below. And their voracious appetite and varied diet pushes their average size to a whopping 6.5 feet (two metres) in length and 550 pounds (250 kilograms), although much larger specimens are not uncommon.

They are among the most ambitiously migratory of all fish, and some tagged specimens have been tracked swimming from North American to European waters several times a year.

Flat-bottomed boats

Tuna Flats are native to St. Margaret's Bay. They're the squat, green boats that are towed behind the larger vessels that fish mackerel and tuna.

The boats got their name from the fact that three or four burly men could all stand on one side and haul a one thousand pound tuna over the side without capsizing the boat.

Due to their low, wide design, they are very cumbersome to row.

Amelia Earhart lands in Nova Scotia

By the time of her disappearance in 1937, Amelia Earhart had logged thousands of miles and hundreds of hours of airtime. In an age when men dominated the sky, Earhart was a household name. She was the first woman to fly across the Atlantic — a feat she accomplished in June of 1928.

En route to infamy, Earhart was forced to make an unexpected stopover in Eastern Passage, here in Nova Scotia on June 23, 1928. She was a passenger on a Fokker Trimotor floatplane called Friendship. Before it could complete its transatlantic flight, it ran into heavy fog over Halifax.

Halifax journalist and author Dean Jobb says the three crew members on board, including Earhart, didn't want to stay, but weather conditions left them no choice.

"They had no intention of coming to Halifax," Jobb says in an ATV news item recalling the historic visit. "In fact, it sounds like they were beyond Halifax when they really had to turn back and reground and get more fuel and wait for the weather to break."

The crew of the Friendship was forced to spend the night. Earhart tried to keep to herself, but Jobb says it was tough.

"She was here in Halifax for a day, didn't leave the plane at first and then finally went to a hotel in Dartmouth and stayed there the whole time," he says. "She did pose for a picture with two of the crew, but it was the pilot and navigator that ended up talking to the press and holding them at bay."

Earhart would go on to greater things, inspiring generations of female aviators and trailblazers.

On May 20, 1932, Earhart was in Harbour Grace, Newfoundland, just before the world's first transatlantic solo flight by a woma.

Ameila Earhart stops over in Eastern Passage on June 23, 1928, en route to becoming the first woman to fly across the Atlantic. Pictured with Earhart are Wilmer Stultz and Slim Gordon.

Other solo flights would follow, including her attempt to circumnavigate the globe in 1937, cementing Earhart's place in the history books.

Starting in California, she and navigator Fred Noonan began their journey. They left Miami on June 1, travelling from South America, to Africa, and to Northeast Asia. Finally, 22,000 miles later, they landed in New Guinea.

With 7,000 miles to go, they took off again, heading to a small island about 2,500 miles away between Australia and Hawaii. But they never made it, launching one of the most enduring mysteries of all time.

The search for Earhart's plane has been ongoing for generations.

Hindenburg flies over Nova Scotia

On July 4, 1936, the German airship Hindenburg flew over Nova Scotia, possibly taking pictures for German intelligence.

It appeared to fly low over Halifax and the province in general but especially low over Shelburne, Chester and Hazel Hill.

The Halifax Herald reported in bold print that perhaps "those aboard the Hindenburg were taking pictures of Halifax and other places, for the files of the German air ministry."

The airliner flew at an altitude of about 1000 feet, but due to its size the dirigible seemed to be just above the tree line. Military authorities said photographs could easily be taken up to 10,000 feet and would be impossible to thwart.

The next year would be the Hindenburg's last as it came to an abrupt end in 1937 when it exploded while attempting to dock at the Naval Air Station Lakehurst in Manchester Township, New Jersey.

The Hindenburg caught fire, igniting the flammable gas within, killing 35 of the 97 people on board   13 passengers and 22 crewmen. One member of the grounds crew also died in the tragedy.

The incident shattered public confidence in the giant, passenger-carrying, rigid airship and marked the abrupt end of the airship era.

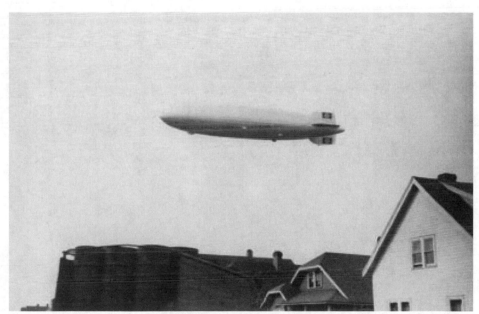

Hindenburg flying over Halifax Citadel in 1936 before the disaster. The Hindenburg came straight up from Halifax to Blomidon, and then went straight down the middle of the Bay.

5 FAST FACTS

1. Annapolis Royal was settled in 1605 by Samuel de Champlain and Pierre Du Gua de Monts. It is the oldest continuous European settlement north of St. Augustine, Florida. Port Royal was retained by France during most of the 17th century but was subject to frequent capture by the British. It would be returned to France by recapture or treaty negotiations,. In 1713, the Treaty of Utrecht returned Port Royal to the British for the last time. Annapolis Royal was the capital of Nova Scotia from 1710 until the founding of Halifax in 1749.

2. Shipping magnate Sir Samuel Cunard was born November 21, 1787, in Halifax. The son of a master carpenter and timber merchant who had fled the American Revolution and settled in Halifax, Samuel founded the Cunard Line in 1840.

3. Adopted as the provincial berry in January 1996, the wild blueberry is native to Nova Scotia — one of the five regions in Canada in which the berries grow naturally. Originally hand-picked in the wild, the blueberry is now cultivated throughout Nova Scotia and harvested by machines. Once popular primarily as market fare, the blueberries are now grown, frozen and exported to a number of countries around the world.

4. Adopted as the provincial tree by an Act of the House of Assembly in 1988, the red spruce represents the strength and resiliency of Nova Scotians. Able to survive in virtually any terrain and condition, the red spruce is the anchor of Nova Scotia's economy and is the province's number one lumber product. During early settlement, the twigs of the red spruce were brewed into a tea, which made an effective cure for scurvy. It has been a staple of the shipbuilding industry for centuries.

5. Adopted as the provincial bird of Nova Scotia in 1994 by an Act of the House of Assembly, the osprey is a bird of prey sized between the larger eagle and the smaller hawk. Their main source of food is salt-water or fresh-water fish, depending on where they roost and hunt, and can often be seen hovering above the ocean, rivers and lakes looking for a meal. Then, in a spectacular display of aerobatics, they dive feet first, skimming the water's surface, and then rise majestically into the air with a fish clasped in their talons.

Historically Speaking

All-black hockey emerges in Halifax

Windsor, Nova Scotia, is widely accepted as the birthplace of hockey, but the province is also home of Canada's first all-black hockey league.

In the late 19th century, Baptist Church leaders believed all-black hockey would be a great way to attract young black men to the Church to strengthen their religious path. Games became community events that brought mixed audiences together in the stands while post-game meals united black players from different communities.

There was no predetermined game schedule. Rather, teams challenged each other to matches by telegraph or by placing ads in local newspapers. Organizers, players and newspapers of the day called the ultimate prize the Colored Hockey Championship, a term not in use today.

Some of the game's early developments, such as the earliest recorded uses of down-to-the-ice goaltending, were later adopted by players in "white-only" leagues, including profes-sional leagues. At that time, hockey goalies in other leagues stood upright.

The first record of an all-black hockey game in the Halifax area dates back to March 1895 and involved the Dartmouth Jubilees and the Halifax Stanleys. Six more teams would soon form, including one from Prince Edward Island. There were the Halifax Eurekas, Africville Sea-Sides, Truro Victorias, Hammonds Plains Moss Backs, Amherst Royals and Charlotte-town West End Rangers.

The all-black league began 23 years before the National Hockey League was founded and has been credited with some innovations which exist in the NHL today. Most notably, it is claimed that the first player to use the slapshot was Eddie Martin of the Halifax Eurekas.

The golden era of all-black hockey was between 1900 and 1905, when games often outdrew those of "white-only" leagues, but teams continued to play for the Colored Hockey Champi-onship until the 1930s.

Hitting the ice

Hockey was not invented, nor did it start on a certain day of a particular year.

Historical records suggest that hockey originated around 1800, in Windsor, where boys of Canada's first college, King's College School established in 1788, adapted the exciting field game of hurley to the ice of their favourite skating ponds. The new winter game was called ice hurley.

Over a period of decades, ice hurley gradually developed into ice hockey.

A man who is still North America's most quoted author, Thomas Chandler Haliburton, born in Windsor in 1796, told of King's boys playing "hurley on the ice" when he was a young student at the school around 1800. This is the earliest reference in English literature of a stickball game being played on ice in Canada.

Haliburton, who wrote the first history of Nova Scotia, was the first Canadian to acquire international acclaim as a writer, and the account of his recollection is therefore of great significance.

Soon after the boys of King's College School adapted hurley to the ice, the soldiers at Fort Edward in Windsor took up the new game. They carried the game to Halifax where it, in turn, gained momentum as it was played on the many Dartmouth Lakes and frozen inlets of Halifax Harbour.

The development of ice hurley into ice hockey during the 19th century is chronicled in the newspapers of Nova Scotia.

Though the origins have been widely debated, there's no question that hockey is Canada's game — whether it was first developed in Windsor or Kingston, Ontario, or in Montreal where, on March 3, 1875, modern hockey was first established during an indoor game at Victoria Skating Rink in Montreal.

It was there that Halifax native James Creighton organized the game with mainly McGill University students. The nine-member teams played on the ice with a flat wooden puck.

By 1877, some basic rules were established which included no forward passing and seven players on the ice. The first hockey team, the McGill Hockey Club, was established two years later. From there, the Amateur Hockey Association of Canada was formed in 1886, which included members from Ottawa, Quebec City, as well as Montreal.

Hockey quickly gained in popularity and in 1892 Governor General Lord Stanley donated the Dominion Challenge Cup, now known as the Stanley Cup. In 1895, the Coloured Hockey League was established in Nova Scotia, and women's teams formed at McGill a year later.

In 1909, the National Hockey Association was established which, in 1917, became the National Hockey League. Hockey went on to debut at the 1920 Summer Olympics in Antwerp.

From there hockey grew and evolved into the sport we know today.

This street sign is proof that at one time Liverpool was home to Gorham College.

Give It the old college try

Did you know there is a College Street in Liverpool, but no college?

It's true, but there used to be.

The story starts with Jabez Gorham who was born in 1707 and produced a son of the same name in 1726. He married Mary Burbank at Plymouth, Massachusetts, on November 16, 1750. Six children were born to the couple; four died in infancy.

Gorham moved to Liverpool in 1760 and became one of the proprietors of the township. Another six children were born here. James, the second son, was to become Liverpool's first and most generous philanthropist. In the 80 years of his life here, he saw the settlement grow from a mere fishing village to a prosperous sea port.

James Gorham amassed a fortune through trading on the high seas. During the War of 1812 he was a shareholder in the privateer *Retaliation*. When James Gorham died on August 5, 1841, his widow endowed $12,000 to Gorham College, a boarding school that out-of-town scholars could attend.

With the $12,000 bequest from the Gorham estate, Congregationalists began a movement throughout the membership to establish an institution here. Gorham also willed a large tract of land where the new college would be erected. The site selected was a plot of rising ground commanding a view of Liverpool Harbour and the town.

In 1848, Mrs. Gorham laid the cornerstone of the institution that would bear her husband's name, as requested in his will. The college was a long, plain building without ornamentation. The building was of wood construction and painted white. The structure was so designed that at the front ground level, wings could be added later to enhance its appearance. The long dining hall also served for study during evening hours.

Apartments for the college president and his family were located on the second storey, as were the dormitory rooms for the students who were boarding at the college. These were plainly decorated and furnished. The structure stood 300 feet back from what was to become College Street. A wide, gravelled walk, half-circle in shape, formed the approach.

In the summer of 1851, notices about Gorham College appeared in Maritime and New England newspapers promoting the first and second terms. A Junior School was included in the system and boys were admitted who could read and write. The students came from Nova Scotia, New Brunswick, and the states of Maine and Massachusetts. There was also a quota for Milton, Brooklyn and Bristol (now Bristol Avenue) and it was filled at once.

A large sum of money had been collected through the efforts of the Clements family of Yarmouth. It was to be applied to finishing the college's third storey, which was to be an auditorium for public recreational purposes. The room was to be named Clement's Hall.

Work had started on this project early in the New Year and it neared completion. However, at the noon hour on February 7, 1854, when faculty and students were gathered for dinner, fire was discovered in the assembly hall. Flames spread rapidly due to the highly inflammable paints and varnishes present, and by nightfall, the entire structure was a smouldering ruin. The life of Liverpool's Gorham College (1848-1854) was tragically brief.

In grand style

Freemasonry is the largest and oldest men's fraternity in the world.

Nova Scotia is the birthplace of Freemasonry in Canada where, in 1738 at Annapolis Royal, Nova Scotia, the first Masonic Lodge was founded in Canada.

Since then, the Fraternity has developed a rich history in the province. One of the most famous Nova Scotia Freemasons was Alexander Keith who was a famous beer brewer and mayor of Halifax.

The first Masonic Lodge in Canada was founded in 1738 at Annapolis Royal, Nova Scotia.

Today, the Fraternity operates under the Grand Lodge of Nova Scotia Ancient Free and Accepted Masons.

Historic Halifax

Founded in 1749, the city of Halifax is surrounded by a number of historic sites, most notably Georges Island.

According to Parks Canada, the British military forces occupied Georges Island in 1750. Its strategic position in the middle of Halifax Harbour catapulted it to the heart of seaward defences for one of the principal naval stations in the British Empire in the 18th and 19th centuries.

The island came under the command of Prince Edward in 1794 amidst tensions between the United Kingdom and the United States. Home to Fort Charlotte and later its two powerful, seaward-facing batteries and underground tunnel complex, the island is also the site of one of Canada's first fully automated lighthouses.

Georges Island was also used as a prison in the early years. Between 1755 and 1763, during the deportation of the Acadians, known as Le Grand Dérangement (The Great Upheaval), the island became a holding area for large numbers of Acadians.

Thanks to its complex of subterranean passages and tunnels, this mysterious island has been the subject of local folklore for generations.

Halifax Citadel is another historic strategic military location. It's obvious why this hilltop location with a commanding view of the Halifax harbour was chosen in 1749 for the fort destined to protect the city.

The Halifax Citadel's star shaped architecture is equally as impressive from the inside and out. It is part of a series of forts — each one showcasing changes over time to its defenses, each significantly different than its predecessor — that protected Halifax Harbour from 1749 to 1906.

The fort was so strategically important that it was rebuilt three times yet it was never once attacked.

Another historic Halifax structure is the Prince of Wales Tower whose constructed began in the 1790s.

The first tower of its type ever built in North America, the Prince of Wales Tower is part of the robust Halifax Defence Complex which included nearby Halifax Citadel to protect British sea batteries from a French landward attack.

This solid, thick walled Martello tower stands guard on the highest point of Point Pleasant Park. Today, interpretive panels portray the tower's history, architectural features and significance as a defensive structure from more than two centuries ago in an era of military clashes between British and French forces.

Almost three times as wide as it is high, with eight-foot thick walls, the Prince of Wales Tower is the oldest Martello tower in North America. While other locations within the defence complex were in use until after the Second World War, changing military technology rendered the Prince of Wales Tower obsolete by the time the surrounding land was leased to the city for a park in 1866.

Built in the 1880s, Fort McNab is another important military fixture. At one time, it was the most powerful guardian of Halifax, thanks to its powerful breech-loading guns.

Fort McNab served as an important counter-bombardment battery in the two World Wars before being decommissioned in 1959 and becoming a national historic site in 1965.

Because of its strategic location and advanced technology, Fort McNab was the gatekeeper of Halifax Harbour for many decades. Located at the southern end of McNabs Island, the fort was once part of Canada's front line of seaward defence.

Today, the remains of the fortifications can be accessed by rough trails and former military roads on the island. The guns, shelters and searchlight emplacements are an enduring reminder of the importance of this once-formidable fort.

5 FAST FACTS

1. Charles Dickens, the celebrated novelist and seasoned traveller, visited Halifax in 1842. Dickens was anxious to begin the trip in spite of the prospect of a stormy crossing, so he and wife, Catherine, departed Liverpool, England, on the steamship Britannia on January 2, 1842. After a rough voyage during which he said the little vessel was often "stopped, staggered and shivered by the angry sea," they arrived in Halifax on the 19th.

2. At four kilometres, the Halifax Harbourwalk is the world's longest downtown boardwalk. It stretches along the waterfront for 10 city blocks from Casino Nova Scotia to the Canadian Museum of Immigration at Pier 21.

3. Located in the 1820s Keith's Brewery Building, the Halifax Farmers' Brewery Market is the old oldest farmers' market in Canada.

4. The Halifax-Dartmouth ferry, established in 1752, is the oldest salt water ferry service in North America.

5. Canada's oldest newspaper and the third oldest in North America is the *Halifax Gazette*. The first issue, a half sheet with bits of news and some advertising, was published on March 23, 1752. The Halifax Gazette lives on today as the Nova Scotia Royal Gazette, official government publication for legal notices and proclamations.

Samuel Mack died at the age of 47 and was buried in the Old Port Medway Cemetery in 1783.

A history built of wood

The first pulpwood mill in Nova Scotia was built in 1880 at Salter's Falls in Charleston, Queens County, and it was called the Nova Scotia Wood Pulp and Paper Company.

After the first mill was razed by fire in June 1903, the second Nova Scotia Wood Pulp and Paper Company mill was built soon after but that mill also burned in 1947. It never reopened.

The story of lumbering in Nova Scotia starts with Samuel Mack who came from Connecticut in 1764 and made his home in the new settlement of Liverpool. Life was difficult for the Mack family when Sam was born in 1737 but fortunes changed for him when he married Lydia Brainerd from a prosperous farming family.

It is believed that Samuel's father-in-law may have funded an earlier trip for Samuel to Nova Scotia to assess the timberlands here. The Mack family was notable for their ability in milling and dam building, having built a substantial dam across the Connecticut River; it's reasonable to assume he would be scouting new areas for potential investment.

Samuel had two daughters by his first wife, Lydia, who died soon after in 1760. He moved to Nova Scotia about two years later, and purchased a share in a lumber mill that had recently been built by Lodowick Smith along with his partner Dr. Thomas Mosely, and funded by six other Liverpool proprietors.

The location of that mill was first called Port Medway Mills, (or Port Mills) then Mills Village and now Mill Village, Queens County.

In time, Mack soon bought this mill from the other owners and built another mill nearby (both mills perhaps on a small island in the Medway River). He had a good business from this location and enjoyed a regular association with Simeon Perkins, another notable Nova Scotian.

Samuel was married in 1766 to Desire Cohoon, the daughter of one of the original founders and proprietors of Liverpool. Samuel and Desire had several children; their sons also continued in the lumber business well into the 1800s.

By all accounts, Samuel and his progeny became respectable mill owners and businessmen expanding their lumbering operations into nearby Bridgewater.

Samuel Mack died at the age of 47 and was buried in the Old Port Medway Cemetery in 1783. Eventually, Mrs. Mack remarried and her new husband took over the business and proceeded to operate a modest milling operation along the river.

Worthy of note here is the fact that Samuel Mack was the great uncle of Joseph Smith Jr. who became the prophet and founder of the Mormon Church. Joseph's mother, Lucy, was the daughter of Solomon who was Samuel's brother.

At 4.5 metres in height and 7.5 metres in length, "Marvin" the Mastodon is one of the biggest statues in the province.

Marvin the Mastodon

When you are at Mastodon Ridge in Stewiacke you are halfway between the equator and the North Pole.

Mastodon Ridge started to come to life January 1995 with the unveiling of a life-size mastodon replica that was commissioned in 1994 following the discovery of mastodon bones in nearby Milford in 1991.

At 4.5 metres in height and 7.5 metres in length, "Marvin" the Mastodon is one of the biggest statues in the province.

Evidence that mastodons roamed the forests and grasslands of the Maritime provinces comes from the discovery of partial skeletons and teeth.

In 1991, a partial skeleton of an adult male was unearthed in the Gypsum Quarry in Milford, Nova Scotia. About 80,000 years ago this male mastodon fell into a sinkhole, broke its leg and drowned. Thousands of years passed and the sinkhole filled with vegetation and sediment, preserving the mastodon in dark clay.

Archaeologists at the Nova Scotia Museum recovered the mastodon skeleton from the Milford quarry and studied the bones.

More recently, in May 2014, mastodon bones were found at Little Narrows gypsum quarry in Cape Breton. This important find is further evidence that mastodons existed throughout Nova Scotia.

Although mastodons were big by human standards, (about three metres tall at the shoulders), they were only about two-thirds as large as an average elephant. But they had imposing tusks, up to three metres long, that swept forward rather than downward. They weighed between four to five tonnes.

Mastodons that did not succumb to disease or injury could live for about 55 years.

That's electric

By 1897, the town of Parsboro had electric lights making it the first place in Nova Scotia to have electricity.

The first hydro plant in Nova Scotia was installed in 1903 by mining interests on the Liscomb River in Guysborough County.

The Nova Scotia Power Commission was formed in 1919 by the provincial government, following the lead of several other Canadian provinces in establishing Crown corporation electrical utilities. The commission constructed and opened its first hydro plant at Tantallon the following year.

Throughout the 1920s-1960s, the commission grew as private and municipal owned hydro plants and electrical utilities went bankrupt or sold their assets. In 1960, Nova Scotia was connected to the New Brunswick Electric Power Commission in the first electrical inter-connection between provinces in Canada.

The Nova Scotia Power Commission underwent unprecedented expansion during the late 1960s when five new thermal generating stations were constructed to meet the growing residential and industrial demand in the province.

On January 27, 1972, the Government of Nova Scotia acquired Nova Scotia Light and Power Company, Limited, leasing its assets to the renamed Nova Scotia Power Corporation. In 1984, NSPC opened the world's first tidal power generating station on the Annapolis River at Annapolis Royal.

In 1992, NSPC was privatized by the provincial government of Premier Donald Cameron in what was then the largest private equity transaction in Canadian history. This privatization created Nova Scotia Power Incorporated (NSPI).

On the rocks

Nova Scotia can claim the questionable distinction of having more shipwrecks off its coast than any other province in Canada.

The statistics are not surprising, given Nova Scotia's position projecting into the North Atlantic Ocean, closeness to major shipping routes, rocky shores and frequent fog banks.

By the end of the 20th century, there were some 9,600 recorded wrecks off Nova Scotia, followed by Newfoundland with 7,000. Prince Edward Island had the least with 700, followed by New Brunswick with 1,800.

Halifax's Maritime Museum of the Atlantic maintains an on-line searchable database of some 5,000 shipwreck records, one-fifth of the estimated 25,000 shipwrecks along the province's shores.

The worst shipwrecks in our history include:

RMS *Titanic*: White Star liner that sank 1,300 kilometres southeast of Nova Scotia on April 15, 1912, with 1,517 lives lost in the tragedy including 40 Canadians. Purists may not agree that *Titanic* qualifies as a Nova Scotia shipwreck, but the recovery operation was mounted out of Halifax and this resulted in 209 bodies being brought to the city where 150 are buried.

RMS *Atlantic*: White Star liner that ran aground and sank near Prospect on April 1, 1873, with the loss of 562 lives. This was the deadliest civilian maritime disaster in the North Atlantic Ocean prior to the loss of *Titanic*.

Chameau (or *Le Chameau*): A French Navy armed transport ship that sank off Louisbourg on August 27, 1725. An estimated 216 to 316 people were lost in the wreck of which 180 bodies washed ashore.

Sibylle: An immigrant ship that sank off St. Paul's Island — known as "The Graveyard of the Gulf" with more than 350 recorded shipwrecks — 23 kilometres northeast of the northern tip of Cape Breton Island on September 11, 1834. While the exact number of victims is not known, there is evidence that more than 300 were lost in this tragedy.

HMS *Tribune*: This Royal Navy frigate sank off Herring Cove on November 16, 1797, taking 238 souls with her.

SS *Hungarian*: Allan Line steamship wrecked off Cape Sable Island on February 19, 1860, killing 205 people.

Sovereign: British troop transport stranded on St. Paul's Island on October 18, 1814, killing 202 people.

HMS *Acorn*: A Royal Navy 18-gun sloop wrecked off Halifax on April 4, 1828, resulting in the loss of 115 lives.

Maria: Immigrant ship that sank in Cabot Strait, 80 kilometres from St. Paul's Island on May 10, 1849, killing 109 people.

HMS *Feversham*: A Royal Navy 32-gun warship wrecked on Scatarie Island off the east coast of Cape Breton Island, October 7, 1711. A total of 102 lives were lost.

Hanna: When this immigrant ship sank in the Gulf of St. Lawrence on April 29, 1849, an estimated 49 perished.

Spanish flu ravaged province in 1918

No one would have ever believed that by the end of the summer of 1918, Nova Scotians would be grappling with the Spanish flu — a terrible virus that would eventually kill more than 2000 men, women and children of all ages.

Not surprisingly, the Spanish flu arrived in Nova Scotia by sea, carried on ships with sick seamen, whether it was New England fishing schooners that sailed into various ports, or First World War troop carriers returning from Europe.

According to the renowned Halifax historian Allan Marble, the first known soldier who arrived back in Canada with the influenza was a young man from Inverness County. Within two weeks, 17 people in the Inverness area had died.

No one can say for certain when the flu case arose in Nova Scotia. It may have been when HMHS *Araguaya*, a hospital ship returning from overseas with Canadian soldiers, arrived in Halifax on July 17, 1918. It was immediately placed in quarantine, with 175 influenza-stricken men among the 763 wounded soldiers aboard.

5 FAST FACTS

1. Edward Cornwallis granted the first divorce in British North America in Nova Scotia. The year was 1750, a hundred years before the British House of Commons passed legislation of this kind for England.

2. Nova Scotia ended prohibition in favour of government control of liquor October 30, 1929.

3. Canada's first post office opened in Halifax on December 9, 1755, with subsidized direct mail to Britain. Nova Scotia issued its first stamp on September 1, 1851.

4. The 1,280-metre Canso Causeway linking Cape Breton Island to Nova Scotia mainland opened on December 10, 1954. It is the deepest causeway in the world.

5. On January 12, 1868, Nova Scotia voted to leave Confederation unless it was ensured better terms.

As the Spanish flu started to really spread across the province, newspapers in Halifax began publishing daily reports, listing new cases, infected residents' addresses and, sadly, deaths.

Both Dartmouth and Halifax opened hospital beds at the quarantine facility on Lawlor's Island, and in unused wards at the Victoria General Hospital. But the authorities also quickly built a facility in Willow Park.

Men began wearing facemasks and health officials from Halifax ordered all bodies to be buried immediately, without church services. Some people lost several members of their immediate family, and the community was shaken with anxiety, fear and economic hardship.

Halifax and Dartmouth's boards of health also took other initiatives to stop the flu from spreading. They ordered all public gathering places, including churches, theatres, schools and restaurants, to reduce their open hours, or to close completely.

The public was told about "how to dodge flu" by avoiding crowds, and protecting their nose and mouth in the presence of "sneezers."

Since absolutely no treatments were available for the flu, strange remedies were promoted, like turpentine and beef tea — treatments that may have caused more harm than good.

The flu struck quickly and without warning. Victims suddenly began to shiver, suffered severe headaches and back pain and then collapsed. They then developed a high fever, a hacking cough and aching joints. Most victims survived for three or four days, after which they developed pneumonia and cyanosis (a blue tinge to the skin caused by low blood-oxygen levels), which brought on their deaths.

Women were hit particularly hard by the virus; the highest mortality was seemingly in healthy people, including those in the 20 to 40 year old age group — a unique feature of this pandemic.

The first recorded death from the pandemic was reported in September 1918, in Belle Cote, Inverness County, when 26-year-old Marjory MacDonald succumbed to the disease. Seventeen deaths followed.

The first confirmed influenza death in Halifax County was in Beechville, where a 13-month-old boy named Murray Dorrington died on September 12, 1918.

Only a few days later, the first death in Yarmouth was reported after the influenza was brought to the South Shore by fishermen from Gloucester, Mass.

The mayor of Halifax at the time, Dr. Arthur Hawkins, realized how important it was for people in Nova Scotia to learn to isolate themselves from others. He ordered that every public venue in Halifax had to be completely closed for six weeks, and that the public health officer publish in the newspaper 14 preventive measures that residents should heed.

His main message, however, was the same as it is today: "Make sure you wash your hands frequently."

By the end of December 1919, at least 1,984 Nova Scotians had died from the pandemic, while at least another 281 died between January and April 1920, for a total of some 2,265 dead.

Still, what proved to be quite remarkable is the fact that the lowest death rate in Canada from the Spanish flu was in Nova Scotia.

Who were the Acadians?

The name Acadia originally applied to an area that included part of southeastern Quebec (the Gaspé), eastern Maine, New Brunswick, Nova Scotia and Prince Edward Island. Some say the name came from the Greek "Arcadia" meaning "rural contentment."

Others give it Algonquian roots, according to the website, *A Country by Consent*.

The heart of early Acadia was Port Royal on the Bay of Fundy. Early French settlers lead by Samuel de Champlain established a small settlement here in the winter of 1605. The settlers built houses, planted gardens, established a theatre and began the Ordre de Bon Temps.

The settlement was abandoned two years later, but attempts were made to resettle it in 1610. The English, in the meantime, had founded Virginia in 1607, and tried to lay claim to the whole eastern seaboard of the new world.

Throughout the 1600s, Acadia passed back and forth between England and France several times. During one of its English periods in the 1620s, James I, a Scottish King, granted the land to a poet and fellow Scot, William Alexander, who named it New Scotland or Nova Scotia.

The first serious attempt to colonize Acadia began in 1632 after another treaty restored the area to France. The French wanted to build a buffer against expansion from the New England colonies to the south and Governor Isaac de Razilly, a cousin of Louis XIII's powerful advisor, Cardinal Richelieu, brought about 300 men and some women to begin the settlement.

The French settlers drained the flood lands around the Bay of Fundy using sod dikes at first. These were later replaced with more permanent dikes and sluices to drain water. By building their houses around the bay rather than clearing forestland, the settlers didn't disturb the local Indigenous people and were able to enjoy an unusually peaceful co-existence with the Mi'kmaq and Malecite.

These reclaimed lands were also extremely fertile for farming crops such as wheat, oats and apples, which were grown in abundance. The main Acadian centres were Port Royal (later named Annapolis Royal under the English) and Grand Pré.

The Acadians also had quite an active trading relationship with the English colonies to the south, selling their surplus grain and buying manufactured products like cloth, dishes and tobacco and West Indian imports like rum and molasses.

British Governor Charles Lawrence and the Nova Scotia Council decided on July 28, 1755, to deport the Acadians. Although Grand Pré to this day is the most well known symbol of the expulsion, it actually began at Fort Beauséjour on August 11.

Fort Beauséjour is a large, five-bastioned star fort on the Isthmus of Chignecto in eastern Canada, a neck of land connecting the present-day province of New Brunswick with that of Nova Scotia.

Between 1755 and 1763, approximately 10,000 Acadians were deported. They were shipped to many points around the Atlantic. Large numbers were landed in the English colonies, others in France or the Caribbean. Thousands died of disease or starvation in the squalid conditions on board ship.

The British evicted the Acadians from their land because they refused to take an oath of allegiance to the Protestant British King.

Remembering Africville

Africville was a small, African Nova Scotian community located on the shores of the Bedford Basin, founded in the mid-18th century.

The first two landowners in Africville were William Arnold and William Brown. Clergyman Richard Preston established the Seaview United African Baptist Church in Africville in 1849, after starting with the Cornwallis Street Baptist Church in 1832.

The population of Africville grew to 400 residents after the Second World War. In the wake of the 1917 Halifax explosion, Halifax wanted to redevelop Africville for industry, which meant kicking out the poor, black people living there.

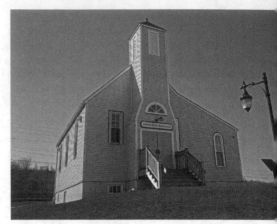

Peter Arsenault photo
In 2012, the Africville replica church museum opened and the area was renamed Africville Park.

The City of Halifax forcibly demolished the community for the purpose of urban renewal, forcing residents to relocate with little compensation for their homes and land. The city demolished the houses as residents were evacuated one by one. This made resistance much harder, after most of the residents had left.

The final property in Africville was expropriated 1967. The church of Africville was torn down in 1969 for fear of controversy and the last house was destroyed on January 2, 1970.

In 2010, Halifax Regional Municipality Mayor Peter Kelly apologized for the destruction of Africville with a commitment to build a replica church.

The two banks of Liverpool

During the 1870s, Liverpool had two (short-lived) banks — Bank of Acadia and Bank of Liverpool. Both banks issued their own currency.

According to the Queens County Museum, the Bank of Acadia was only open for approximately 120 days between 1872 and 1873. That makes it the shortest-lived bank in the history of Canada.

Its president, Thomas Robert Pattillo, was a prominent Liverpool businessman. The bank was located on the Main Street of Liverpool across from the current Town Hall Center.

From its beginning, the Bank of Acadia was focused on economic development and made several large loans to local lumberman and shipbuilders. The bank ran into difficulty when the world economy suddenly panicked and the debtors were unable to repay their loans.

At the time, there were many rumours of shifty business practices. However, the poor economic climate was the true cause of the bank's failure. The bank tried to reimburse its customers but did not have the liquid assets to meet that desire.

The failure of the Bank of Acadia took a toll on the health of Pattillo, who died the next year of a heart attack.

Information from the Queens County Museum suggests that that the corporate life of The Bank of Liverpool was from 1871 to 1879.

The bank was actually closed from April 1873 until 1878. It was also located on Main Street, Liverpool, near the present day Dixie Lee, at 254 Main Street.

After its closure in 1873, it reopened in 1878 for a fruitless attempt to regain its business. However, the same economic panic that caused the failure of the Bank of Acadia proved fatal for the Bank of Liverpool.

The Bank of Nova Scotia took over took over the meager assets of the defunct Bank of Liverpool.

Queens County Museum explains denomination of the bank notes: "Many ask why a four dollar bank note. We must go back to the time they were printed; a skilled carpenter could be making about two dollars per day for an eight to 10 hour workday. A shop girl may make less than a dollar a day. Therefore four dollars would be a week's wages for that shop girl and two notes would equal the carpenter's wages for the week."

During the 1870s, Liverpool had two (short-lived) banks — Bank of Acadia and Bank of Liverpool. Both banks issued their own currency.

A historic battle

Battle of the Atlantic was Canada's longest continuous military engagement of the Second World War, making it one of the defining conflicts of the war.

The battle lasted 2,075 days between 1939 and 1945. In May 1943, the Allies gained the upper hand in battles with German U-boats, though skirmishes continued until the end of the war.

In total, Battle of the Atlantic claimed the lives of more than 4,000 men and women of the Royal Canadian Navy, the Royal Canadian Air Force and the Canadian Merchant Navy.

Where was Beechville?

A 31-hectare area of Crown land known as Beechville located just outside of Halifax once housed black refugees from the War of 1812.

The first settlers in Beechville were among the 2,000 black refugees that arrived in the Maritimes between 1813 and 1815 from the Chesapeake Bay area of the U.S. Most of those refugees were escaped slaves from southern American colonies.

In November 1815, 23 refugees were settled at Refugee Hill near the Northwest Arm on land conveyed to them by the Crown. Initially, 23 men were each given a licence to occupy a four-hectare lot at Refugee Hill.

A year later, about 76 blacks lived there. They stayed only a short time before they were moved further back into the woods in the Chain Lake area along St. Margarets Bay Road. The new settlement was called Beech Hill and later, Beechville.

In June 2017, the Nova Scotia Department of Natural Resources transferred the 31 hectares of land to the Department of Communities, Culture and Heritage to ensure that the cultural and historical significance of the land is preserved.

Canada's first all black battalion

Although black men were not altogether welcome in the armed forces, there were those who served in a number of combat units during the First World War. This includes the 106th Battalion, Nova Scotia Rifles, which was authorized on November 18, 1915.

Recruits were drawn from Nova Scotia, Prince Edward Island, New Brunswick and Newfoundland. As the 106th Battalion began the recruitment process, protest erupted over black volunteers.

According to an article on the Canadian Encyclopedia website written by Lindsay Ruck, Samuel Reese, a black man from British Guiana living in Truro, was told he would only be accepted to the armed forces if he first recruited a certain number of black soldiers. "At the same time, Reese was referred to Commanding Officer Lieutenant-Colonel W.H. Allen for enlistment in the 106th Battalion," Ruck writes. "Reese also reached out to Reverend William A. White for assistance. White was pastor of Zion Baptist Church in Truro, and he in turn appealed directly to Allen to assist young black men with the enlistment process. Reverend White made a verbal agreement to put his efforts into recruiting Black men throughout Nova Scotia."

In December 1915, the federal government declared that enlistees could not be refused based on their race. This proclamation did not sit well with several white volunteers, who refused to sign up and fight alongside black soldiers.

"As there was no official policy for discrimination, recruiting officers were ultimately responsible for selection. Allen felt strongly that a segregated battalion would be the best solution; however, from December 1915 to July 1916, approximately 16 Black volunteers were accepted into the 106th Battalion," writes Ruck.

The black soldiers were dispersed throughout the battalion's four companies. On July 15, 1916, the battalion left for England aboard the RMS *Empress of Britain*. As was common practice at the time, the 106th Battalion was divided to provide reinforcements for front-line battalions that had suffered heavy casualties in France.

Other CEF combat units containing black volunteers included the 25th Battalion, the 102nd Battalion, the 1st Quebec Regiment and the 116th Battalion. There are a number of battles in which black Canadians fought, including the Battle of Vimy Ridge and the Battle of Passchendaele.

Black milestones in Nova Scotia

The first recorded instance of a black presence in Canada was that of Mathieu de Costa. He arrived in Nova Scotia sometime between 1603 and 1608 as a translator for the French explorer Sieur DeMonts. This expedition founded Port Royal.

The following is a list of black milestones throughout Nova Scotia's history:

1774: Born March 13, 1774, into slavery in the British Colony of Virginia, Rose Fortune, came to Annapolis Royal with the Black Loyalists when she was 10 years old. She went on to become a successful businesswoman and the first female police officer not only in Canada but in all of North America.

1859: William Hall of Horton's Bluff becomes the first Canadian to be awarded the Victoria Cross.

1890: George Dixon of Halifax wins the World Bantamweight boxing title. This is the first time a black man has won a world boxing title in any weight class.

1898: Nova Scotia's first African Nova Scotian lawyer, James Robinson Johnston, was called to the Bar.

1949: Nova Scotian William Andrew (Bill) White, III, was born February 7, 1915, in Truro. He was a well-known composer, educator and social activist, but he earns his place in history for being the first black Canadian to run for federal office in Canada. He stood as the Cooperative Commonwealth Federation candidate in the Toronto electoral district of Spadina in the 1949 election, although he was not elected.

1960: Rev. W.P. Oliver is chosen to serve as president of the United Baptist Convention of the Maritimes — the first black to be so honoured.

1967: Isaac Phils of Sydney becomes the first black appointed to the Order of Canada.

1984: Daurene Lewis is elected mayor of the town of Annapolis Royal. This is the first time in Canadian history that a black woman is elected mayor of a town in Canada.

1992: George Boyd becomes the first black anchor of a national news show, when he becomes an anchor on CBC Newsworld. He was born and raised in Halifax.

1993: Born 1943 in Halifax, Wayne Adams was first elected to the Halifax Municipal Council in 1979 and was re-elected five times. He was deputy mayor from 1982 to 1983. A Nova Scotia Liberal, he was elected in the 1993 Nova Scotia general election in the riding of Preston. He was the Minister of the Environment, Minister responsible for the Emergency Measures Act, and the Minister responsible for the Nova Scotia Boxing Authority in the governments of first John Savage (1993–1997) and then Russell MacLellan (1997–1998). Adams was Nova Scotia's first black MLA and cabinet minister. He was defeated in 1998 by the NDP candidate, Yvonne Attwell.

1998: Born in 1943 in East Preston, Yvonne Atwell was Nova Scotia's first black woman MLA. In 1996, she ran unsuccessfully for the leadership of the Nova Scotia New Democratic Party. She won a seat for the NDP in the Nova Scotia House of Assembly in 1998 for the riding of Preston, becoming the first black woman MLA in the province. She lost her seat in the 1999 provincial election.

2001: George Elliot Clarke wins the Governor General's Award for Poetry. He is the first black Canadian writer to win this prestigious award.

A historic place

The Old Burying Ground, founded in 1749, the same year as the settlement, is the oldest cemetery in Halifax. It was originally non-denominational and for several decades was the only burial place for all Haligonians.

The burial ground was also used by St. Matthew's United Church in Halifax and in 1793 it was turned over to the Anglicans of St. Paul's Church. The cemetery was closed in 1844.

The site steadily declined until the 1980s when it was restored and refurbished by the Old Burying Ground Foundation, which now maintains the site and employs tour guides to interpret the site in the summer. Ongoing restoration of the rare 18th century grave markers continues.

The Old Burying Ground, founded in 1749, the same year as the settlement, is the oldest cemetery in Halifax.

Over the decades some 12,000 people were interred in the Old Burial Ground. Today there are roughly 1,200 headstones, some having been lost and many others being buried with no headstone.

The Old Burying Ground was designated a National Historic Site of Canada in 1991. It had been designated a Provincially Registered Property in 1988.

This monument located in the Garrison Cemetery is dedicated to Rose Fortune, a Black Loyalist who has the distinction of being the first female police officer in what we now know as Canada. The exact location of her grave is not known.

Rose's final resting place

The Garrison Cemetery in Annaoplis Royal is noteworthy as the final resting place of Rose Fortune (1774-1864), a Black Loyalist who has the distinction of being the first female police officer in what we now know as Canada.

Rose Fortune was born into slavery in Philadelphia, PA, March 13, 1774, her family subsequently being relocated to Virginia by the Devones family. Escaping slavery during the American Revolution, the family was relocated to Annapolis Royal, as part of the Black Loyalist migration, when Rose was 10 years old.

In 1825, she started her own business, carting luggage between the ferry docks and nearby homes and hotels. She became entrusted with safeguarding property and maintaining order on the wharves and warehouses of Annapolis Royal, acting as the town's waterfront police officer.

Rose Fortune died on February 20, 1864, in the small house she owned at the engineer's lot near Fort Anne. The business she founded was continued by her grandson-in-law Albert Lewis as the Lewis Transfer Company and continued for several generations, remaining in business until 1980.

Rose Fortune was buried in Annapolis Royal in the historic Garrison Cemetery. Her grave is unmarked, but a plaque in Petite Parc, now named Rose Fortune Plaza, on the Annapolis Royal waterfront commemorates her life and contribution to Nova Scotian history.

A headstone found in the Garrison Cemetery adjacent to Fort Anne in Annapolis Royal is the oldest English gravestone in Canada.

The oldest marker in the land

The Garrison Cemetery is located on the grounds of Fort Anne in Annapolis Royal. It is located next to the old Court House, at the intersection of George St. and Nova Scotia Highway 1.

Initially used as a burial ground for French military forces, it has since been used by Acadians, the British military and the parish of St. Lukes.

The earliest remaining tombstone is from 1720, that of Bethiah Douglass who died October 1, 1720, in her 37th year. Incidentally, the Douglass marker is the oldest English gravestone in Canada.

Robert Ross rests here

Halifax's Old Burying Ground is also historically important because Robert Ross is interred there.

Born in 1766, Ross was a British Army officer who is most well known for the Burning of Washington, which included the destruction of the White House and United States Capitol in August 1814. The invasion was retaliation for the destructive American raids into Canada, most notably the Americans' burning of York (Toronto) earlier in 1813.

After a very distinguished career in the Napoleonic Wars, Major-General Robert Ross was given command of the British troops that were sent to America in 1814 after Napoleon's default to relieve the military pressure on Canada in the War of 1812.

His troops were met by the American Army at Bladensburg, fives miles north of Washington. Ross used Congreve rockets, which the Americans had never seen before. The British won the battle and marched in Washington where they set fire to a number of public buildings, including the president's mansion. The building was so badly stained with smoke that it had to be painted — white.

The following month the British attempted to land at Baltimore, but were defeated. According to legend, a young lawyer named Francis Scott Key, after watching the red glare of Ross' rockets, was moved to compose "a national anthem for his country to celebrate the sight of the Stars and Stripe flying bravely in the dawn's early light to signal British defeat."

General Ross was killed at the Battle of North Point near Baltimore before the infamous Bombardment of Fort McHenry. His body was brought back to Halifax where it was buried in the Old Burying Ground on September 19, 1814, with full military honours. His grave is marked with a formal, high, flat tombstone.

Commemorating the Crimean War

The last erected and most prominent structure in Halifax's Old Burying Ground is the famed Welsford-Parker Monument, a Triumphal arch standing at the entrance to the cemetery commemorating British victory in the Crimean War. This is the second oldest war monument in Canada and the only monument to the Crimean War in North America.

The arch was built in 1860, 16 years after the cemetery had officially closed. The arch was built by George Lang and is named after two Haligonians — Major Augustus Frederick Welsford and Captain William Buck Carthew Augustus Parker.

Both Nova Scotians died in the Battle of the Great Redan during the Siege of Sevastopol (1854-1855). This monument was the last grave marker in the cemetery.

Embracing Titanic victims

Considered one of the greatest marine disasters in recorded history, the story of RMS *Titanic* begins in Southampton, England, on April 10, 1912, when the vessel left on her maiden voyage. For some of those who lost their lives aboard the ill-fated ship, Halifax is where the story ended.

On Sunday, April 14 at 11:40 p.m., *Titanic* struck a giant iceberg and by 2:20 a.m. on April 15, the "unsinkable ship" was gone. The first vessel to arrive at the scene of the disaster was the Cunard Liner RMS *Carpathia* and she was able to rescue more than 700 survivors. On Wednesday, April 17, the day before the *Carpathia* arrived in New York, the White Star Line dispatched the first of four Canadian vessels to look for bodies in the area of the sinking.

On April 17, the Halifax-based Cable Steamer *Mackay-Bennett* set sail with a minister, an undertaker and a cargo of ice, coffins and canvas bags. She arrived at the site on April 20 and spent five days carrying out her grim task. Her crew was able to recover 306 bodies, 116 of which had to be buried at sea. On April 26, the *Mackay-Bennett* left for Halifax with 190 bodies. She was relieved by the *Minia,* also a Halifax-based cable ship.

The *Minia* had been at sea when *Titanic* sank, but returned to Halifax in order to collect the necessary supplies before sailing from the Central Wharf on April 22 for the scene of the disaster. After eight days of searching, the *Minia* was only able to find 17 bodies, two of which were buried at sea.

On May 6, the Canadian government vessel CGS *Montmagny* left Halifax and recovered four bodies, one of which was buried at sea. The remaining three victims were brought from Louisbourg to Halifax by rail. The fourth and final ship in the recovery effort was the SS *Algerine,* which sailed from St. John's, Newfoundland and Labrador, on May 16. The crew of the *Algerine* found one body, which was shipped to Halifax on the SS *Florizel.*

The majority of the bodies were unloaded at the Coal or Flagship Wharf on the Halifax waterfront and horse-drawn hearses brought the victims to the temporary morgue in the Mayflower Curling Rink.

Only 59 of the bodies placed in the morgue were shipped out by train to their families. The remaining victims of *Titanic* were buried in three Halifax cemeteries between May 3 and June 12. Religious services were held at St. Paul's Church and at the Synagogue on Starr Street. Burial services were held at St. Mary's Cathedral, Brunswick Street Methodist Church, St. George's Church and All Saint's Cathedral.

Various individuals and businesses expressed their sympathy by donating flowers and wreaths. The coffins of the unidentified victims were adorned with bouquets of lilies. Most of the gravestones, erected in the fall of 1912 and paid for by the White Star Line, are plain granite blocks. In some cases, however, families, friends or other groups chose to commission a larger and more elaborate gravestone. All of these more personalized graves, including the striking Celtic cross and the beautiful monument to the Unknown Child (who has since been identified), are located at Fairview Lawn Cemetery.

The three Halifax cemeteries where *Titanic* victims are buried are Fairview Lawn (121 graves), Mount Olivet (19 graves) and Baron de Hirsch (10 graves). Each cemetery has informational panels indicating the location of the gravesites.

Two of the Halifax cemeteries where Titanic victims are buried: Fairview Lawn and Mount Olivet.

Bayview Cemetery is valued for its particular association with the "foreign Protestant" settlers and their rare Germanic gravemarkers.

The German connection

Bayview Cemetery is situated on a hillside above Edgewater Street at the head of the harbour in Mahone Bay. Some grave markers date from the late 1700s, including several rare Germanic gravestones.

Bayview Cemetery is located close to seven other heritage properties on the main route leading into the town from the east. Municipal heritage designation applies to the land at the corner of Main Street and Clearland Road.

Bayview Cemetery is valued for its tangible associations with the early history of Mahone Bay; for its particular association with the "foreign Protestant" settlers and their rare Germanic gravemarkers; and for its continuous use as a community burial ground since the late 1700s.

The historic value of Bayview Cemetery is evident in its late 18th and early 19th century gravestones. Several of the earliest stones mark graves of foreign Protestants, mainly German-speaking Europeans, who immigrated as part of the British initiative to colonize the area.

Initially based in nearby Lunenburg, they began claiming their farm land grants at Mahone Bay in 1754. Burials took place in Lunenburg until 1774, by which time the settlers had established a burial ground at Mahone Bay. The "burying ground at Mush-a-Mush," so-called after the nearby river, eventually became Bayview Cemetery.

The early gravestones at Bayview Cemetery are valued as an expression of the austere life experienced by the settlers and as testament to their faith and fortitude. The primitive quality of the earliest markers and the use of Germanic symbols and language evoke a sense of the settlers' isolation within the colony.

Bayview Cemetery is also valued for its rare early Germanic gravestones marking the graves of foreign Protestant settlers.

Lunenburg County's oldest surviving German inscription — that of Ana Catherina Zwicker (d. 1780) — is here. Her stone is roughly crafted of soft, local slate with touchingly awkward and uneven block letters in German. Other hand-carved stones have Gothic script. Some depict traditional Germanic images — a tulip on the 1805 Eisenhauer marker, or a heart on an infant's stone.

By 1872 when the community was well-established, the burial ground was named Bayview Cemetery. The Bayview Cemetery Company, whose volunteers managed ongoing operations, was incorporated in 1925. When the Company disbanded in 2007, operations were assumed by the Town of Mahone Bay.

You'll find Howe here

Camp Hill Cemetery is the final resting place of Joseph Howe, journalist, politician and writer who is largely considered as the father of the free press. Howe is often ranked as one of Nova Scotia's most admired politicians and his considerable skills as a journalist and writer have made him provincial legend.

He was born in Halifax, the son of John Howe and Mary Edes. He inherited an undying love for Great Britain and her Empire from his Loyalist father. At age 23, the self-taught but widely read Howe purchased the *Novascotian,* soon making it into a popular and influential newspaper. He reported extensively on debates in the Nova Scotia House of Assembly and travelled to every part of the province writing about its geography and people.

In 1835, Howe was charged with seditious libel, a serious criminal offence, after the *Novascotian* published a letter attacking Halifax politicians and police for pocketing public money. Howe addressed the jury for more than six hours, citing example after example of civic corruption. The judge called for Howe's conviction, but swayed by his passionate address, jurors acquitted him in what is considered a landmark case in the struggle for a free press in Canada.

The next year, Howe was elected to the assembly as a liberal reformer, beginning a long and eventful public career. He was instrumental in helping Nova Scotia become the first British colony to win responsible government in 1848. He served as premier of Nova Scotia from 1860 to 1863 and led the unsuccessful fight against Canadian Confederation from 1866 to 1868.

Having failed to persuade the British to repeal Confederation, Howe joined the federal cabinet of John A. Macdonald in 1869, and played a major role in bringing Manitoba into the union.

He resigned his Cabinet post to become the third Lieutenant Governor of Nova Scotia post Confederation in 1873. He died June 1, 1873, at aged 68, only three weeks after his appointment. He is buried in Camp Hill Cemetery.

Oldest military burial ground in Canada

The Royal Navy Burying Ground is part of the Naval Museum of Halifax and was the Naval Hospital cemetery for the North America and West Indies Station Halifax. It is the oldest military burial ground in Canada.

The cemetery has grave markers to those who died while serving at Halifax and were treated at the Naval medical facility or died at sea. Often shipmates and officers had the grave markers erected to mark the deaths of the crewmembers who died while in the port of Halifax.

The number of burials that took place there is estimated at over 400, however, there are only 89 stone markers remaining. There was a register of deaths established in 1860 for the burial ground. As well, surgeons of a ship registered the deaths of crewmembers, including how the person died and where they were buried.

These reports were entered in the official register, with a detailed account sent quarterly to the Medical Director-General, Admiralty, England. There is no local record of who is buried. The four most common causes of death for those buried there are, in order, disease, falling from the topmast, drowning, and death as a result of naval battles.

Along with two monuments that commemorate casualties of the War of 1812, the most prominent markers are for the crew that died on the flagships of the North American and West Indies Station — HMS *Winchester* (1841), HMS *Wellesley* (1850), HMS *Cumberland* (1852), HMS *Indus* (1859), HMS *Nile* (1861), HMS *Duncan* (1866) and HMS *Royal Alfred* (1869).

There were many buried during the wars of the 18th century (American Revolution, French Revolutionary War and Napoleonic Wars) that do not have grave markers.

Nova Scotia man appears on D-Day coin

The identity of a soldier engraved on the back of a Canadian silver dollar commemorating the 75th anniversary of D-Day is that of a Queens County man.

According to information released by the Canadian Mint, working with local historians and officers of the Bathurst, New Brunswick-headquartered North Shore Regiment, the Royal Canadian Mint solved the mystery of the identity of the soldier whose face is dramatically portrayed on its 2019 Proof Silver Dollar commemorating the 75th Anniversary of D-Day.

The image of Private George Baker can be seen in this close up of D-Day 75th anniversary coin.

That soldier, the Mint says, was identified as Private George Herman Baker, a member of No. 3 Platoon, A Company, of the North Shore Regiment who landed with his comrades at Juno Beach, between Courseulles and St-Aubin-sur-Mer, France, on June 6, 1944.

"Private Baker lived through the Second World War and returned home to Liverpool, Nova Scotia where he raised a family in peace time," the information from the Mint reads. "Like so many other brave Canadians on D-Day, Private Baker risked everything to help restore an Allied foothold on the Western Front and eventually win the Second World War for Canada and its allies."

Private Baker's image was adapted from several frames of archival film footage loaned to the Mint by the Juno Beach Centre in Normandy, France. The 75-year-old film provides a rare and unique perspective of the North Shore Regiment landing at the Nan Red sector of Juno Beach.

In consulting a number of experts to ensure the accuracy of its coin design, the Mint says it learned of Private Baker's identity thanks to the invaluable assistance of Brandon Savage, historian and teacher at Miramichi Valley High School, as well as Dr. Marc Milner, military historian at the University of New Brunswick, amateur historian Bruce Morton of Barrie, Ontario, and North Shore Regiment Commanding Officer Lieutenant Colonel Renald Dufour.

George Baker was born in Nova Scotia on August 31,1923, and died in South Brookfield, Queens County, on July 23, 2003. He was only 20 years old when he made history at Juno Beach.

"The North Shore men fought valiantly securing their landing objectives at the end of D-Day but suffered heavy losses which totalled 120 casualties of which 33 were fatal," said North Shore Regiment Commanding Officer Lieutenant-Colonel Renald Dufour in the information from the Mint.

"The D-Day landing was one of the most significant events in Canadian military history and our regiment was at the centre of it, with three other assaulting units," he said. "Honouring and recognizing nationally our soldiers' legacy and their families' sacrifices on the eve of the 75th anniversary with a commemorative coin is a remarkable and world-class act."

Designed by Simcoe-area artist Tony Bianco, the 2019 Proof Silver Dollar vividly depicts Canadians coming ashore under enemy fire. It is a poignant testament to the brave soldiers who risked all to help Canada and its allies win the Second World War.

Multiple engravings of the letter "V" for victory in Morse Code further illustrate the magnitude of an incredible moment in the life of Private George Baker and of all those who fought alongside him at Juno Beach.

Port Mouton: the other Loyalist settlement

Shelburne's place in history as Nova Scotia's Loyalist town is well established, but a lesser-known fact is that another South Shore community also has ties to the Loyalist immigrants.

In 1783 and 1784, a township was laid out along the north shore of Port Mouton Bay by British officials. This was immediately after the end of the Revolutionary War, and out of loyalty to the Crown, 20,000 people would come from the former colonies to Nova Scotia. Over half of those would find themselves at the new town of Shelburne, located approximately 50 kilometres south along the coast from Port Mouton. The new Guysborough Township was therefore created in order to accommodate some of the Loyalist refugees from the American Colonies.

The township was situated immediately west of the Liverpool Township that had been established 14 years earlier and settled by Planters from New England.

The first Loyalists were members of Tarleton's Legion. They arrived in Port Mouton on October 10, 1783, and there were 125 men, along with 175 women and children. On October 17, 1783, some 70 African American Loyalists arrived at Port Mouton. It is believed that over 2,000 additional people arrived in Port Mouton through the rest of October and November.

The settlers struggled to survive throughout the winter on the rocky shore of Port Mouton Bay. In May of the following year, only six months after their arrival, many people left Port Mouton and went on to found the towns of St. Stephen, New Brunswick, and Guysborough, Nova Scotia.

All that remains of the Loyalist movement in Port Mouton are a stonewall and a cemetery that are believed to date back to 1783.

Shelburne race riots

On July 26, 1784, a mob of Loyalist settlers stormed the home of a black preacher in Shelburne, armed with hooks and chains seized from ships in the harbour.

An article written by Jesse Roberston and published on the website, *Canadian Encyclopedia*, says the confrontation ignited a wave of violence in Shelburne County that lasted approximately 10 days.

The Shelburne Riot has been described as the first race riot in North America since the majority of the attacks targeted the county's free black population.

Roberston writes, "In Shelburne County, white dissatisfaction towards British administrators was often directed towards neighbouring Black communities. Arriving with little money, white refugees often faced significant delays in receiving the land allotments that had been promised to them."

She notes that many were forced to hire themselves out as labourers in order to earn a living. Those who did resented the fact that free blacks were willing to work for far less than white labourers deemed acceptable.

Under such conditions, it didn't take long for racial animosity to arise. Tensions reached a breaking point in Shelburne on July 26, 1784, when a group of about 40 white Loyalists demolished the home of Baptist preacher David George.

George had chosen to establish his church in Shelburne rather than Birchtown where many Black Loyalists and former slaves had relocated in 1783, and had challenged the established racial hierarchy by baptizing white Loyalists. The mob also tore down the houses of about 20 other free blacks living on George's property.

Despite threats, George continued to preach from his church in Shelburne. The mob returned, beating the pastor with sticks and chasing him into a swamp. The riot spread, Roberston writes.

"While Black Loyalists were the primary targets, rioters also attacked white settlers that were believed to be colluding with the incompetent British authorities. Surveyor Benjamin Marston fled to the army barracks, where his remaining friends convinced him to slip away on a boat to Halifax."

Shelburne County's Black Loyalists had no such refuge, writes Roberston. Rioting continued for at least 10 days, and incursions into Birchtown were reported for up to one month.

Four companies of the 17th Regiment were dispatched to maintain order in the weeks following the riot. Governor John Parr visited Shelburne on August 23. Marston, despised by Shelburne's white Loyalists, provided a convenient scapegoat and was subsequently fired.

Evidently concerned that violence might again emerge, Parr also dispatched a naval frigate to support the 17th Regiment. Only one individual was charged in connection with the riot.

The Shelburne Riot was emblematic of the broader racial prejudices encountered by black Nova Scotians in the years following the American Revolution. It had little immediate effect on the county, Roberston writes.

However, within several years the region soon faced a faltering economy and declining population. Many Black Loyalists eventually relocated to other parts of the province.

In 1791, Birchtown residents were given the option of sailing to a new colony in Sierra Leone. At least half of the town's families agreed to depart the following year, preferring an uncertain future on a new continent to the conditions they had found in Shelburne County.

Wreck of the SS Atlantic

The biggest shipwreck in Nova Scotia history, second biggest in Canadian history, and the largest marine disaster in the North Atlantic before the *Titanic*, occurred on the shores of Nova Scotia on April 1, 1873.

In the early hours on that date, the SS *Atlantic,* a member of the White Star Line and considered the greatest liner of her era, ran aground on the rocky shores of Lower Prospect.

Heralded as one of the most modern steamships afloat, *Atlantic* was on her 19th voyage across the Atlantic Ocean, leaving Liverpool, England, en route to New York. There were some 975 passengers, crew and stowaways on board the vessel.

With his ship running short of coal, Captain James Williams feared they might not make it to New York, so he diverted to Halifax to refuel. This was on the night of March 31, 1873.

Williams, who had never previously sailed into Halifax, was unaware of the strong currents of the Western Atlantic caused by the 50-foot tides of the Bay of Fundy. While he believed the ship was close to Halifax, it was, In fact, almost 20 kilometres to the west and close to Lower Prospect, a small fishing community about a half hour from the port city.

At 3:15 a.m. on April 1, 1873, as the captain slept, the *Atlantic* smashed at full speed into the rocky shores and was wrecked. The forceful impact resulted in the deaths of around 550 people (the exact number has never been established) including all the women and all the children.

The tragic loss of life may have much higher but for the heroic fishermen of Lower Prospect, who quickly launched their boats to rescue survivors clinging to life on the wreck of the crippled ship.

At the same time, the residents of the local communities struggled to care for those that managed to make It to shore.

During the following days, bodies were collected. Of those recovered, 277 were not claimed and were buried in St. Paul's Anglican Cemetery. Another 150 were buried In the Star of the Sea Roman Catholic Cemetery.

In 1905, the family of Thomas Henry Ismay, who was the founder of the White Star LIne, donated a monument in memory of the victims of the SS *Atlantic*.

The monument reads:

> **Near this spot
> was wrecked the
> S.S. 'Atlantic'
> April 1st, 1873
> When 562 persons
> perished, of whom 277
> were interred
> in this church yard.**
>
> **This monument is
> erected as a sacred memorial
> by a few sympathetic friends.**
>
> **Jesus said
> I am the resurrection and the life.**

The historic CSS Acadia

The century-old CSS *Acadia,* known as Halifax's Grand Old Lady, is an important piece of Nova Scotia history.

The vessel is permanently moored at the Maritime Museum of the Atlantic wharf where restoration and repair work is underway to maintain the CSS *Acadia* as a floating exhibit.

The CSS *Acadia* is the only surviving ship to have served the Royal Canadian Navy during both world wars and the only vessel still afloat that survived the Halifax Explosion.

The CSS Acadia is the only surviving ship to have served the Royal Canadian Navy during both world wars and the only vessel still afloat that survived the Halifax Explosion.

The ship is named *Acadia* in honour of Nova Scotia's name in the French colonial era. CSS stood for, at different times, "Canadian Scientific Ship" and "Canadian Survey Ship."

According to information on the museum's website, *Acadia* was launched in 1913 at Newcastle-upon-Tyne, England, at the yards of Swan, Hunter and Wigham Richardson Ltd. She was the first vessel specifically designed and built to survey Canada's northern waters, and her career took her from the dangerous, ice-infested waters of Hudson's Bay to Nova Scotia's South Shore.

"In her early years, *Acadia* was responsible for pioneering hydrographic research in Canada's Arctic waters. At the end of her career, she was used to chart the coast of Newfoundland after it joined Confederation in 1949, creating entirely new charts and updating some that were nearly a century old."

Acadia also holds the distinction of being the only surviving ship to have served the Royal Canadian Navy during both world wars. She served as a patrol and escort vessel from 1916 to 1919. She received minor damage in the Halifax Explosion in 1917 while acting as a guard ship in Bedford Basin, making her the only vessel still afloat today to have survived the Halifax Explosion.

Acadia was recommissioned as a warship in 1939, serving first as a patrol vessel and later as a training ship until the war's end in 1945.

After 56 years of service, *Acadia* was retired in 1969. For the next 12 years, she remained berthed at the Bedford Institute of Oceanography. Further recognition came in 1976 when she was designated a National Historic Site.

In 1982, she moved to the wharves behind the Maritime Museum of the Atlantic and became part of the Museum's collection where she is the subject of a program of continuous restoration and maintenance.

Hector delivers the Scots

On September 15, 1773, the ship *Hector* brought the first wave of almost 200 emigrants from Scotland to Nova Scotia, landing at what is now the town of Pictou. The landing of this famous ship is widely recognized as one of the earliest arrivals of Scottish settlers to Canada.

While their arrival in this new land ended 11 hard weeks at sea that included severe storms and disease that resulted in the death of 18 people, the voyage of the *Hector* started a wave of emigration from Scotland that resulted in Pictou being declared "the birthplace of New Scotland."

According to Mike Thorburn, who writes for a website known as *Scotland Is Now*, there is a deep Scottish connection to Pictou and the rest of Nova Scotia, that has been fostered since the *Hector* docked upon the shores of Canada.

It's also a wonderful coincidence that even the name "Pictou" brings forth allusions of Scotland, he writes.

"An ancient race of Scottish warriors known as the Picts lived in Scotland during the Dark Ages. These Caledonian combatants were famed for fighting off the invasion of the Roman Empire in Scotland."

The significance of the Hector and her passengers has been immortalised in the town of Pictou to commemorate the ship's contribution to Nova Scotia's Scottish history. After several years of construction, the replica Hector opened to the public in September 2000.

For the Scots on board the *Hector*, the decision to leave their native land wasn't an easy one to make. Many families were forcibly removed from their ancestral lands during the brutal Highland Clearances and given nowhere else to go.

"Stranded in their own country with no place to call home, many looked across the Atlantic hoping for a brighter future. When a Scotsman named John Ross showed up offering a fresh start in Canada, many jumped at this new opportunity."

Ross was a recruiting agent working on behalf of Scottish businessmen in North America. The group had purchased land rights in Pictou and charged Ross with finding willing settlers back in Scotland.

He was actively encouraged to deceive vulnerable families and use any means necessary to convince people on board, writes Thorburn. He offered cheap transport and promised a year's worth of supplies and a large piece of coastal farmland to anyone willing to make the journey.

In total, 189 people boarded the *Hector* from two different points in Scotland — 10 at Greenock and 179 at Lochbroom.

Though it was mainly families and young male labourers, the passenger list also included a last minute addition. An unnamed piper came on board the ship hoping for passage. It's believed that the musician was initially ordered ashore by the captain, as he had not paid a fare, Thorburn writes.

"However, the wailing refrain of his bagpipes so affected the passengers on board that they pleaded with the captain to let him stay. The ship's occupants even offered to share their own rations with him in exchange for his music."

The piper's tunes no doubt helped raise spirits during a long and arduous trip. The ship and its cargo of people faced several difficulties throughout the journey. Sadly 18 people, mostly children, died during the voyage and were at sea. Amongst the causes of death were smallpox and dysentery due to the poor and cramped conditions on board the *Hector*.

As well as this, the ship also ran into a huge storm off the coast of Newfoundland, causing a 14-day delay, according to Thorburn.

"This wasn't the only delay and in total the voyage that was supposed to take six weeks ended up taking nearly double that amount of time. The increased time at sea also meant that their already stretched food rations were completely exhausted by the time they docked at Pictou."

The West Novies

The West Nova Scotia Regiment, a Primary Reserve infantry regiment of the Canadian Forces, is one of the oldest elements of the Canadian Forces. It has seen active service in both world wars and is considered one of the finest regiments to ever engage in combat on behalf of this country.

The regiment was formed in 1936 by a merger of the 69th (Annapolis) Regiment, formed in 1717, and the 75th (Lunenburg) Regiment, formed in 1870. Both of these descend from the 40th Regiment of Foot (Prince of Wales Volunteers), raised in 1717 at Fort Anne, Annapolis Royal. It also combines the 112th and 219th Battalions of Infantry of the World War I Canadian Expeditionary Force.

Two of the four rifle companies were posted on the South Shore, with "A" company and were stationed at the exhibition grounds in the Town of Bridgewater. In fact, the exhibition has taken place every year since 1891, with the exception of 1939, when the Canadian military took over the grounds to train the regiment for combat in the Second World War.

When the Second World War broke out on September 1, 1939, the West NSR was mobilized as an active service force battalion. The active service battalion left Halifax and disembarked at Gourock, Scotland, shortly after Christmas in 1939; they immediately entrained for Aldershot, England.

On June 15, 1943, the regiment embarked from England in the first part of "Operation Husky," the invasion of Sicily. The West Nova Scotia Regiment was the first allied unit to land and stay on the continent of Europe for the entire duration of the war.

The Regiment continued to fight in Italy until February 9, 1945, when the 1st Canadian Corps was transferred to Northwest Europe. The Regiment moved to Marseilles, France, by sea and arrived in Holland where it remained until the German surrender on May 5, 1945. During this time the Regiment won 26 theatre and battle honours, in addition to the Distinguished Service Order, the Military Cross, Distinguished Conduct Medal and many others.

From Sicily to Holland there are 352 graves of West Novas who paid the final sacrifice during the war. There were also 1,084 wounded and missing. Since the Second World War the West Nova Scotia Regiment has been a unit of the Canadian Armed Forces (Reserves). It has contributed soldiers to UN peacekeeping tours in countries such as the former Yugoslavia, Cyprus and the Middle East.

VE Day riots in Halifax

The Halifax VE Day riots, of May 7 and 8, 1945, in Halifax and Dartmouth began as a celebration of the Second World War Victory in Europe.

This rapidly evolved into a rampage by several thousand servicemen, merchant seamen and civilians, who looted the City of Halifax.

Although a subsequent Royal Commission chaired by Justice Roy Kellock blamed lax naval authority and specifically Rear-Admiral Leonard W. Murray, it is generally accepted that the underlying causes were a combination of bureaucratic confusion, insufficient policing, and antipathy between the military and civilians, fuelled by the presence of 25,000 servicemen who had strained Halifax wartime resources to the limit.

A vote for women's rights

April 2018 marked 100 years of women being extended the vote in Nova Scotia — allowing many women to vote for the first time, according to the Nova Scotia Archives.

"While this did not extend to all women, they won the same terms as those granted to men at the time," says information from the archives.

The campaign for the rights granted in 1918 involved the dedicated efforts of women and men from across the province. Suffragettes, as they were known, gathered signatures to submit to the Provincial Government calling for "an acting granting the provincial franchise to women upon the same terms as those upon which it is granted to men."

The petitions of 1918 were not the first attempt to pass this legislation, as earlier attempts in 1894 and 1895 had failed. It took the societal shake up of the First World War, leading to the extension of the franchise to military family members, to refuel the drive for universal extension.

At least 3,865 names on 18 petitions, representing areas from across the province, were presented to the House of Assembly and on April 26, 1918, the legislation was passed.

The names on the petitions represented a cross-section of Nova Scotia society, men and women from all over and with a variety of occupations demonstrating the issue's importance to "regular folk" — homemakers, tailors, music teachers.

Julie Matisoo, a direct bloodline descendent of early Liverpool settler Simeon Perkins, now lives in New Zealand but on July 12, 2015, she was the first Perkins family member to enter the historic home since 1822 when her great-great-great-great grandmother, Elizabeth Perkins, left Liverpool and moved to New York.

History and present collide

Not since 1822, when Elizabeth Perkins, the widow of famed diarist Simeon Perkins, left Liverpool and went to live with her daughter in New York, had a descendant of Perkins walked the historic grounds.

But on July 12, 2015, after almost 200 years, a direct descendant of Perkins not only visited the town that her great-great-great-great grandfather helped to build in the wilderness and establish as a bustling seaport, but she also had the unique opportunity to explore the historic home of her ancestors built in 1766.

Julie Matisoo, accompanied by her husband, Andy, travelled all the way from New Zealand to see the home of her ancestors, Simeon and Elizabeth Perkins. They made the stop following a cross-Canada train trip from Vancouver to Halifax and made a detour to Liverpool before heading to Boston and then onto Maine to visit with family there.

It was their first time in Liverpool and Julie, a native of Indiana, admitted during the visit that the experience was more than a little overwhelming; until a few years ago, she had no idea that her ancestor was such an important historical figure in this part of the world.

A genealogist who spent many years researching her family tree, Matisoo had known the name Simeon Perkins but it wasn't until she was contacted by people at the Queens County Museum a few years earlier, that she came to learn of and really understand Perkins' role in Nova Scotian history.

"I had read a lot about Simeon Perkins, but it really didn't sink in until I began exchanging e-mails with Linda [Rafuse] at the museum, that I finally understood how important he was," she said.

It was strange being in the centuries-old structure, she admitted, following a tour of the historic home where her great-great-great grandmother, Lucy Perkins, was born and raised. Walking through the place was very emotional and educational at the same time, she said.

"It brought my family's history to life," she explained. "After reading about these people for so many years on paper, it gave their story more meaning."

Linda Rafuse, curator of the Queens County Museum, explained that until about five years earlier it was widely believed that there were no direct living descendants of Simeon Perkins anywhere in the world.

However, about five years ago she said they went to an Internet site called the World Connect Project where they made an entry stating that they were looking for anyone who had a direct bloodline to Simeon Perkins. Within a short time they connected with a woman in Kentucky named Ann Prothos who is also a genealogist with a direct family line to Perkins.

"It was she," Rafuse explained, "who told us we should contact Julie Matisoo in New Zealand and so we did and we were pleased to learn that Julie had done a lot of the family research and she could plug many of the gaps that we had regarding the family members after they left Liverpool."

She said they were overwhelmed to finally be in touch with a direct descendant of Simeon, someone whose linage can be traced back to his daughter, Lucy.

Lucy was born in 1780 and was the third of eight children born to Simeon and Elizabeth Perkins. She is Matisoo's great-great-great grandmother and Rafuse said the idea that one of Simeon's descendants has actually now been in the historical house after so many years, was a bit surreal to herself as well as to the members of the Queens County Museum board of directors and members of the local historical society who met her during the momentous visit.

The gap was closed, she said, following the personal tour on July 12 that was given by local historian and Queens County Museum assistant Kathleen Stitt.

The historic home of settler and famed Nova Scotian diarist, Colonel Simeon Perkins, is located on Main Street, Liverpool. Recovered in 1897, the Perkins' diary is considered to be one of Canada's most valuable historic documents as it is essentially a 40-year testimonial to colonial life in Liverpool through his eyes and from his hand.

A native of Connecticut, Perkins immigrated to Nova Scotia in 1762, during the Planter migration, participated in privateering, and soon became one of Liverpool's leading citizens. He established himself as a successful businessman active in West Indian trade and the fisheries.

Perkins was involved in many areas of local and colonial government, conducting business and entertaining royal governors, naval officers, private captains and wandering preachers in his home.

From 1767 until his death in 1812 at age 78, Perkins recorded in his diary the experiences and events of everyday colonial life in Liverpool. Copies of the diary can be seen at the Queens County Museum, located next to the Perkins' House Museum.

As for his former home, Perkins House was restored to its pre-1812 condition from descriptions in the diary. The Cape Cod was built in 1766 for Perkins and it is the oldest house in the Nova Scotia Museum collection.

Matisoo said it was an absolute honour to be in the home as it allowed her to identify with how her ancestors lived and worked. To see where they ate, slept and worked was, she said, an amazing experience for her.

5 FAST FACTS

1. The classic Christmas song, *It's Beginning to Look a Lot Like Christmas* was written in 1951 by American composer and songwriter, Meredith Wilson. Originally titled *It's Beginning to Look Like Christmas*, the song has been recorded by many artists, but was first a hit for Perry Como. Bing Crosby recorded a version on October 1, 1951, which is still widely played today. According to local legend, Wilson wrote the song while visiting Nova Scotia and staying in Yarmouth's Grand Hotel. The song makes reference to a "tree in the Grand Hotel, one in the park as well...". The park is Frost Park, directly across the road from the Grand Hotel, which still operates in a newer building on the same site as the old hotel.

2. Canada's oldest English gravestone is located in the Garrison Cemetery at Fort Anne. It belongs to Bethiah Douglass who died on October 1, 1720.

3. Wolfville Harbour is the smallest harbour in the world.

4. At 2 a.m. on Sunday, April 15, 1923, the "rule of the road" changed in Nova Scotia. After that date, all traffic moved to the right-hand side of the road. Previously, automobiles, streetcars, horses, bicyclists, and all other vehicles and travellers adhered to the left-hand side of the road.

5. The Town of Digby became the first jurisdiction in Nova Scotia to impose a speeding limit when, on July 29, 1910, it was decreed that, "No automobile shall be driven through the streets of the Town of Digby at a speed exceeding six miles per hour [10 km/h] and the drivers of automobiles shall keep the horn sounding while approaching and passing any person driving, walking or standing upon the streets. The penalty for a violation is $30.00 or sixty days in jail."

Important Landmarks

The Battle of Bloody Creek
The Battle of Bloody Creek at Carlton Corner was fought December 8, 1757, during the French and Indian War.

An Acadian and Mi'kmaq militia defeated a detachment of British of soldiers of the 43rd Regiment at Bloody Creek (formerly René Forêt River), which empties into the Annapolis River at what is the present day Carleton Corner.

The battle occurred at the same site as a battle in 1711 during Queen Anne's War.

Halifax Dockyard
Created in 1758 under the supervision of Captain James Cook, the Halifax Dockyard was the earliest Royal Navy dockyard in North America and is still in use by the Royal Canadian Navy.

King's College
The first university to be established in the Dominions of the British Empire was King's College in Windsor. The original site of the oldest university in what was to become Canada (campus now located in Halifax).

Little Dutch (Deutsch) Church
A small, wooden church surrounded by an 18th century burying ground and a stone wall in Halifax is the oldest known surviving church in Canada associated with the German Canadian community.

Marconi National Historic Site
The isolated site in Glace Bay where Guglielmo Marconi received the first transatlantic radio telegraph message; comprises the remains of two telegraph towers that once supported Marconi's antennae and the foundation walls of his receiving room and powerhouse.

Marconi Wireless Station
This 350-hectare (860-acre) site in Cape Breton Regional Municipality contains the foundations of aerial towers and three abandoned buildings; the wireless station, which, along with a sister station in Ireland, was the first to provide regular public intercontinental radio service commencing in 1908.

Old Barrington Meeting House
This wood-frame building was erected by settlers from New England. It is one of the oldest surviving buildings in English-speaking Canada, and a good example of a New England-style colonial meeting house.

St. Paul's Anglican Church
A small, wooden church with a gable roof and central steeple in Halifax is the first building erected in Canada in the Palladian style, and the first church outside Great Britain to be designated an Anglican cathedral.

Thinkers' Lodge
Located in Pugwash, Thinkers' Lodge is the birthplace at the height of the Cold War of the Pugwash Movement, a transnational organization for nuclear disarmament and world peace.

Wolfe's Landing
Wolfe's Landing in Cape Breton Regional Municipality is the site where British forces in James Wolfe's brigade launched their successful attack on the French forces at the Fortress of Louisbourg during the Seven Years' War.

5 FAST FACTS

1. Dr. Daurene Lewis of Halifax, a seventh generation descendant of black slaves who settled in Annapolis Royal in 1783, became the first black woman mayor in North America when she was elected mayor of Annapolis Royal 1984. In 1988, she became the first black woman in Nova Scotia to run (albeit unsuccessfully) in a provincial election. She has received numerous awards for her community service including the Order of Canada.

2. Located north of Sutherland's River, Pictou County, Big Cove YMCA Camp was founded in 1889. It is the longest running and oldest residential camp in North America.

3. Nova Scotians have been called "Bluenoses" or "Bluenosers" since the 1700s because of the blue marks left on the noses of fishermen by their blue mitts. It's also the nickname given to the Nova Scotia British troops, which occupied New York City and Boston during the American Revolution.

4. It is reputed that famed American gangster Al Capone, who was also known as Scarface, was a regular visitor to Riverport, a small fishing village on the province's South Shore, during the era of prohibition where he was said to hole up at the former Myrtle Hotel. Given the secluded location and the fact that the area was heavily immersed in rum running, the legend seems very likely to be true.

5. The Halifax Common, or the Commons as most people call the area in Halifax, is Canada's oldest urban park, with the North Common and the Central Common still in use as a public park area.

Legends

Bridge over troubled waters

When European newcomers suggested that a bridge over The Narrows linking present-day Halifax and Dartmouth would make life a lot simpler, a Mi'kmaw chief warned that this would not be a good idea.

The chief said to build such a bridge would result in three failures — the first would take place during a great wind; the second would happen during a great quiet; and the third catastrophe would result in great death.

In 1887, a hurricane caused the collapse of a railway bridge that had been built across the harbour. Then the temporary bridge to replace the railway bridge fell down on a calm and quiet night.

The Angus L. Macdonald Bridge has now been operating for more than half a century. What fate awaits this existing link is unknown.

Who is Glooscap?

According to Mi'kmaw (Mi'kmaq) legend, Glooscap, the first human, was created out of a bolt of lightening in the sand. These legends are stories that are passed down from generation to generation and tell of the Mi'kmaq culture.

Much of what we know today about the traditional stories, myths and legends of the Mi'kmaq originate with books published in the late 1800s by a Nova Scotia Baptist missionary clergyman, Silas Tertius Rand, an accomplished linguist who became fluent in Mi'kmaq. The stories Rand documented were all told to him in Mi'kmaq, which he then translated and wrote down in English. To increase their accuracy, he then read the translated stories back to the storyteller.

Glooscap's wondrous powers are impressive throughout a number of the Mi'kmaq legends. As demonstrated in many legends, Glooscap even had the power to shape the environment

These legends of Glooscap are passed down from generation to generation and tell of the Mi'kmaq culture.

around him. Since the late 1800s, many authors became entranced by the stories of the Mi'kmaq and with this increase in awareness Glooscap's accomplishments grew. Yet he still embodies the fundamental attribute of wisdom and hope.

In one version of the Mi'kmaq creation myth, Glooskap lay on his back, with arms outstretched and his head toward the rising sun for 365 days and nights; then Nogami, the grandmother, was born as an old woman from the dew of the rock. The next day, Nataoansen, Nephew, was born from the foam of the sea. On the next day was born the Mother of all the Mi'kmaq, from the plants of the Earth.

Glooscap was said by the Mi'kmaq to be great in size and in powers, and to have created natural features such as the Annapolis Valley. In carrying out his feats, he often had to overcome his evil twin brother who wanted rivers to be crooked and mountain ranges to be impassable. In one legend, he turns the evil twin into stone.

Another common story is how he turned himself into a giant beaver and created five islands in the Bay of Fundy by slapping his huge tail in the water with enough force to stir up the earth.

When Glooscap slept, Nova Scotia was his bed and Prince Edward Island, his pillow.

Glooscap is remembered for having saved the world from an evil frog-monster who had swallowed all the Earth's water. Glooscap killed the monster and the water was released. Some animals, relieved at the resurgence of water, jumped in, becoming fish and other aquatic animals.

Of course, this legend like many others, did have some basis in fact. A massive earthquake converted a mountain on the east side of the Penobscot River into a new channel through a split in that mountain. The eastern side of this mountain became Verona Island.

Later, when explorers asked about the location of the stone Fort Norumbega, they were told that it lay on the eastern side of the river (which it did prior to the earthquake), and so could never find the new location. It is presently located in the northwest corner of the Sandy Point Animal Enhancement Area in Sandy Point, Maine.

Glooscap is also believed to have brought the Mi'kmaq stoneware, knowledge of good and evil, fire, tobacco, fishing nets, and canoes, making him a cultural hero. In addition to being a spiritual figure, Glooscap also became a major figure of regional identity for the Bay of Fundy region with everything from steam locomotives, the ship Glooscap, schools, businesses and the Glooscap Trail tourism region named after the heroic figure.

Shag Harbour on Nova Scotia's South Shore is the site of one of Canada's most famous and mysterious UFO incidents.

Are we alone?

That depends upon who you ask, but if you were in the tiny village of Shag Harbour on Nova Scotia's South Shore on the night of October 4, 1967, you might be inclined to answer in the negative.

Shortly after 11 p.m., witnesses reported that a UFO, estimated at 60 feet in diameter, was seen hovering over the water. Those who saw the object reported that they saw four bright lights and those flashed in a uniform pattern. After hovering for several minutes, witnesses said the object tilted and quickly descended toward the water.

Witnesses who immediately called the nearby RCMP detachment located in Barrington Passage reported a bright flash and an explosion. The immediate thought was than an aircraft had plunged into the icy Atlantic. The rush was on as there could be survivors.

With the calls coming in, three RCMP officers were dispatched to the scene, two approaching from east of the site, while a third who was on highway patrol on Highway #3, headed to the impact site from the west. When the three officers met they found that the object was still floating on the water about a half-mile from shore.

It was glowing a pale yellow and was leaving a trail of dense yellow foam as it drifted in the ebb tide. Witnesses later reported that the object had changed shape several times before hitting the water.

Neither the rescue co-ordination centre in Halifax nor the nearby NORAD radar facility at Baccaro had any knowledge of missing aircraft, either civilian or military. Also, a coast guard lifeboat dispatched from nearby Clark's Harbour along with several local fishing boats were sent to the crash site, but the UFO had submerged before they reached the location.

However, the sulphurous-smelling yellow foam continued to bubble to the surface from the point where the UFO went down. In a matter of time, a 120 by 300 foot slick developed. Search efforts continued until 3 a.m. and then resumed at first light the next day, as it was clear that something had gone into the water.

The next morning a preliminary report was sent to Canadian Forces Headquarters in Ottawa. After communicating with NORAD, Maritime Command was asked to conduct an underwater search as soon as possible for the object. Seven navy divers from the HMCS Granby searched for several days throughout the daylight hours until October 8. On October 9, Maritime Command cancelled the search saying nothing was found.

In time, the Shag Harbour UFO became Case #34 in the infamous Condon Committee Report, but whatever the object was remains a mystery even today. This incident is the only UFO crash recorded and recognized by the Canadian Government.

The mysterious Runic (or Yarmouth) Stone was discovered by Dr. Richard Fletcher in 1812 on his property at the head of the Yarmouth Harbour.

What is the Runic Stone?

Ever since 1812, when Dr. Richard Fletcher discovered the Runic (or Yarmouth) Stone on his property at the head of the Yarmouth Harbour, this artifact has been the subject of academic and popular controversy. Many theories have been proposed as to the origin and content of the 13-character inscription on the face of the 400-pound stone.

After Dr. Fletcher discovered the stone near a path that led to a primitive ferry dock, he moved it to a spot near his home, where it stayed for the next 60 years. Around 1872, the stone was moved to the grounds of a local hotel, and later put on display at the library.

Shortly before the First World War, the Runic Stone travelled to Christianna (now Oslo), Norway, where it was shown at an international exhibition. It was then taken to London,

England, where it would remain in storage at the offices of the Canadian Pacific Railway, as ocean travel during the war was hazardous, and it was deemed too risky to transport the stone. It finally returned to Yarmouth sometime after the Armistice of 1918.

After some debate in the 1960s over who actually owned the Runic Stone, the artifact was eventually granted to the Yarmouth County Historical Society, and moved to its current location at the museum.

Although the nature of the mysterious inscription is still a matter of debate, the Norse rune theories remain the most persistent, thus giving the Yarmouth Stone its common name, the Runic Stone.

What really happened on Sacrifice Island?

A few kilometres off the shore from Lunenburg, a small piece of land protrudes from the Atlantic Ocean and is known as Sacrifice Island.

According to legend, the island was named when early settlers, mostly of German and French descent, moved into what is now known as Lunenburg County. Conflict quickly erupted between the settlers and the Indigenous people.

It is said that one summer evening, local Aboriginals carried away several white children from a small settlement that had sprung up along the mainland somewhere in the area of what is now Mahone Bay.

From the shore, the legend goes, the white children where taken to Sacrifice Island where they met their untimely demise. As time rolled on the island became known as Sacrifice Island.

Since no documentation can be found to support this claim, the story is understood to be more folklore than fact. However, locals vehemently believe something tragic did happen there.

Throughout the past two centuries, local seamen have reported seeing lights from Sacrifice Island. As no one lives on the island, they concluded the lights must be the spirits of the children killed there.

How did that bloody handprint get on that rock?

On May 8, 1756, on a 108-acre island strategically stationed in what is today known as Mahone Bay, Louis Payzant was murdered and scalped, but not before leaving his mark on the landscape of local folklore. At the same time, a 12-year-old boy, a servant and her child also met their untimely fates on Covey Island, once known as Payzant Island.

The legend that surrounds the killings on the island is best known locally for the bloody handprint that is emblazoned on a rock that sits a fair distance from where it is believed the Payzant homestead was located more than 250 years ago.

5 FAST FACTS

1. The Fishermen's Exhibition, which ran from 1947 to 1996 in the historic town of Lunenburg, was the only festival of its kind in Canada to celebrate the fishing industry. For 49 years the Festival was held in September, and marked the end of the fishing season. It finished, if the season had been death-free, with a service of thanksgiving; otherwise, with one of remembrance. The Queen of the Sea Pageant was one of the highlights of the weeklong event.

2. Here's a little known fact: there is a Medal of Honour recipient buried in central Halifax in Holy Cross Cemetery, just across the path from Sir John Thompson, one of two Canadian Prime Ministers buried in Halifax. Three of Robinson's shipmates, Ordinary Seaman Peter Cotton, Captain of the Forecastle, Pierre Leon, and Boatswain's Mate John McDonald, also received the medal for their part in the expedition, which took place in Mississippi.

3. An excerpt from an early issue of *The Halifax Chronicle Herald* reads: The wooden structure still overlooks the Avon River at Windsor, but nothing suggests the connection between Fort Edward and the modern-day State of Israel. Nor is there any sign of a link between the small rural community of Nova Scotia's Annapolis Valley and the man known as the father of that Jewish state. But here, almost a century ago, a Zionist leader arrived with hundreds of other Jewish men to train for the newly formed Jewish Legion, a fighting force of the British Army's Royal Fusiliers created to liberate Palestine from Turkish rule during the First World War. That man was David Ben-Gurion (born David Green), who would lead the struggle for an independent Jewish state and, in 1948, become Israel's first Prime Minister. Who knew Nova Scotia's connection with the State of Israel?

4. The Crowley Memorial was erected in 1870 in the Town of Pugwash by the Legislature of Nova Scotia in honour of Mary E. Crowley, who died October 1869 at 12 years of age after rescuing her younger brother and sister from a house fire. This is believed to be the first public monument ever erected to a woman in Canada.

5. Born in Halifax in 1915, Edward Francis Arab was the grandson of the first Lebanese settlers in Halifax. He enlisted in the army on the outbreak of the Second World War and was killed in the 1944 Battle of the Scheldt Estuary in Holland.

Science suggests that the markings are the result of iron deposits that have rusted in the rock. However, the folklore is much more fascinating. The story of the bloody handprint begins with the epic journey of Marie Anne Payzant when, as a Huguenot, she fled from France to Jersey to escape religious persecution. In Jersey, Marie Anne met and married Louis Payzant, who had also fled to Jersey to escape Catholicism.

In 1753, the couple and their four children left a comfortable life on the island of Jersey and sailed across the Atlantic to settle in Lunenburg and, in 1755, built a home on Payzant Island, now Covey Island, in Mahone Bay. Within a year, a Maliseet raiding party, which was loyal to the French, landed on the island, killed and scalped Louis and the three others previously mentioned and took a pregnant Marie Anne and her children captive.

It is said that in the last few minutes of his life, Louis grabbed his bleeding chest, and in one last act of desperation, fell back onto a rock beside the front door, bracing himself with his bloody hand. The intense heat from the burning cabin seared the handprint into the boulder, where it can still be seen today. The rock has since been moved down the hill, where it sits near the beach.

As for Marie Anne and the Payzant children, the Maliseet raiders took the family to Quebec by canoe. Marie Anne was kept as a prisoner of war for four years, and the children were adopted by the Maliseet tribe and the Jesuits. Marie Anne and her children survived the ordeal and eventually made their way back to Nova Scotia. They settled in Falmouth, where Marie Anne remarried and lived to be 85.

Who pulled off the Red Ruse?

Legend has it that in 1782 the women of Chester saved their small settlement from invading forces by reversing their scarlet lined garments and appearing as a British regiment.

It was a defining day of events for the Village of Chester. Capt. Jonathan Prescott, a doctor and one of the educated men who had been among the original settlers who populated Timothy Houghton's community in 1759, then known as Shoreham, had laid the plans for what would be perhaps one of the greatest combat maneuvers that Nova Scotia has ever seen.

In the morning hours, three large vessels identified as American had been spotted entering the mouth of the harbour. Within a short time, the intentions of the invaders were made quite clear as shots rang out in the direction of the blockhouse. Capt. Prescott, one of the few men present, grabbed arms and began returning fire at the vessels.

The bulk of the militia had, in fact, removed to Lunenburg for training; when the American ships appeared, the village was essentially unguarded. Capt. Prescott, realizing that the fate of the community lay in the balance, resisted, firing back at the American vessels, and eventually hitting one. Prescott's efforts appeared fruitful as the vessels hailed, requesting permission to bury their dead.

While it may have been an attempt by the American captains to gather information, Prescott allowed the attackers to proceed under the condition that they be unarmed. Prescott later invited the captains to dine ashore, knowing full well that he needed to buy time, either until the militia returned or until he could come up with a plan.

Meanwhile, as the Americans prepared to depart their vessels, Prescott made arrangements with the women and elderly in the community who had remained behind when the militia departed for Lunenburg. Before dawn, anyone with a redlined cape was to report to the blockhouse where once the sun rose, they would parade about, as if soldiers on guard against an invading force. As the day grew long, the American captains eventually came ashore and met with Prescott for the proposed dinner.

The next morning before the break of dawn, just as planned, the townspeople gathered, cloaks turned inside out, the red of the lining facing outward. Prescott's hope was that the Americans, undoubtedly spying on the blockhouse in the early morning from a distance, would see the women and elderly in red, parading around with brooms, and mistake them for the militia.

It was a dangerous gamble for Prescott. Not only had he lied about the presence of the militia in Timothy Houghton's barn, but he had also used townspeople to create his fictitious militia. If the Americans detected the deceit, they would surely land soldiers and the blockhouse would be instantly overwhelmed and the town ransacked. The worst outcome would be that prisoners would be taken back to New England.

Worse yet, if the Americans failed to detect the deceit but decided nonetheless to pursue an attack on the blockhouse, it would mean the women of the town would be in the line of fire and much blood would be shed. As the sun rose that morning, Capt. Jonathan Prescott held his breath, waiting and hoping. Finally, after many tense moments, Prescott and his garrison of townsfolk watched as the American vessels, having weighed anchor, slowly disappeared from site.

The gambit had paid off and the American privateers had left, not to return. The village had been spared by the clever plan of a doctor-turned-tactician. Unfortunately for the people of Lunenburg, Chester's victory was to their detriment. The American vessels subsequently rolled into Lunenburg harbour and attacked the town, pillaging it and leaving the settlement in chaos.

Is that The Young Teazer you see?

Legend has it that a ghostly burning pirate ship named *The Young Teazer* haunts Mahone Bay. It is said that on summer nights when the moon is full, a flaming ghost of the ship can be seen moving across Mahone Bay.

In 1813, *The Young Teazer* was trapped by a British warship in Mahone Bay. The ship's captain, Frederick Johnson, knew that the game was up. He and his crew faced either imprisonment or death by hanging. Rather than allowing their ship to be captured, the pirates threw a torch into the ship's powder magazine, causing a huge explosion. The ship was blown out of the water in a fiery blaze, killing the captain and the entire ship's crew.

The chase of *The Young Teazer* had come to an unexpectedly abrupt end, apparently at the hands of her own crew. Eight survivors out of the 36-member crew were plucked by the British from the waters near Naas Island on June 27, 1813.

A year after the explosion, locals began reporting sightings of a ship resembling *The Young Teazer*, burning on the horizon. Whenever rescue boats were sent out to investigate, the burning ship simply vanished into thin air.

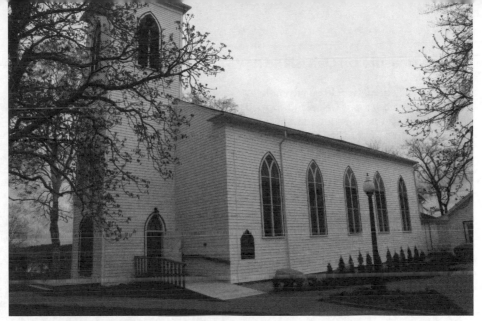

St. Stephen's Anglican Church, built in 1840, is located at the top of a knoll near the corner of Regent and Central Streets in Chester. The church has a unique connection to the story of The Young Teazer.

Over the years, hundreds of people have seen a burning ship out on the bay. Those who saw *The Young Teazer* up close, claimed there were men moving about on her decks, engulfed in flames and running back and forth in a panic. Others even reported hearing the tortured cries of the dead pirates who have been trying to escape their burning ship for more than a century.

But one small detail dealing with the final resting place of the little marauder has been lost in the development of the modern mythology surrounding the ship. While the chase itself did indeed take the vessel through the vast, sprawling waters of Mahone Bay, the fiery end of the adventure actually occurred some distance from what would become the town of Mahone Bay, in the waters off Chester.

A footnote

Here's an interesting footnote to both *The Red Ruse* and *The Young Teazer* legends. St. Stephen's Anglican Church, built in 1840, is located at the top of a knoll near the corner of Regent and Central Streets in Chester.

In 1836, the parish determined that the congregation of St. Stephen's Church had outgrown the original building and four years later it was demolished. Within a week, the new church was sufficiently advanced in its construction and regular service began there in June 1840.

One of the church's early historic associations is with Captain Jonathan Prescott, who was a veteran of the second siege of the Fortress of Louisbourg and was one of the congregation's first wardens. He is buried in St. Stephen's cemetery, which surrounds the church on its north and east elevations.

The church also has a unique historical association that pre-dates its construction. Tradition maintains that the small wooden cross that hangs in the church is made from a section of the keel of *The Young Teazer*, an American privateer that was set on fire by its captain to avoid capture by the Royal Navy during the War of 1812 in Mahone Bay.

Is there treasure on Oak Island?

A collection of legends would be incomplete without the world-famous Oak Island, located just off the rugged, yet picturesque coast near Western Shore, Lunenburg County. This mysterious place has attracted treasure seekers from around the world for centuries. The mystique and aura that surround Oak Island date back to 1795, when the hunt for an elusive treasure began.

Theories abound as to what is buried beneath the rocky, course soil of this small island that has spawned dozens of books and countless ghost stories. Many men have lost fortunes and their lives trying to solve the clues, hoping to ultimately unlock the treasure vault, but to date, the island has refused to give up its secret.

Perhaps the most popular of those theories is that it is a rich booty buried there by a band of blood-thirsty pirates, most notably Captain Kidd, who plied the waters of the Atlantic Ocean hundreds of years ago. Other theories suggest the stash is ancient Inca treasure or that it is the lost manuscripts of William Shakespeare. Some even theorize that the treasure is the Arc of the Covenant, hidden there by the Knights Templar, who were known to have visited the New World long before other early European explorers. The theories are as limited as one's imagination.

The world-famous Oak Island, located just off the rugged, yet picturesque coast near Western Shore, Lunenburg County, has attracted treasure hunters since 1795.

Legend has it that the mystery of Oak Island began in 1795 when a young Daniel McGinnis set out in the early morning hours to row to the island to investigate lights that had been reported there. Some locals said it was restless spirits while others whispered of pirates and buried treasure.

While on the island, McGinnis discovered a clearing in the midst of an oak tree stand. Someone had clearly cut down several trees. The boy also noticed that there was a visible depression in the centre of the clearing, about four metres in diameter, where the soil had obviously been disturbed, replaced and then allowed to settle. A block and tackle, attached to an oak branch hanging from a nearby tree over the centre of the depression, deepened the mystery.

McGinnis immediately became convinced that he had stumbled upon the location of a long forgotten deposit of pirate bounty. Hurrying back to shore, he convinced two friends to return to the island with him. Almost immediately, their efforts were rewarded. Two feet into the depression, they found a layer of intentionally placed flat stones. Digging further they saw that a shaft, about seven feet wide and walled with clay, had been sunk into the surface of Oak Island.

And so began the great Oak Island treasure hunt but the truth is, whatever treasures are buried beneath the ground on the fabled Oak Island remains just as much a mystery today as it did over 200 years ago. Now that's a local legend.

Who was Jerome and what happened to his legs?

Although the mysterious story of Jerome isn't exactly a legend in the traditional sense, its unusual place in the annals of Nova Scotia history and folklore has earned it the right to be included in this collection. As you read on, you'll see why.

In the early morning hours of a fine September day in 1863, near Digby, Nova Scotia, a fisherman busily gathered rock weed along the shore in a place called Sandy Cove on the Bay of Fundy. It wasn't long before he noticed a dark figure nestled alongside a big rock on the beach.

At first, he thought it was a seal because they are common in the area. However, as the fisherman got closer, he saw that the figure was that of a huddled man, his legs wrapped in bloodied cloth. Upon inspection, he found that both of the man's legs had been amputated just above the knees by a skilled surgeon, but the stumps were only partially healed and bandaged. The man was also suffering from cold and exposure.

Beside the man in the sand was a jug of water and a tin of biscuits, placed there by whoever had deposited this bloodied stranger. There were footprints on the beach, and blowing about were a few strips of linen that could have been bandages.

There were no other clues and no clue as to the man's identity except that when he moaned and tried to speak, it was in a foreign language that the fisherman did not understand. The fisherman later recalled he had seen a ship passing back and forth the day before, about a kilometre offshore in St. Mary's Bay. Residents of the area concluded the man must have been brought in from the ship after dark and left on shore. No one knew why.

The castaway, who was about 25 years of age, was carried to the home of Mr. Gidney in nearby Mink Cove, where he was wrapped in warm blankets and given hot drinks. Through the moaning and muttering, only one word was understood. Witnesses said they heard him whisper, "Jerome." Thinking that might be the name of the mysterious man, that is what local residents began to call the stranger who had been deposited without explanation in their midst.

Following a physical examination, it was discovered that Jerome's hands were not calloused, which implied he was not of the working class. As well, the stranger's clothing was curious. His waistcoat was delicately lined and was unmistakably of a foreign pattern. His shirt was of the finest linen, while his knee-length pants were made of a material unknown to the people of Digby.

Speculation up and down the bay soon led many to believe he had attempted a mutiny on one of the foreign ships that pass the bay on their way to and from Europe, and was punished by amputation. Others suggested the mysterious man had been tossed from a pirate ship, perhaps as retribution for some unspeakable deed. Most thought, however, that he was heir to a fortune and had been crippled and cast away to make way for someone else seeking his inheritance. None of the stories has ever been proven.

Although Jerome was almost terrified of most adults, he seemed fond of children. He spent most of his time with children and seemed to enjoy watching them play. Fitting into the community, Jerome conducted himself with dignity, and when offered money, he would appear humiliated, as if too proud to take a handout.

However, he would accept gifts of candy, tobacco and fruit. He was wary of strangers, but in appearance and manner, he was a gentleman and easy to care for. Eventually, he could move nimbly on his stumps but he still sat most of the time.

It was clear that with no clues to his identity and nowhere else to go, Jerome was there to stay in the tiny seaside village on the northern shore of Nova Scotia. To help cover his expenses, the provincial government contributed two dollars per week toward his keep.

5 FAST FACTS

1. The Sambro Island Lighthouse is the oldest lighthouse in Nova Scotia. In fact, built in 1758, it is the oldest continuously working lighthouse in the Americas. The tower height is 82 feet and it stands 140 feet above sea level. The lighthouse was built during the Seven Years War by the very first act passed by Nova Scotia's House of Assembly on October 2, 1758, which placed a tax on incoming vessels and alcohol imports to pay for the lighthouse. Located at the entrance to Halifax Harbour, the Sambro Light has been upgraded over the years, but predates New Jersey's Sandy Hook Light by four years, and Virginia's Cape Henry Light, Maine's photogenic Portland Head Light and Long Island's Montauk Point Light by three decades.

2. On July 17, 1749, Governor Cornwallis granted a license to sell beer and liquor to John Shippey, making it the first liquor license to be issued in New Scotland (Nova Scotia). Shippey named his tavern The Spread Eagle, as its sign was taken from the German coat of arms — The Double Eagle. Shortly after opening, the tavern became affectionately known as The Split Crow.

3. The Split Crow, located at the southwest corner of Salter and Water Street, was a second home for sailors, mariners and travellers. There they could expect comfortable lodgings, hearty platters of food and generous mugs of grog. In the tradition of the day, music was played, ladies entertained, politics were discussed and, inevitably, fights broke out. One of these fights resulted in the first ever murder charge in Nova Scotia.

4. The first charted bank in Nova Scotia opened on August 29, 1832, when the first branch of The Bank of Nova Scotia opened for business in Halifax at the corner of Granville and Duke streets.

5. The second branch of the Bank of Nova Scotia opened in 1839 in Yarmouth, but its real claim to fame is that it is said to have been the site of the first recorded bank robbery in North America in 1861.

Throughout the years, sailors from many countries around the world were brought to Jerome to see if he would speak their language. He still did not speak, but some observers believed that he was familiar with European languages. He would become very angry when any such visitor mentioned Trieste, a city in northeast Italy.

Some people believed that he was of noble stature and that he once must have been an officer. From his looks and complexion, they felt he must be French or Italian. In time, Jerome was taken to the home of John Nicholas in Meteghan, who spoke several European languages.

Mr. Nicholas tried to break Jerome's silence but failed. Jerome spent seven years with Mr. Nicholas and the remaining 42 years of his life with Deider Comeau and his family at Alphonse de Clare.

As the years went by, Jerome would make his way down to the water's edge on fine days. There he would sit for hours, gazing toward the sea as if he were expecting visitors from beyond the horizon. The locals became and remained convinced that the legless man lived in constant fear of someone or something.

In time, residents noted that Jerome withdrew further into himself. He would often spend days in his room gazing from his window toward the sea. Other times he would sit on the floor, his head bowed and his hands folded. Close to the last 30 years of his life were spent in absolute silence. His eyes held a tortured look, as if some terrible burden rested on his soul.

On one occasion, as if in payment for some evil done in the remote past, he pressed his hands against a hot stove. His hands were horribly blistered, but Jerome did nothing to acknowledge the pain.

Many attempts were made to find an identity for this mystery man, but none succeeded. When Jerome died on April 19, 1912, he took with him the secret of his mutilation and of his mysterious arrival on the Bay of Fundy shore.

Who was Jerome? Where had he come from? What macabre circumstances had led to his mutilation and abandonment?

Those who knew him best believed Jerome had carried within his heart a secret too terrible to divulge. And if silence had been his pledge, he had kept it well. For almost 50 long and monotonous years he had waited for death, and when it came, it found a silent and inscrutable Jerome. A large stone marker bearing the only name "Jerome" can be found in the Meteghan parish cemetery where he was buried.

In summer 2006, Jerome's story made headlines once again when it was declared that the mystery of how the legless, mute man came to the Nova Scotia shore in 1863 may have been solved. Historian John Lutz of the University of Victoria said in August that new information, found in a New Brunswick archive, could hold the key to the mystery. It told of a man who was "exhibiting strange behaviour and couldn't speak. Members of his community rid themselves of the eccentric by tossing him into the sea, but not before surgically amputating his legs."

They then set him adrift, hoping he would eventually make it New England. John Lutz believes this is the same man who ended up in the remote Nova Scotian village near Digby.

Has the mystery of Jerome been finally solved? Not likely, say many of the locals. Not likely.

The Mystery Walls of Bayers Lake

The Bayers Lake Mystery Walls are a series of stone structures and walls of unknown origin and uncertain age located in Halifax.

The ruins consist of walls outlining a small, five-sided building and a 150-metre wall with ditches, both made with flat-surfaced ironstone slate rocks on the slope of a hill overlooking the Bayers Lake Park.

The mysterious ruins pose many unanswered questions for archaeologists and historians. The most simple and humble explanation suggests a sheep pen, but some suggest they were built for a military purpose, either a training installation or a

The mysterious walls located at Bayers Lake pose many unanswered questions for archaeologists and historians.

defensive work. The walls are a protected archaeological site designated under Nova Scotia's Special Places Act.

The site is included within the historic limits of one of the nine original Dutch Village grants issued in 1762 — a 150-acre grant assigned to Johann Gotlieb Shermuller. Schermuller sold the property in 1770 and moved to Philadelphia, where he became a butcher.

The site changed hands many times after 1770. However, given its ground conditions, it is unlikely to ever have been farmed. A 1918 map depicts a building standing in approximately the location of the site steps, the only structure on the property for which there is known documentary evidence.

In October 1990, Jack McNab contacted local media regarding this site, as it was about to be cleared for the newly developed Bayers Lake Business Park. His effort helped protect the area. In 2013, the Nova Scotia Archaeology Society set up a committee called Bayer's Lake Walls Historical Site Advocacy, as a result of recent vandalism to the site.

In December 1998, a lichenologist examined the masonry of the wall and identified patterns of lichen growth that indicated that the stonework had not been disturbed since around 1798.

The Legend of Boxing Rock

Boxing Rock is a shoal off Hartz Point in Shelburne Harbour that's exposed only at low tide.

Legend has it that centuries ago, sea captains sailing their vessels into the still fledgling settlement known as Port Roseway which is present day Shelburne, found a special way to use the rock.

According to information on the website for Boxing Rock Brewery located in Shelburne, sailing ships spent weeks or months at sea. Crews ate, slept and worked within inches of each other — seeing, smelling, hearing and jostling one another every moment of every day. Inevitably, they became irritated with their fellow sailors and when some men reached the end of their patience, captains dealt with bickering crew by assigning them opposite watches or even throwing them in the hold together until they sorted out their differences. Sometimes, Boxing Rock was the only answer.

In an age when most sailors couldn't swim, a disagreement that set a couple of crewmembers on Boxing Rock forced a quick resolution. Imagine the captain calling over the gunwales, "Here's the deal, boys. Shake hands and share a beer or box until one of you drops. We'll be back before high tide to pick up one or both of you."

More often than not, the two would duke it out, only the winner returning to the ship. But every now and then a pair would appreciate the dry land beneath their feet — however modest a chunk — and the break from their labours and the jug of beer they agreed to share.

They would sit together, laugh together, and drink together, breathing the fresh air and watching the waves lap at their feet while awaiting the ship's return.

Yo Ho Ho and a good pirate story

Nova Scotia is rich in pirate folklore where imagination takes over from history. Pirate legends exist for almost every major island in the province.

In Halifax alone, Georges Island is said to be haunted by two young pirates hanged there in 1785. And Hangman's Beach is supposed to be haunted by hanged mutineers near the lighthouse. Also on the island, strange noises and lights were seen in 1845 near Finlay Cove beside a mysterious hole in the ground.

Pirate legends exist for almost every major island in the province.

Navy Island, in Bedford Basin, is also home to treasure legends, including a whole crew of pirate ghosts who stand guard over the treasure there. At Oak Island in Mahone Bay, home to one of the world's greatest and longest running treasure hunts, searchers have been unsuccessfully digging for more than two centuries.

The "Golden Age of Piracy" occurred from 1690 to 1730. Nova Scotia was largely unsettled by Europeans, making it a possible location for pirates to hide or refit, according to Dan Conlin, former curator of marine history at the Maritime Museum of the Atlantic.

5 FAST FACTS

1. The oldest tree ever found in Nova Scotia — a 418-year-old eastern hemlock — was discovered by a university student studying environmental science. While its exact location has never been publicly revealed to protect the tree, it is known that it stands somewhere in southwestern Nova Scotia. With 418 rings, the hemlock beat the previous record in Nova Scotia by 20 years. The eastern hemlock, like many of the oldest trees in the world ever found, was not very large. Despite its age — the 11th-oldest eastern hemlock in the world — the tree is only 30 centimetres in diameter. It is the third oldest ever found in Canada. The two older eastern hemlock trees were both located in southern Ontario.

2. Stewiake is halfway between the Equator and the North Pole.

3. Halifax is closer to Dublin, Ireland, than it is to Victoria, British Columbia.

4. The Order of Good Cheer was established by Samuel de Champlain in Port Royal (then known as Acadia) in the winter of 1606-07. It was the first gastronomic society in North America. The Order of Good Cheer provided good food and good times for the men to improve their health and morale during the long winter. Although it lasted only one winter, the society was a great success.

5. The Town of Antigonish is home to the oldest continuous Highland Games outside of Scotland. Highland games are events held throughout the year in Scotland and other countries as a way of celebrating Scottish and Gaelic culture and heritage, especially that of the Scottish Highlands. Certain aspects of the games are so well known they have become emblematic of Scotland, such as the bagpipes, the kilt and the heavy events, especially the caber toss. While centred on competitions in piping and drumming, dancing, and Scottish heavy athletics, the games also include entertainment and exhibits related to other aspects of Scottish and Gaelic culture.

The governor of Fortress Louisbourg in the mid 1720s was so afraid of pirate attacks in Cape Breton that he asked for extra naval protection, Conlin writes.

One of the nastiest pirates of the Golden Age was Ned Low. He raided fishing fleets that used Nova Scotian harbours as shelters and fishing stations. Low's exploits include an incident in which he terrorized a New England fleet in Shelburne in 1720.

There is some speculation that Low hid treasure somewhere in Nova Scotia, adding to the many legends that suggest that untold riches of unclaimed pirate booty remain buried somewhere in the province.

Conlin explains that centuries ago the law required that pirates be executed with their bodies displayed in public as a warning to other sailors.

"The body was covered in tar and hanged from chains in an iron cage called a gibbet," he writes. "The Royal Navy used the same treatment on mutineers."

Two pirates were hanged this way on Georges Island in 1785. Another, Conlin says, named Jordan the Pirate, was hanged at Point Pleasant Park, near the Black Rock beach in 1809.

At the same time, the Navy hanged six mutineers at Hangman's Beach on McNab's Island; any ship entering Halifax Harbour in 1809 had to pass between hanging and rotting corpses.

The last major piracy trial in Nova Scotia was in 1844 when a gang of six pirates were brought to Halifax in 1844 when their ship, the barque *Saladin*, was shipwrecked on the Eastern Shore.

"*Saladin* had a cargo of silver bars and a large shipment of coins. They had mutinied and killed the captain and half the crew before falling out among themselves," Conlin writes. "Initially charged with piracy, they were subsequently convicted of murder. Four of them were hanged near the old VG hospital on South Park Street."

According to legend, two of the bodies are believed to be under the sidewalk at the library on Spring Garden Road.

While they were not pirates, Conlin explains naval sailors and privateers (sailing licensed private warships) personally profited from capturing enemy ships in wartime as they received a share called "prize money" from each capture. Sometimes their aggressive captures gave them a "piratical" reputation.

Another popular legend has it that the pirate William Kidd hid treasure somewhere in what is present day Nova Scotia before he surrendered to authorities in 1699.

Kidd is the only pirate known to have actually hidden treasure. However, only one location was ever verified, Gardener's Island near Long Island, New York. While there are theories and speculation that Nova Scotia may have been one of his hiding places, there is no real evidence to suppose this.

Stories of pirates and pirate treasure run throughout Nova Scotia including Mira River in Cape Breton where it is believed a pirate shipyard was once located.

In an article in on the *goCapeBreton.com* website, Richard Lorway writes Mira River is the site of pirate legends that go back hundreds of years to the time before Fortress Louisbourg was constructed.

Lorway says historic records indicate that Bartholomew Roberts known as Black Bart, one of the most successful captains during the Golden Age of Piracy from 1650 – 1730, once used the Mira as an operating base.

During the course of his career, Roberts captured more than 400 ships. His reputation was so fierce that when Roberts sailed into the bay and hoisted his colours (flew his flag), the other captains and crews abandoned their ships and hid ashore.

Why did pirates establish a shipyard on the Mira River? In an article published in *Cape Breton's Magazine* in 1977, writer and historian David Dow explained that its location was strategic. Mira was very near the Great Circle Route, and mostly uninhabited at that time. "Treasure ships, bound for Spain using the Gulf Stream and the trade winds, would pass a few hundred miles off of Cape Breton. Ships travelling up the St. Lawrence were less than a day's sail away, and Newfoundland was similarly placed."

The shipyard itself was set in a little cove off the side of the gut that cannot be seen from the bay. It was out of range of ship cannons and easily defended by gun batteries on the cliffs that tower 50 feet above the cove entrance.

When in operation, the stream feeding the inlet was dammed to create a millpond, and the sluiced water likely used to drive a stamp mill for ironwork.

As the Fortress of Louisbourg was developed, the increased activity of the French and British navies in the area made the location less attractive, and the shipyard was eventually abandoned. During the last century, the mouth of the cove filled with silt, and it can now only be accessed by canoe or kayak.

For centuries, the thought of finding buried treasure in Nova Scotia has intrigued and inspired the imagination of locals and others worldwide. Dozens of areas throughout this province and seacoast claim to shield the stolen booty of pirates, sunken money ships and the confiscated cultural cashes from long-lost cities.

An article published in July 2015 on the SaltWire Network says Pictou County has had accounts reported of buried treasure within its seacoast and landmass. Some are very well known, such as the buried gold of Caribou Island. The story has been passed down for generations and attempts have been made over the years to retrieve the riches.

Supposedly, in 1755, a French frigate buried a large cache of gold destined to pay the soldiers at Quebec. They built a "well of stone" and deposited the bullion deep within its rock walls. Over the years, attempts have been made to recover the fortune, but have proved unsuccessful. Ghostly sightings at night have been reported of French sailors walking about the beach near Gullrock Lighthouse protecting their stash.

Another well-known buried treasure story was reported in Rev. George Patterson's *A History of the County of Pictou, 1877*. A French war ship containing salvaged treasures had escaped the British attack on Louisburg in 1758.

The French vessel was chased into Caribou Harbour and eventually beached at a little inlet off the Little Caribou River. Instructions were left with the Mi'Kmaq First Nation people that if discovered by the English, the craft was to be burned.

The father and uncle of Pictou Deputy Sherriff Thomas Harris found the abandoned French ship. When they returned with implements to move her, she had been torched.

Some 44 years later, a vessel was reported travelling up the Caribou River at night and in the morning the people of the area discovered a shallow hole dug at the head of tidewater. All clues point to a buried treasure dig.

Another relatively unknown buried treasure story occurred in the French River area of Pictou County. In the latter part of the 1800s a family story had been passed down about a cache of riches hidden "a few miles east of the river under a tall tree."

In 1902, an attempt was made to unearth the hoard but proved unsuccessful. As reported, "an unknown schooner sailed down the French River" and the local people found a "big hole under the tree with an imprint of a very heavy box and a hurried excavation."

Did the Chinese settle in Cape Breton?

It was in 2002 when Cape Bretoner Paul Chiasson, a Yale-trained architect and amateur historian, went hiking up Kelly's Mountain on Cape Breton Island and waded into a controversial story that has subsequently morphed into legend status.

As Joe O'Conner reported in an article appearing in the *National Post* on December 2, 2010, it was during this hike that Chiasson stumbled upon an old road bordered by stone walls, which has put him on a quest to prove that the Ming Dynasty Chinese discovered North America, and settled in Cape Breton in the 15th century long before the voyages of Christopher Columbus.

After that first hike he kept going back to Kelly's Mountain, and kept finding evidence, that in his mind, confirmed human habitation.

O'Conner wrote, "Stone pilings, slabs of slate, mounds that appeared to be graves and rocks with curious markings. He had aerial photos taken, dove in to the history books and produced his startling theory, packaged in book form."

The Island of Seven Cities: Where the Chinese settled when they discovered North America hit the shelves in 2006, and was immediately met with a landslide of scepticism.

The Chinese were ancient mariners. They built ocean-going vessels that documentation shows sailed as far as South Africa. But there is a whole lot of ocean between South Africa and Cape Breton, wrote O'Conner.

To the skeptics, Mr. Chiasson's great wall looked suspiciously like a mid-20th century firebreak, while his road — his "emblem of civilization"— was once a fire road and then a gravel road built by a company surveying the area as a possible site for a gravel pit.

Despite the sceptics he pushed on.

His story eventually attracted the interest of Stephen Ellis of Ellis Entertainment, a long-standing player in the Canadian documentary field. He was responsible for *Mysterious Ruins: Cape Breton*, a 44-minute look at Mr. Chiasson's lonely pursuit that aired on History Television in December 2010.

The documentary explored Chiasson's theory and included interviews with an archeologist and a geologist from the area who viewed the site that Chiasson theorizes was the location of a pre-Columbian Chinese community. Both stated that they found no evidence of any human settlement on the site.

As part of the investigation, a film crew was sent to China to interview several architectural historians. They showed them aerial photographs and extensive footage from the top of Kelly's Mountain.

"I feel that what he has found is not yet enough to prove that it is ruins of a Chinese settlement," stated Dr. Zhu Guangya, Professor of Architectural History at Southeast University. "But it is possible."

Possible, as in — maybe — instead of a resounding "no."

Mr. Chiasson's book has been published in China. His Chinese pen name is Xia Yay Song.

"There is no easy explanation for what is there," Mr. Chiasson says. "So the easy explanation is that nothing is there."

Chiasson challenges his critics in his second book, *Written in the Ruins: Cape Breton Island's Second Pre-Columbian Chinese Settlement*.

What's that under the street?

There is a long-held legend in the privateering seaport of Liverpool, located on Nova Scotia's South Shore, that the bodies of two dearly departed men are buried beneath two of the town's streets.

And, in fact, there is some historical documentation to confirm these legends, that while strange, are actually more fact than fiction.

It is recorded in the famous Simeon Perkins diary that William Brocklesby died on December 13, 1799. Brocklesby, a reformed alcoholic, worked as a mason and had quit drinking two and a half years prior to his suicide.

But he got "in with privateers people at Mrs [sic] Boyles," Perkins writes and he was on a drinking binge of about one week before his death.

He died by hanging himself in John Robert's barn, located near Weir Lane behind the building at what is now 325-327 Main Street.

In those times, people who died by their own hands were not permitted to be buried in hallowed ground.

According to local legend, a man by the name of William Brocklesby is buried under this Liverpool street. Now known as Old Bridge Street, the road forms the border of the town's historic old burying ground.

Following Brocklesby's death, a coroner's inquest was held and Brocklesby was subsequently "buryed [sic] in the lane by the burying ground."

Today, this lane is known as Old Bridge Street.

While explicit details of the second body are not as well known or documented as the first, according to legend a young soldier reportedly hanged himself in Perkins' apple orchard located near the top of Hop Toad Hill after receiving a Dear John letter from the woman he loved. (He was perhaps a member of the famed King's Orange Rangers who defended the privateering port at this juncture in history.) Today, this area is the location of Queens General Hospital and the Queens RCMP detachment.

Because the young soldier took his own life, it is said that his body was buried under the road located at the foot of the hill. Several hundred years ago, the road would have been nothing more than a wagon path. Based on today's coordinates, however, that location would be somewhere in the area of the four-way intersection of School and Waterloo Streets.

So what's the story here?

The centuries-old practice of burying bodies under the streets and roads of early settlements originated in Europe and came with the settlers of the new world. As it was a sin to take one's own life, the deceased could not be buried in hallowed ground and furthermore, because of the nature of the death, it was believed the spirit of the deceased would be restless and would want to roam. It was believed that the traffic from the street (path or trail) would force the spirit to remain planted in the ground.

In some instances, the practice of burying the deceased in the streets also included burying the body face down and in more extreme cases, driving a wooden stake through the body to keep the spirit pinned in place.

The body of a man who committed suicide hundreds of years earlier, is said to be buried somewhere near this intersection and under the pavement.

The Legend of the Lunenburg werewolf

While the origins of this story are not clear, a detailed chronicle of the events that earned him a place in the darker side of the town's past were written by author Theodore Hennigar and published in the *Progress Enterprise* on April 12, 1963.

According to an item published on Facebook page, *Maritime Monsters and Weird Stories*, the tale begins in December 1755 when a French girl named Nanette managed to escape to the woods after British troops had invaded and destroyed the village where she lived in the Cornwallis Valley, now the Annapolis Valley.

After a period of wandering, she came upon a Mi'kmaq settlement where she was taken in, cared for and treated as one of their own. Days later, Nanette appeared with a female Mi'kmaq elder at a small German settlement on the outskirts of present-day Lunenburg where they encountered an old woman who took an immediate liking to the young girl, expressing a desire to adopt her.

An agreement was struck and, after Nanette was traded for a crimson handkerchief, she again was back in a white family where she grew into "a charming young woman with a beautiful face, manner, amiable disposition and a magnetic power of making friends among both young and old."

While those qualities attracted a variety of suitors, Nanette's affections fell to one Hans Gerhardt, "a finely built German lad of the community who had a particular temper."

According to the article, the two were wed and for a time enjoyed an idyllic marriage in which they were "extremely devoted to each other."

Soon they were blessed with a baby daughter, an event which rather than enhancing their affections for each other, had a strangely opposite effect.

"It seemed Hans was incapable of understanding the love of Nanette for her daughter," Hennigar wrote. "He became jealous and moody, falling into violent fits of temper over nothing, feeding his peculiar mind with fuel for the fires of self-pity which raged within."

Occupied with her newborn child, Nanette did not realize for some time that something was amiss with her husband. When she finally did, she took it for granted that he had become ill, perhaps from working too hard on their farm.

Hans then began to display even more erratic behaviour, and began sleeping in the kitchen, apart from his wife, saying he was being disturbed by the baby as he tried to rest.

He also took to wandering from their home at night, a practice that became more and more regular and one which he would not discuss with his wife when she questioned him of his activities.

It was at that time that strange tales of a mysterious nightly presence, manlike, but able to run swiftly on all fours, began circulating in the community.

Farmers started finding their lambs "lying dead in the morning with their throats torn from ear to ear, and the blood gone from their bodies."

At first, bears were suspected as the culprits, but it was reasoned that that could not be the case since the meat of the animals was not taken nor was it consumed. Hans joined the hunters who were trying to find whatever beast was killing the lambs, but no guilty party could be identified.

That summer, with the blueberries in full ripeness, Hans left the family home one afternoon with a basket to harvest the fruit. After rocking the baby asleep, Nanette left the child at home and joined her husband in the fields.

His basket full, he returned to the house to empty it.

Soon realizing that her husband had been gone a long time and thinking that something might have happened to the baby, Nanette raced home where she discovered that both daughter and husband were missing.

A search party was hastily arranged, and those men entered the woods where they came upon a gurgling brook, [and] Hans Gerhardt crouching low over the water.

"At their approach, he sprang up with a snarling cry and turned upon them with animal fury," Mr. Hennigar wrote. "The strong men soon subdued him, however, and tied him. There were bloodstains on his arms, and a wet spot on his blue linen blouse.

"'Mon Dieu! He has killed her,' shrieked Nanette, and Hans tried to spring at her, but the men had done a good job of tying him and his struggle was in vain."

Hans was taken to Lunenburg, jailed, and sentenced to die for his alleged crime, but that eventuality never took place.

When his cell was opened the next morning, he lay dead on the floor, the veins of his arms ripped open by his own teeth, which caused him to bleed to death.

He was buried in a nameless grave on Gallows Hill.

5 FAST FACTS

1. Evan Farmer was the last person in Nova Scotia to be executed in 1937. He was from Shelburne and had killed his step-brother after an argument. This came almost 30 years before Canada abolished capital punishment. The last executions in Canada were in 1962.

2. The oldest courthouse in Canada is the Argyle Township Courthouse and Gaol located in Tusket. Gaol is an old British word for jail. It's no longer used as a jail though, as it was decommissioned in 1944. It later became government offices for the municipal government from 1944 to 1976. In 1982 it became a museum.

3. The first courthouse in Canada was built in 1797 at the corner of Brunswick Street and Main Street in Liverpool. In 1853, Chief Justice Brenton Halliburton publicly reprimanded Liverpool Township for the deplorable conditions of their courthouse. At the time, Liverpool hosted the Supreme Court and the Court of General Sessions of the Peace. In response, representatives from Queens County gathered in 1854 to plan the building of a new courthouse.

4. Wayne Adams was the first African Nova Scotian elected as a member of the provincial legislature. He served from 1993 to 1998.

5. Nova Scotia's first Acadian cabinet minister was Gerald Doucet in 1964.

The legends of Seal Island

Seal Island is a small piece of rocky land in the North Atlantic situated just off the southern-most tip of Nova Scotia. One of the oldest wooden lighthouses in Canada is located there.

In earlier times, Seal Island was the home of a small number of French Acadian settlers who fished for a living. Today, the island is abandoned, except for the few summer residents who visit and, possibly a few spirits; according to local legend, Seal Island is home to a ghost named Annie.

Known for the treacherous waters that surround the island, over the centuries an untold number shipwrecks occurred around the shoals and rocks, leaving scores of humans either dead or missing.

History records that those who were lucky enough to have reached the island's shores alive often died of starvation and exposure during the harsh winter months. The early years of the 19th century spawned a grim spring tradition: preachers and residents from Yarmouth and Barrington would head to the island where they found the remains of those who had perished during the preceeding winter, and then proceeded to bury the dead.

Some say that on one occasion, 21 people were buried in shallow graves in a single day. In 1823, two families, the Hichens and the Crowells settled on the island in the hopes of assist-ing the unfortunate souls cast ashore during the winter storms.

The story of Annie goes back to October 31, 1891, when the newly built steamer SS *Ottawa*, on voyage from London, England, departed Halifax for Saint John, New Brunswick.

It was a dark and stormy night and the seas were boiling, the swells driven by a strong southwest gale. Resulting problems at the Seal Island light set the *Ottawa* on a course for destruction as it hit a large rock located just off the shores of Seal Island.

Information from the Nova Scotia Museum and Nova Scotia Lighthouse Preservation Society says that, in the midst of the storm, the steamer struck Blonde Rock at 5 a.m. on Sunday, November 1, at low tide and ran aground.

The resulting impact ripped a large, gaping hole in the ship's bottom, flooding the engine compartment. With the starboard side being broadside to the sea and with a strong list to starboard, the sea became worse and broke heavily over the ship.

With her stern submerged, the lifeboats were launched, and in one of those boats were three men along with the ship's stewardess, Mrs. Annie Lindsay.

When the boat was about two ships' lengths from the steamer, it was overturned by a tre-mendous wave, throwing its passengers into the sea, trapping them all underneath the boat, except for one man who managed to climb on to the keel. After a few minutes the mate also managed to climb on to the keel, leaving Annie and the third man trapped under the boat.

Strong tides and waves made it difficult for the other lifeboat to rescue those in the water, but as their boat drifted in the heavy sea, the waves eventually turned the boat upright again, and the two men got back in the boat. Surprisingly, the man that was trapped under the boat managed to survive, but Annie was dead.

After seven hours of hard rowing against the wind and sea, the crew of the ill-fated *Ottawa* made it safely to Seal Island.

Once on shore, Annie was buried beside the East End church. Her grave was marked in later years by a concrete headstone made by the family of the lightkeeper. Some believe that when the coffin was later disinterred, it showed evidence that she was buried alive.

Today, according to legend, the spirit of Mrs. Annie Lindsay still haunts the shores of Seal Island.

The story of Annie is but one of many that centre on Seal Island. Another local legend revolves around the brig *Triumph* that was en route from New York to Halifax loaded with a cargo of flour and passengers. The brig ran ashore at Seal Island in November 1861.

Records suggest that in total 10 people died in the tragedy but only three bodies were recovered, those being the remains of three supposedly naked women that washed ashore following the crash.

By this time, Seal Island was inhabited by a number of families and according to local legend, the unclothed remains of three women were found floating in the water by several young boys who had been out exploring the shores following the shipwreck on the southern end of the island.

Adults were quickly summoned to the scene and the youngsters were immediately sent home to protect them from a heinous scene. The adults pulled the bodies ashore, lined them up on the beach and then buried them there in three graves, side by side.

While the graves are clearly marked with headstones, the great mystery remains — who were these women? Why were they naked? Where were they from? Where were they headed?

No one knows.

These three graves contain the remains of three unknown women who were lost when the brig Triumph ran aground on Seal Island in November 1861.

According to local legend, every seven years the wreckage of a mysterious vessel on Summerville Beach shows itself to the curiosity seekers. These images were taken in the summer of 2018 when the wreckage was visible for about two weeks.

The ghost ship of Summerville Beach

There is a beautiful beach located on the South Shore of Nova Scotia where according to local legend, every seven years the wreckage of a mysterious vessel shows itself to curiosity seekers.

Known as the 'Ghost Ship of Summerville Beach' (in the Region of Queens) it is believed the pieces of the wooden vessel have been buried under the shifting sands for several centuries. Throughout the years, they have been noted in local historical documents, including the famous diaries of early Liverpool settler and privateer Simeon Perkins.

Today, the Perkins Diaries are considered the definitive historical record of colonial settlement in Nova Scotia. Several passages in Perkins' diary (1766 1780) may hold the secret of the ghost ship of Summerville Beach.

On September 20, 1778, Perkins recorded, "There was an engagement between a Halifax cruiser — (perhaps *TRUBLU*) — and a privateer sloop from Dartmouth (probably Dartmouth, Mass.) at Port Mouton. The sloop ran near the shore, brought her guns to bear on the ship to keep off the enemy."

The next diary entry concerning shipping was made by Perkins on September 24, 1778. "It was recorded that the privateer burned their vessel and saved the guns."

But a more probable solution is this entry from October 25, 1778: "Mr. Hallett Collins reported a ship and sloop came into Port Mouton. The privateer sloop ran ashore and they set fire to her themselves. The schooner went out."

While it is possible that one of the vessels Perkins refers to in his diary is the one that rests below the shifting sands of Summerville Beach, the truth is that no one really knows the truth about the mysterious wreckage. However, there are lots of theories about its identity, including the possibility that it could be the remains of an early Viking vessel or a Spanish galleon that once sailed in the waters off what is now the province of Nova Scotia, or a Privateer vessel that patrolled the troubled waters of the North Atlantic.

Historical records show that many vessels met their demise off Little Hope Island, located just off Port Joli Point. It is highly possible that wreckage from any one of these ships could have floated down the coast into Port Mouton Bay and come to rest onto Summerville Beach.

Over the decades, visitors to Summerville Beach have observed several pieces of oak planks in the sand at low water, near Broad River at the far end of the beach. The planks are secured to members just below by wooden pins at each joint. These planks were visible again during several weeks in July 2018.

One local researcher with a piqued interest in the Summerville Beach wreckage, David Pottier, shares his theory of the mysterious vessel that comes and goes with the shifting sands.

"The wooden wreck has been on the beach all of our lives," he says, noting that local lore says that the ship may reappear about every seven years before vanishing into the sands once more.

The summer of 2018 saw her return and Pottier says not having seen her in 40 years, he felt locals needed to protect the wreck and try to learn where she was built and her age.

These are the facts, he says — she was built from solid oak, stitched together with wooden treenails. American naval vessels were oak but there are no records of such a wreck in these waters. Bronze nails came into use around 1553. A metal detector found nothing — no metal — so the wreck is older, possibly much older, than the 16th century.

"An Israeli friend of mine, both Naval architect and archeologist, gave me a direction about what to look for. He was right, our wreck matched 16th century French naval specifications. Champlain arrived in Port Mouton Bay in 1604 but there are no records of a lost naval vessel since then."

The exposed oak keel, not reported previously, had the letter Y carved by the final dovetail. Working towards the bow, 25 letters X distance to next exposed dovetail, the local wreck had a keel length over 60 feet long.

"From the letter 'Y' carved into the keel, the exposed structure we are familiar with is the stern castle, which is in a capsized position."

What could the ghost ship have been, Pottier wonders? Where did she come from?

"Spanish Galleons were known to have transited and sunk in our waters in the early 17th century, but bronze nails were used to set their treenails, so that can't be it," Pottier explains. "She could be Basque, whose fishery existed off Newfoundland as early as 1525, but there are no records of Basque whaling in this area. The Basque fishery ended in 1625."

The Basque whaling industry in North America lasted from 1525 until 1625. To date, the oldest shipwreck ever discovered in Canadian waters is the Basque whaling galleon *San Juan*, which sank near the shore of Red Bay, Labrador, in the autumn of 1565. The *San Juan* was a 52-foot, three-masted, 250-ton ship.

Pottier says the marine archeologist who retrieved the whaler *San Juan* told him she was built using bronze nails.

"This fits within what we know about this period in shipbuilding. Nails came into use in 1553. The Summerville wreck has been scanned with a metal detector and has no nails.

Or, he continues, "She could also be part of the lost Knights Templar treasure fleet that sailed from La Rochelle, France, and vanished. Today, clues to the Templar fleet's final destination all point to Oak Island."

Our ghost ship needs to be aged, identified and preserved. It is our heritage, he says, adding that until definitive research is complete, the mystery of the Summerville ghost ship will remain.

5 FAST FACTS

1. The donair was named the official food of Halifax in 2018 with December 8th being named National Donair Day.

2. The unofficial world record for most donairs eaten in an hour is held by Joel Hansen from Halifax who ate 19 donairs in 60 minutes on January 1, 2019.

3. According to the Guinness Book of World Records, the record for the largest documented lobster goes to one caught off the coast of Nova Scotia on February 11, 1977. It weighed 20.14 kilograms (44 pounds, 6 ounces) and was estimated to be over 100 years old!

4. Nova Scotia celebrated its first official Lobster Day on February 28, 2020, honouring the province's lobster fishery heritage and culture, as well as its economic importance.

5. The largest man made explosion (before the Atomic Bomb) happened in Halifax on December 6, 1917, resulting in almost 2000 deaths and an estimated 9000 injuries.

The Great Amherst Mystery

The Great Amherst Mystery was a notorious case of reported poltergeist activity in Amherst between 1878 and 1879.

It was the subject of an investigation by Walter Hubbell, an actor with an interest in psychic phenomena, who kept what he claimed was a diary of events in the house and which was later expanded into a popular book.

The Amherst Mystery centred on Esther Cox, who lived in a house with her married sister Olive Teed, Olive's husband, Daniel, and their two young children. A brother and sister of Esther and Olive also lived in the house, as did Daniel's brother John Teed.

According to Hubbell's account, events began at the end of August 1878 after 18-year-old Esther was subjected to an attempted sexual assault by a male friend. This left her in great distress, and shortly after, it is said the physical phenomena began.

That activity included knockings and bangings in the night, and Esther herself began to suffer seizures in which her body visibly swelled and she experienced unexplained fevers and chills. Then objects in the house took flight.

The frightened family called in a doctor. During his visit, bedclothes moved, scratching noises were heard and the words "Esther Cox, you are mine to kill" appeared on the wall by the head of Esther's bed.

The following day the doctor administered sedatives to Esther to calm her and help her sleep, whereupon more noises and flying objects manifested themselves. Attempts to communicate with the "spirit" resulted in tapped responses to questions.

The phenomena continued for some months, and became well known locally. Visitors to the cottage, including clergymen, heard banging and knocking and witnessed moving objects, often when Esther herself was under close observation.

In December, Esther fell ill with diphtheria. No phenomena were observed during the two weeks she spent in bed, nor during the time she spent recuperating afterwards at the home of a married sister in Sackville, New Brunswick. However, when she returned to Amherst the mysterious events began again, this time involving the outbreak of fires in various places in the house.

Esther herself now claimed to see the "ghost," which threatened to burn the house down unless she left.

In January 1879, Esther moved in with another local family, but the manifestations around her continued and were witnessed by many people, some of whom conversed with the "ghost" by questioning and rapped answers. Some were curious and sympathetic; others believed Esther herself to be responsible for the phenomena, and she met with some hostility locally.

Esther was frequently slapped, pricked and scratched by the "ghost," and on one occasion was stabbed in the back with a clasp knife.

Interest in the case grew as the news spread, and in late March Esther spent some time in Saint John, New Brunswick, where she was investigated by some local gentlemen with an interest in science.

By now, several distinct "spirits" were apparently associated with Esther and communicating with onlookers via knocks and rappings.

Bob Nickle, the original "ghost," claimed to have been a shoemaker in life, and others identified themselves as Peter Cox, a relative of Esther's, and Maggie Fisher.

After the visit to Saint John, Esther spent some time with the Van Amberghs, friends with a peaceful farm near Amherst. She returned to the Teeds' cottage in the summer of 1879, whereupon the phenomena broke out again. It was at this point that Walter Hubbell arrived, attracted by the publicity surrounding the case, and moved into the Teed cottage as a lodger to investigate the phenomena.

Hubbell spent some weeks with Esther and her family, and reported having personally witnessed moving objects, fires and items appearing from nowhere. He claimed that he saw phenomena occur even when Esther herself was in full view and obviously unconnected with them.

He also claimed to have witnessed attacks on Esther with pins and other sharp objects, and to have seen her in several of her fits of extreme swelling and pain. He communicated with the various named "spirits" by rapping, and listed three others: Mary Fisher, Jane Nickle and Eliza McNeal, who were also manifesting themselves as part of events.

With Hubbell's professional help, Esther embarked on a speaking tour, attracting audiences who paid to see her and hear her story. However, she met with some hostile reactions and after she was heckled one night and a disturbance broke out, the attempt was abandoned.

Esther returned to Amherst once more, working for a man named Arthur Davison, but after his barn burned down he accused her of arson and she was convicted and sentenced to four months in prison, although she was released after only one.

After this, the phenomena gradually ceased for good. Esther Cox subsequently married twice, having a son by both of her husbands. She moved to Brockton, Massachusetts, with her second husband and died on November 8, 1912, at the age of 52.

Hubbell's book was published in 1879 and proved popular, selling at least 55,000 copies.

At arm's length

When trying to keep their children from misbehaving, stressed parents will sometimes tell their offspring embellished stories or exaggerated tales of the fantastical as if to shock or frighten them into listening and settling down.

Often spine-chilling, some of these stories take on their own life, ultimately becoming urban legends.

One of the most popular of those urban legends is about a young boy about six years old. The boy was in the back seat of a car when his mother told him to keep his arm inside the window or a truck may come along and hit it.

Like most impetuous young children, the boy never listened to his mother and kept his arm outside. And as the small, fragile arm was flailing in the wind, a truck sped by the car and hit the appendage.

Naturally, because he hadn't taken heed of his mother's warnings, the young boy didn't tell her what had happened, fearing she would be angry and punish him for not listening. Instead, he just yanked it back inside the car and became very quiet.

His mother sighed, thinking that her young son had finally taken her warnings to heart. With the usually energetic boy hunkered down in the back seat, the remainder of the trip home was uneventful.

However, the story goes that when the boy got home and took off his jacket, his arm just fell off and hit the floor.

While there is no record to support this story, the events that resulted in this urban legend are said to have happened sometime between 1974-1976 in Nova Scotia.

(Author's confession: I remember doing this as a youngster. If I had only known.)

5 FAST FACTS

1. Ethel Ruby Keeler, born in Dartmouth on August 25, 1909, was an actress, dancer and singer most famous for her on-screen pairing with Dick Powell in a string of successful early musicals at Warner Brothers, particulary 1933's 42nd Street. From 1928 to 1940, she was married to actor and singer Al Jolson. She retired from show business in the 1940s, but made a widely publicized come-back on Broadway in 1971. She died on February 28, 1993 in California.

2. Cabot House, an 18-storey building built in 1970 and located in Sydney, is the tallest building in Cape Breton.

3. One of Canada's most acclaimed painters, Alex Colville, was born in Toronto but is largely considered a Nova Scotian. He died at the age of 92 on July 16, 2013 in Wolfville. In July 2020, Colville's 1976 canvas "Dog and Bridge" shattered a price record for a work by the Canadian master at a live auction selling for $2.4 million.

4. At one time, cabbage was rarely grown in Nova Scotia and was difficult to find across the province except in Lunenburg County.

5. Mi'kmaw stories refer to Kejimkujik as the "land of the fairies."

Noteworthy People

First mayor of Halifax

On April 19, 1841, the town of Halifax was incorporated as a city by an act of the Provincial Legislature.

Stephen Binney was elected as the first Mayor of Halifax that same year, but it was an office he would not hold for long.

On January 3, 1842, Mayor Binney embarked for England. At the Halifax City Hall, Alderman Kenny acted as mayor until the middle of March, when Binney's leave of absence expired. Subsequently, his seat was declared vacant and Kenny was sworn in as mayor to complete the first mayor's term.

In turn, Mayor Stephen Binney passed out of the picture and into the annals of history with the distinction of being the first mayor of Halifax.

Joseph Barss: the greatest of the privateers

Joseph Barss Jr., born February 21, 1776, in Liverpool, was the son of sea captain Joseph Barss Sr. and Elizabeth Crowell.

Barss' parents were married in 1773 and were one of the first families to settle in Liverpool. Barss was the second of their 14 children. In 1798, the Barss family built one of the largest homes in Liverpool. The house still stands today and is part of the Lane's Privateer Inn.

The home of privateers Captain Joseph Barss Sr. and his son Captain Joseph Barss Jr. The original structure was built in 1797 and is today operated as Lane's Privateer Inn on Bristol Avenue.

Barss gained experience as a privateer against the French in the 1790s, serving in several privateer vessels, as an officer on the ship *Charles Mary Wentworth* and in command of the privateer schooner *Lord Spencer*. The schooner sank after striking a reef in the West Indies but Barss and his entire crew survived to be rescued by other Nova Scotian privateer vessels.

Barss briefly served as commander of the brig *Rover*, a noted privateer vessel from Liverpool, famous for its voyages commanded by Alexander Godfrey, another colonial Nova Scotian privateer.

In 1812, Barss took command of the *Liverpool Packet*, a captured slave ship originally named the *Severn* and sometimes nicknamed *The Black Joke*. Within a year, he had captured at least 33 American vessels.

He was known for his excellent use of intelligence on American shipping movement, due in large part to his brother, John Barss. He was also known for his fair treatment of prisoners.

In 1813, following pursuit by the schooner *Thomas* of Portsmouth, New Hampshire, which ended in a short battle, Barss surrendered the *Packet*. This defeat brought no embarrassment upon Barss, as the *Thomas* was over twice the size of the *Packet*, not only in gross tonnage (143 tons vs. 67 tons), but in firepower (12 guns vs. 5) and crew (80 vs. 45) as well.

After several months of harsh imprisonment, Barss was set free and paroled so long as he did not command a privateer vessel again. He was briefly captured a second time during the war in command of a merchant vessel.

In 1804, he married Olivia DeWolf, the daughter of Judge Elisha DeWolf. After the War of 1812, Barss settled near Kentville. He had nine children and lived there the rest of his life.

Barss died on August 3, 1824, near Kentville and was buried in the Oak Grove cemetery at Kentville.

Edward Jordan's skull

Edward Jordan was a 'Black Irishman' originally from County Carlow, Ireland. He had been involved in the events that prepared the way for the Irish rebellion of 1798. During the rebellion he was captured, tried, and sentenced to death; he managed to escape, only to be caught again.

Curator Dan Conlin tells Jordan's story in a 2007 exhibit at Maritime Museum of the Atlantic Ethical Considerations of Display of Human Remains: The Jordan Pirate Skull.

Turning informer, Jordan received a King's Pardon and married, but was forced to flee Ireland when his past contacts discovered his betrayal. He and his wife, Margaret, landed in New York in 1803, moved to Montréal, Quebec, and finally to Gaspé, Newfoundland, where he settled as a fisherman with the help of a creditor.

The heart of Jordan's livelihood as a fisherman was his schooner *Three Sisters*, named for his three young daughters at the time. However, distressed by consistent bad luck, Jordan fell into debt with his creditor and sought help from Halifax merchants J. & J. Tremain.

After a series of more woeful events, Jordan eventually became indebted to J. & J. Tremain.

In late 1809, Captain Stairs was sent by these Halifax merchants to retrieve the 1000 quintals (1 quintal being approximately 100 kilograms) of fish promised by Jordan to repay his debt.

Once in Gaspé, Stairs instead found only 100 quintals and was forced to take *Three Sisters* from Jordan to repay the debt. Still, Stairs offered Jordan and his family passage to Halifax aboard their ship, where he might find employment more easily than in Gaspé.

On September 10, 1809, *Three Sisters* sailed for Halifax with Captain Stairs, three crew members (John Kelly, Tom Heath and Ben Matthews), Edward Jordan, his wife, Margaret Jordan, and their four children.

Three days later on September 13, Jordan pulled out a pistol and shot at Captain Stairs but missed and killed crew member Heath, standing next to him. A conflict immediately arose pitting Jordan and Margaret against Stairs and Matthews.

It was reported that throughout the entire struggle Kelly continued to navigate and steer *Three Sisters*. Jordan, with the help of Margaret, killed Matthews. After being wounded, Stairs jumped overboard.

Jordan insisted on changing course to "make sure that John was finished." Kelly refused, stating that it was unlikely Stairs would make the swim back to shore in the running sea and that if were they to bring the ship around it would be difficult, if not impossible, to locate Stairs in the bad weather that was coming up around the schooner.

Jordan, his family, and Kelly sailed to Newfoundland with plans to hire a crew and continue on back to Ireland. A schooner heading for Massachusetts, however, rescued Stairs. He then made his way to Halifax, where he reported what had occurred aboard *Three Sisters*.

The British Consul circulated a description of the ship all along the Eastern coast. The instructions to all legal authorities were to "arrest Jordan and Kelly, whenever found, on charges of piracy and murder."

The reason Jordan was charged with piracy and not mutiny was that he was technically a passenger aboard the ship and not a crewmember, though it made little difference as the penalties for both was the same: death.

Once the news of the crime reached the city of Halifax, a reward of £100 was offered for the capture of "the pirate Jordan."

Cruisers were sent out of Halifax Harbour to run down *Three Sisters*. She was eventually captured by the schooner H.M.S. *Cuttle* in Bay of Bulls, Newfoundland. Although Jordan and his family were determined to make their way to Ireland, all were brought to Halifax.

The Court of Admiralty held the trial under the Acts of William and Mary. Jordan was convicted and sentenced to be hanged. His wife, Margaret, was discharged, as the court felt she had acted out of "duress or fear of her husband."

Jordan was executed on November 23, 1809, "on [the beach near Freshwater/ [Bridge] Halifax, being hanged from the neck until dead. After execution, his body was tarred and gibbeted, or hanged in chains, in Point Pleasant Park at Black Rock Beach near Steele's Pond."

Harsh laws developed during the Golden Age of Piracy (1690-1750), such as the British Piracy

Acts that required the bodies of executed pirates to be displayed in public as a warning to other mariners. The same year, the Royal Navy had gibbeted four or six mutineers on McNab's Island at Mauger's Beach (Hangman's Beach), just across the Harbour from Black Rock Beach.

Any ship entering Halifax Harbour in 1809 faced a gauntlet of rotting corpses as their welcome to Halifax. For those citizens of Halifax who walked through Point Pleasant Park, the sight of Jordan's corpse would have been an unavoidable one, as it was located just beside the main road.

Conlin writes, "It remained there for over three decades, slowly deteriorating, dropping into the sea, until only the skull remained. In 1844 the skull was collected from Point Pleasant Park and ultimately it was given to the Nova Scotia Museum (NSM)."

In 2007, it was on display at the Maritime Museum of the Atlantic (MMA) as a part of their "Pirates: Myth vs. Reality" exhibit.

Nova Scotia's first female lawyer

"Everyone called her Frank." That's how one lawyer who had known her all his life remembered her.

According to a short biography by Barry Cahill published on the *NBGS MIRAMICHI* website, Frances Lillian Fish was the middle of five sisters. She was described as "an athletic, husky-voiced woman who played ice hockey into her mid-twenties."

Fish never married, instead becoming a lifelong advocate for women, children and the disadvantaged and in her later years, was famous for her tulip garden.

"A hard-working woman in a man's profession and a man's world, she practiced law continuously for 40 years," Cahill writes. "She was Nova Scotia's first female lawyer, and the first woman in the province to graduate with a law degree."

When Fish was called to the Nova Scotia Bar in September 1918 at age 29, the event made front page news in Halifax.

Born in Newcastle (now Miramichi), New Brunswick, she and all four of her sisters were university educated. Three got degrees at the University of New Brunswick and the youngest — Ruth Foster Fish Davidson — also became a lawyer in North Carolina in 1930.

Upon graduating in classics from UNB in 1910, Fish went on scholarship to the University of Chicago, where she earned an MA. While teaching at the Grammar School in Campbellton in 1913, she became a student-at-law, only the third woman in New Brunswick to do so.

In 1915, she came to Dalhousie Law School, where she received her LLB in 1918. That summer, she worked at what is now Burchells LLP, then with Robert Yeoman, a fellow Newcastle native who was counsel to the Halifax Relief Commission, which was set up in the aftermath of the 1917 Halifax Explosion.

Fish intended to settle here permanently, but it was not to be. At the law firm, she had been hired only to replace junior partner James Layton Ralston until he returned from overseas service.

A.K. MacLean, MP, and head of Burchells, found a post for her in Ottawa at the Department of Finance. She later joined the Canadian head office of Metropolitan Life also in Ottawa, then went to Montreal where her mother and sister were living.

From 1918 to 1934, Fish did not practice law at all. Cahill writes, "Mystery surrounds her sudden and permanent departure from Halifax, which may have had something to do with a broken engagement."

After her father's death in 1933, Fish moved back to Newcastle. Called to the New Brunswick Bar in 1934, she spent the rest of her life practicing in her hometown, at first as a criminal lawyer before turning to divorce and family law.

In the provincial election of 1935, Fish became the first woman to run for the New Brunswick legislature and ran for a federal seat that same year.

In 1947, Fish was appointed Deputy Magistrate for Northumberland County, holding the post until required to retire at age 75 in 1963, when she became a deputy judge of the Juvenile Court. Receiving her QC designation in 1972, she remained in practice until a few months before her death in October 1975.

From Sydney to Hollywood

George Alan Cleveland was a Canadian film actor. He appeared in more than 180 films between 1930 and 1954, and in television shows up to his death in 1957.

Cleveland was born in Sydney, Cape Breton, on September 17, 1885. He moved to Hollywood in 1936 and went on to work in films via acting, producing and directing.

Cleveland is perhaps best remembered today as George "Gramps" Miller in the early years of the long running American television series *Lassie*. The early seasons in which Cleveland appeared were retitled *Jeff's Collie* for syndicated reruns and DVD release.

He played the grumpy but kind-hearted father-in-law of farmwoman Ellen Miller (Jan Clayton) and grandfather of Lassie's owner, Jeff (Tommy Rettig).

Cleveland appeared in the first three seasons (1954–1956) and in the first 12 episodes of the fourth season (1957). His death in July 1957 was written into the 13th episode of the fourth season (1957) and became the storyline motive for the selling of the farm and the departure of the Millers for Capitol City.

Cleveland died of a heart attack on July 15, 1957, in Burbank, California at age 71. He was survived by his spouse Dorothy Melleck, whom he married in 1955.

An American war hero born in Yarmouth

General George Churchill Kenney was born in Yarmouth on August 6, 1889, while his family was on vacation there, but he grew up in Brookline, Massachusetts.

He attended Massachusetts Institute of Technology from 1907 to 1911, but never completed his degree, choosing a career with a railroad company as an engineer instead.

He enlisted in the United States Army Signal Corps in 1917 as a flying cadet, and was commissioned as a first lieutenant in 1917 after earning a reputation as the first man who installed machines guns on the wings of an aircraft.

He had a distinguished career as a United States Army Air Forces general during the Second World War and was commander of the Allied air forces in the Southwest Pacific Area (SWPA) from August 1942 until 1945.

One of Kenney's most successful air operations was the destruction of a major Japanese re-inforcement fleet during the Battle of the Bismarck Sea in 1943. The loss of most of this huge armada, loaded with supplies and troop reinforcements, ended Japanese hopes of retaining control of New Guinea.

Kenney received the four stars of a full general on March 9, 1945, and after the Second World War served in Europe as a staff officer. During a career which spanned over 30 years, Kenney received many honours and decorations.

Kenney wrote three books about the SWPA air campaigns he led during the Second World War. After his retirement, Kenney lived in Florida in where he died on August 9, 1977.

A man of science

Arthur Bruce McDonald, born August 29, 1943, in Sydney, Cape Breton, is a Nobel Prize winning astrophysicist.

McDonald is the director of the Sudbury Neutrino Observatory Collaboration and held the Gordon and Patricia Gray Chair in Particle Astrophysics at Queen's University in Kingston, Ontario, from 2006 and 2013.

He was awarded the 2015 Nobel Prize in Physics jointly with Japanese physicist Takaaki Fajita.

McDonald graduated with a B.Sc. in Physics in 1964 and M.Sc. in physics in 1965 from Dalhousie University. He then obtained his Ph.D. in physics in 1969 from the California Institute of Technology.

McDonald cited a high school math teacher and his first-year physics professor at Dalhousie as his inspirations for going into the field of physics.

Breaking the gender barrier

Bernadette Jordan, Liberal MP for the riding of South Shore-St. Margaret's, is the first woman federal cabinet minster from Nova Scotia.

Jordan was first elected to the House of Commons in Justin Trudeau's Liberal sweep in 2015. She was re-elected to the seat in the 2019 general election.

Jordan was sworn in as the Minister of Fisheries, Oceans and the Canadian Coast Guard on November 20, 2019. Prior to the October 2019 general election, she had served as Minister of Rural Economic Development, a new portfolio created by Trudeau.

Liberal MP Bernadette Jordan is the first woman federal cabinet minster from Nova Scotia.

In her earlier life, Jordan completed a Bachelor's degree in Political Science at St. Francis Xavier University. Before entering politics, she was a development officer for the Health Services Foundation in Bridgewater, where she spent eight years as part of a team raising millions of dollars for health care in the region.

She had been involved in her community for years, holding positions such as President of the Atlantic Community Newspapers Association and Chair of the Earth Day Challenge Committee.

Jordan and her husband, Dave, have raised three children, Isaac, Mason, and Rebecca.

Breaking the colour barrier

William (Bill) Riley, born September 20, 1950, in Amherst, goes down in the sports hockey books as the first black hockey player and the third overall to play in the National Hockey League (NHL).

Riley's mother worked as a cleaning lady, while his father pulled in the minimum wage of $1.25 per hour. In spite of the financial situation, they made the necessary sacrifices to outfit their son with the necessary skates and pads to play hockey starting in peewee.

Riley stuck with the game in spite of the absence of many black role models in the sport. After two seasons with the Amherst Ramblers, a team he would go on to coach many years later, he held no aspirations of pursuing hockey as a big-league career.

In 1973, while working in a factory and playing senior hockey with the Kitimat Eagles senior team in the Pacific Northwest Hockey League in British Columbia, Riley was discovered after putting up 206 points in 80 games across two seasons.

Future NHL coach Tom McVie was in the process of fortifying his lineup for the Dayton Gems of the International Hockey League (IHL). He discovered Riley in Kitimat and invited him for a tryout. Riley accepted and made the club in 1974.

Riley was given a tryout with the Washington Capitals during their inaugural season in 1974-75 and played in one game, but he spent most of his time in the minors, primarily with the Dayton Gems. It was during this time that he was reunited with and played under future Capitals coach McVie.

He would eventually be signed as a free agent by the Capitals during the 1976-77 NHL season and played for the Capitals in parts of the next three seasons.

Riley was claimed by the Winnipeg Jets in the 1979 NHL Expansion Draft, but only played in 14 games before he was sent to the minors, where he played with the New Brunswick Hawks, Moncton Alpines and Nova Scotia Voyageurs, until he retired following the 1983–84 season.

Riley was player-coach and captain of the St. John's Capitals of the Newfoundland Senior Hockey League for three seasons during the late 1980s.

After retiring from professional play, Riley returned to coaching in 1989-90, when he landed a head coaching position with the Amherst Ramblers of the Nova Scotia Junior Hockey League.

Later, he was the head coach, general manager and director of player personnel of the Miramichi Timberwolves of the Maritime Junior A Hockey League. He also served as head coach of the Moncton Wildcats during the 1996-97 season, finishing with a 16–52–2 record.

A Blue Man from Nova Scotia

Blue Man Group is an American performance art company formed in 1987 known worldwide for its various stage productions, which typically incorporate many different categories of music and art, both popular and obscure, in their performances.

Blue Man Group currently has continuing theatrical productions in Berlin, Boston, Chicago, Las Vegas, New York City and Orlando.

A typical Blue Man production employs seven to nine full-time Blue Men who are selected through an audition process. In addition to the stage theatre show, Blue Man Group has had multiple national and global tours, appeared on various TV programs as both characters and performers, appeared on the Norwegian Cruise Line ship *Epic,* released multiple studio albums, contributed to a number of film scores, performed with orchestras around the U.S., and appeared in ad campaigns.

One of the current Blue Men on the roster, Scott Bishop, was born in Kentville. Bishop once lived in Vancouver and now resides in Toronto.

A legendary trailblazer

Carrie M. Best, a black Canadian journalist and social activist, was born March 4, 1903, in New Glasgow.

She was the daughter of James and Georgina Ashe Prevoe. She married Albert T. Best in 1925 and they had one son, James Calbert Best, in 1926. They would later adopt four foster children.

In 1943, Best confronted the racial segregation of the Roseland Theatre in New Glasgow when she purchased two tickets for the downstairs seating of the theatre and attempted to watch a film with her son. Both were arrested and fought the charges in an attempt to challenge the legal justification of the theatre's segregation.

Their case was unsuccessful and they had to pay damages to Roseland's owners. However, the experience helped motivate Best to found *The Clarion* in 1946, the first black-owned and published newspaper in Nova Scotia. It became an important voice in exposing racism and exploring the lives of black Nova Scotians.

In the first edition of *The Clarion* she broke the story of Viola Desmond who also challenged racial segregation at the Roseland Theatre and whose story became a milestone human rights case in Canada.

In 1952, Best started a radio show, *The Quiet Corner*, which aired for 12 years. From 1968 to 1975, she was a columnist for *The Pictou Advocate*, a newspaper based in Pictou.

Her son, James, who helped found *The Clarion*, went on to become a union activist, senior public servant and high commissioner to Trinidad and Tobago.

She published an autobiography, *That Lonesome Road*, in 1977. In 1974, she was made a Member of the Order of Canada and was promoted to Officer in 1979. She was posthumously awarded the Order of Nova Scotia in 2002.

On February 1, 2011, Best was commemorated on a postage stamp issued by Canada Post. Best died in New Glasgow on July 24, 2001, at the age of 98 of natural causes.

Marking a milestone

On January 23, 2017, Catherine Benton, a lawyer with Nova Scotia Legal Aid, became the second Mi'kmaw to serve as a judge in Nova Scotia and the first Mi'kmaw woman to join the judiciary.

Benton was born in P.E.I. circa 1965. Her mother was from Lennox Island First Nation. Prior to going into law, Benton worked as a family support worker in Lennox Island First Nation.

The family moved to Nova Scotia where Benton began her law career. In 1994, she was appointed to the Nova Scotian Bar. In 2017 at the age of 52, she became the first Mi'kmaw woman appointed to the Nova Scotian Bench.

Prior to attaining her law degree, Benton worked as a researcher for the Union of Nova Scotia Indians and the Mi'kmaq Grand Council.

She graduated with her law degree from Dalhousie University Schulich School of Law in 1993. She was appointed to the Nova Scotia Bar a year later.

She practiced poverty law for 22 years, managing the Nova Scotia Legal Aid Bridgewater office. She was also on the board of directors of the Tawaak Housing Association; the Micmac Native Friendship Centre; and the Mi'kmaq Justice Institute, a forerunner of the Mi'kmaw Legal Support Network.

In January 2016, Benton received the Queen's Counsel designation for "demonstrating professional integrity, good character, and outstanding contributions to the practice of law."

The provincial court presides over most indictable offence charges under the Criminal Code and has exclusive jurisdiction over all summary offence charges under provincial and federal statutes and regulations except a charge of murder by an adult.

The family court provides a forum to hear family issues, including maintenance, custody and access and child protection matters.

It is written — on paper

Charles Fenerty, a Nova Scotian-born inventor, goes down in history as the person who invented the wood pulp process for papermaking, which first adapted into the production of newsprint. He was also a poet, writing over 32 known poems.

Fenerty was born in Upper Falmouth in January 1821. He was the youngest of three boys, all of whom worked for their father, a lumberman and farmer. During the winter months, the Fenertys would clear-cut the local forests for lumber, which they then transported to the family's lumber mill at Springfield Lake.

They shipped their lumber to the Halifax dockyards, where it was exported or used locally. The Fenertys had around 1,000 acres (404.6 hectares) of farmland and they shipped most of their produce to the markets in Halifax.

As a young man, Fenerty also began writing poetry. His first (known) poem, written when he was 17 years old, was titled *The Prince's Lodge*, which was later retitled as *Passing Away* and published in 1888. It described an abandoned, decaying home overlooking the Bedford Basin near Halifax. The lodge had been built decades earlier by Prince Edward Augustus, Duke of Kent and Strathearn, who later returned to England.

Each time Fenerty hauled lumber and produce to Halifax, he would pass the local paper mills, and sometimes stopped by to watch the process, since there were many similarities between lumber and paper mills. In those days, paper was made from pulped rags, cotton and other plant fibres, a technique used for nearly 2000 years.

Demand for paper was outstripping the supply of rags, and Europe started cutting down their shipments of cotton to North America. Fenerty had learned that trees have fibres too, through discussions with naturalist Titus Smith.

At the age of 17 (in c.1838) he began his experiments of making paper from wood. By 1844, he had perfected the process (including bleaching the pulp to a white colour). In a letter written by a family member circa 1915, it is mentioned that Charles Fenerty had shown a crude sample of his paper to a friend named Charles Hamilton in 1840 (a relative of his future wife), though the family member in question would have been around eight at the time.

On October 26, 1844, Fenerty took a sample of his paper to Halifax's top newspaper, the *Acadian Recorder*, where he had written a letter on his newly invented paper.

Other inventors had used wood to make paper. In the 18th century, a French scientist by the name of René Antoine Ferchault de Réaumur suggested that paper could be made from trees. His theory caught the interest of Matthias Koops who in 1800 experimented with papermaking by compressing and adhering straw and wood shavings.

In about 1838 German weaver Friedrich Gottlob Keller read Réaumur's report. Unaware of Fenerty across the ocean, he experimented for a few years and in 1845, a year after Fenerty's letter to the newspaper, filed for a patent in Germany for the ground wood pulp process for making modern paper.

In that same year, Henry Voelter bought the patent for about $500 and started making paper. His venture wasn't financially successful, and he later was unable to afford to renew his patent. Voelter has been credited in Germany as the first to make paper from wood pulp.

Fenerty was also a well-known poet of his time, publishing more than 33 (known) poems. Some of the better known titles were: *Betula Nigra* (about a black birch tree), *Essay on Progress* (published in 1866), and *The Prince's Lodge* (about Prince Edward Augustus, Duke of Kent and Strathearn, written around 1838 and published in 1888).

In October 1854, he won first prize for *Betula Nigra* at the Nova Scotia Industrial Exhibition.

Fenerty did extensive travelling throughout Australia between the years 1858 to 1865, living through the Australian gold rushes, and then returned to Halifax. He became involved with the church and held several positions in Halifax including Wood Measurer, Census Taker, Health Warden, Tax Collector for his community, and Overseer of the Poor.

Little attention was given to Fenerty's invention, and he himself never developed his process or took out a patent on it even though it did mark the beginning of a new industry. Today, most people attribute F. G. Keller as the original inventor.

Pulped wood paper slowly began to be adopted by paper mills. German newspapers were the first to adopt the new paper, and then other newspapers made the switch from rags to wood pulp. Soon there were mills throughout Canada, the U.S., and Europe, and later the rest of the world.

A wood pulp paper mill was even erected near Fenerty's hometown and by the end of the 19th century almost all newspapers in the western world were using pulp wood newsprint.

Fenerty died on June 10, 1892, in his home in Lower Sackville, from a flu. He and his wife, Anne Hamilton, had no children.

A sad Nova Scotian link to the Vietnam War

In the Little St. Margaret's Bay United Baptist Church Cemetery, Cpl. Dennis Richard Schmidt is buried. He was 21 years of age when he became the first Nova Scotia man to be killed while serving in South Vietnam.

Denis was the son of Bernard R. Schmidt and Belle A. Schmidt of North Plainfield, New Jersey, USA. He was born on June 6, 1945, in East Chester, Lunenburg County, and lived in Halifax where he attended Tower Road School. He later moved to Kentville with his parents and lived there attending Kentville High School four years before moving to the United States.

While in New Jersey, Schmidt enlisted in the US Marine Corps on August 12, 1964, in New York. Upon completion of Boot Camp at Parris Island in South Carolina followed by Infantry Training at Camp Geiger, he was assigned to his first unit for duty as a Rifleman with Company H, 2nd Battalion, 6th Marines, 2d Marine Division FMF at Camp LeJeune, North Carolina, on December 11, 1964.

After leave on October 8, 1965, he returned to his unit where he received orders for duty in Vietnam and upon arrival in South East Asia April 19, 1966, he was assigned to and served with Company E, 2d Battalion, 4th Marines, 3d Marine Division (Rein) FMF in northern Quang Tri Province.

With the termination of Operation HASTINGS, Operation PRAIRIE began in northern Quang Tri Province. On August 8, a Recon Team on patrol northeast of the Rock pile made contact with an enemy force and a reaction squad was sent to reinforce the team. With the enemy retreating into the heavy undergrowth, both Marine units then moved to a designated location where a helicopter extraction could be made.

Arriving at their destination, the ground units encountered a reinforced NVA Company. A fierce firefight broke out; supporting arms from fixed wing aircraft to artillery were called and began pounding the enemy. By nightfall most of the troops were picked up from the hot LZ (Landing Zone) with 16 men remaining on the ground until morning.

Casualties sustained during the battle were four Marines killed in the action and 18 men wounded. One of the casualties was CPL Schmidt who was killed by hostile rifle fire.

Cpl. Schmidt was returned to Halifax for burial, and he was interred in a family plot at the United Baptist Church Cemetery, Head of St. Margaret's Bay. He was later reinterred at the Elm Grove Cemetery in Kentville.

Nova Scotia's first female doctor was a pioneer

Totally dedicated to serving the medical needs of early Nova Scotians, the province's first female physician, Dr. Maria Angwin, is recognized as a pioneer in caring for the urgent medical needs of poor women and children.

She was also clearly an enlightened innovator since she actively promoted preventive medicine long before it became an essential aspect of medical practice.

Angwin was born in Newfoundland in 1849 at a time when the idea of a woman becoming a physician was considered outrageous. But but as Halifax-based freelance journalist Dorothy Grant writes, it was her destiny to play a significant role in fighting this prejudice.

Shortly after Angwin was born, her family moved to Nova Scotia and settled in Dartmouth.

She graduated from the Wesleyan Ladies Academy at Mount Allison University in New Brunswick in 1869 at the age of 19. However, since the university did not award degrees to women until 1875, Angwin was given a Mistress of Liberal Arts diploma.

At first, Angwin considered becoming a lawyer, but gave up this idea because, as she is quoted as saying, "lady lawyers were unknown and I didn't care about being a pioneer in that direction."

Another kind of "pioneering" pursuit, however, did catch her attention.

According to Grant, this happened when she read a book about Drs. Elizabeth and Emily Blackwell, two eminent American physicians. "I became convinced of the need for women doctors and I saw that earning my living that way, I could help my sex."

At that time, not a single Canadian medical school would accept female students, Grant writes. Nevertheless, Angwin was determined to become a physician. To achieve this goal, she went to the Provincial Normal School in Truro and in 1873, obtained a teacher's licence. For the next five years, she taught school.

Later she admitted, "I didn't like teaching. It didn't agree with my health. Like most other people, I made it a means to an end."

In 1879, with enough money to cover the cost of her tuition, Angwin entered medicine at the Women's Medical College of New York Infirmary for Women and Children. It was one of the few American universities willing to accept female students. She received her MD in 1882.

Before returning to Nova Scotia, she did a year of post-graduate work at the New England Hospital for Children and Women in Boston. During this period, her room and board were provided, but she didn't earn any salary.

The following year, on September 9, 1884, a small ad announcing the opening of her medical practice appeared in the *Halifax Herald*. A few days later, Dr. Angwin earned a lasting place in Nova Scotia history when she became the first woman physician licensed to practice medicine in Halifax.

An article about Angwin's exemplary contribution to medicine in this province written by Lois Yorke, a former provincial archivist at The Nova Scotia Archives, appeared in Volume 43 of the 1991 edition of *Collections of the Royal Nova Scotia Historical Society*.

The article provides a captivating account of the years this extraordinary woman practiced in Halifax and Dartmouth. During these years, Angwin had lived in a number of houses where her office was also always located. In January 1894, she and her unmarried sister, Elizabeth, purchased a house on Spring Garden Road and immediately mortgaged it for $1,500.

Within a year, the doctor had installed a telephone, number 400. (At the time, her male colleagues had also begun to recognize the merit of having the "new-fangled device" in their offices.)

Dr. Angwin, however, became better known not for her telephone but for a pet parrot. The bird apparently loudly squawked, "Someone wants the doctor," every time the front door bell was rung.

Totally dedicated to the urgent medical needs of poor women and children, she directed her tireless efforts mainly to improving their health and wellbeing, Yorke writes. She also became a vocal crusader against alcohol and cigarettes and was a dedicated and vocal member of local temperance groups.

Sadly, as the late 1890s approached, Dr. Angwin's health had deteriorated. Faced with this reality, she notified her patients and colleagues that she felt she immediately needed a change of climate and a rest.

In April 1898, Yorke says Dr. Angwin wrote to the Medical Society of Nova Scotia with the news that she planned to soon resume her practice. She died suddenly that same month from complications from minor surgery.

Without question, Dr. Angwin represents one of this province's most neglected historical figures. As was written about her soon after her death, "she was the pioneer lady doctor in this province, and was greatly respected, not only in her duties as a physician, but also in every work that tended to elevate fallen humanity."

In June 2004, the Nova Scotia College of Family Physicians honoured Dr. Angwin's memory by planting a tree and placing a plaque by her grave in a Dartmouth cemetery.

The South Shore's lumber baron

Born in Mill Village, Queens County, on June 10, 1819, Edward (E.D) Doran Davison built a multi-million dollar business that not only employed hundreds of people during the late 19th century but also exported wood for construction projects from the Maritimes to the Caribbean and South America.

The development of lumbering and milling began along the Medway River in the early 1760s, soon after the county's original settlers had arrived from New England. Over the final three decades of the 18th century, the population of Mill Village grew, with some residents engaged in fishery and farming, while others operated small mills with the most profitable ventures on the river involving the export of lumber.

Davison, who lost both of his parents before he was 12, was raised by an aunt and eventually inherited a modest farm, as well as fish and lumbering businesses from his mother's estate. By 1837, at the age of 18 he had taken control of the operation.

Between the late 1830s and the 1850s, Davison built Queens County's first steam-powered milling operation along the Medway River. He reinvested the surplus money he earned selling his product into acquiring additional land in the interior of the county.

In 1849, a major fire swept through a significant portion of Davison's land holdings, which by that time, had totalled more than 10,000 acres along the Medway River system. By the 1850s, having lost much of his potential harvesting areas to the fire, and with natural regrowth still decades away, Davison was forced to search elsewhere for fertile timbering territory.

He sold his Medway operations and reinvested in lumbering operations in neighbouring Lunenburg County, along the LaHave River in the 1860s. The first mill Davison purchased, the Glenwood Mill located near Bridgewater, had been the victim of flooding during a difficult spring, and a significant amount of equipment had been lost. Davison purchased the property in 1865.

Impressed with the potential the LaHave River area offered, Davison developed a new series of mills. After purchasing a number of the smaller mills and a wealth of land along the upper reaches of the LaHave, Davison's business took off, and the LaHave River came to supplant others — including the Medway — as the chief source of lumber along the South Shore.

By the time the Davison business reached its height in the 1890s, upwards of 250,000 board feet of lumber were being produced daily, and more than 350 men in the county worked in one capacity or another for Davison and his sons.

In the process of this massive expansion, the E.D. Davison and Sons Lumbering Company had acquired more than 200,000 acres of land in southern Nova Scotia, including land along the LaHave, Nictaux and even the Medway River — territory, which Davison had reacquired at a discount some years later.

George Price earns place in history

Private George Lawrence Price of the A Company of the 28th North West Battalion, Canadian Expeditionary Force, was not only the last Canadian soldier to die in battle during the First World War but is traditionally recognized as the last soldier of the British Empire to be killed in action.

The son of James E. and Annie R. Price of Port Williams, Kings County, George was born on December 15, 1892. While the exact date is not known, at some point he relocated to Moose Jaw, Saskatchewan.

He was conscripted into the army in Moose Jaw on October 15, 1917. Private Price died at Mons, Belgium, about two minutes before the signing of the Armistice. He was originally buried in Havre Old Communal Cemetery.

On November 11, 1918, just minutes before the Armistice was due to take effect, Price was part of an advance party that was trying to chase the German fighters out of Ville-sur-Haine in Belgium.

Price and his group had just crossed the Canal due Centre as a German sniper fired upon them. Intent on finding the sniper, the party searched house to house and was still under fire. The group entered the front door of one house only to find that the Germans had exited out the back door.

The Canadians moved to the next house and again found it occupied, but no Germans. The occupant of the house told Price to be careful.

The account of his death in the Mons City Museum states: "Despite this advice, Price went out to attack the enemy with his Lewis machine gun, but he was mortally wounded by a bullet in the region of the heart.

"Art Goodmurphy (a fellow Canadian soldier) recalled that a single shot was heard as he and Price stepped back into the street. Price half turned and slumped into Goodmurphy's arms.

"Art quickly dragged George back into the house. A neighbour, a young Belgian girl, saw Private Price fall. She risked her life to cross the street to come to his aide. The occupants of the house and the neighbour attended to Price, but to no avail. Private George Lawrence Price died at 10:58 a.m., just two minutes before the ceasefire.

"Captain Evans Ross, the commander of 'A' Company, was furious when told of Price's death. 'What the hell did you go across for?' he raged at the other members of Price's patrol. 'You had no orders to go across there.'

"The Captain added, in frustration: 'Hell of a note, to think that that would happen right when the war's over.'"

The official records of the Department of Defense state that Private G.L. Price, regimental number: 256265; rank: Private; died November 11, 1918, and that the cause of death was "killed in action."

It goes on to record that an enemy sniper near the canal killed Private Price at three minutes to 11 o'clock. He was shot through the right breast and died shortly after being hit, although every attention possible was given him and he was buried at the Communal Cemetery in the Town of Havre, just south of Mons. In 1968, on the 50th anniversary of the end of the war, a memorial plaque was placed to commemorate Private Price.

Private Price is considered the last Commonwealth soldier killed in action on the Western Front.

Kentville elects province's first woman mayor

The front page story of *The Berwick Register* on Thursday, February 7, 1946, told the whole story: Mrs. H. W. Porter wins mayoralty contest by biggest majority ever polled in Kentville.

The article continued, Kentville made Nova Scotia history on Tuesday of this week by electing Mrs. H. Wyman Porter as the first woman mayor of a town in this province, adding emphasis to the fact by giving her the highest majority in the town's history, and in the largest vote ever polled there, 970 citizens having marked ballots for the successful candidate, and 442 for her opponent, Ex-Councillor W. C. Vincent.

Mrs. Porter's successful contest was the third in which she has engaged in recent years in the Kentville civic arena. She led the field in the 1942 campaign for election to Town Council, having then a majority of 240 votes, and was re-elected in 1945 with a 300 majority. She resigned as Councillor to run for the Mayoralty, as did her defeated opponent.

Gladys Muriel Porter, Kentville's mayor-elect, who told the voters in her election message that she wanted nobody to vote either for or against her as a woman, but to consider her only as a human being, was born in Sydney, Nova Scotia, daughter of the late Mr. and Mrs. Walter S. Richardson.

She moved to Kentville in 1912, when her father became editor of *The Western Chronicle*, after having suffered his first and only defeat in an election for Mayor of the Steel City. She found a position in the Dominion Atlantic Railway offices as stenographer, and when her father returned in 1913 to successfully contest the Sydney mayoralty, she remained in Kentville where she married and has since resided continuously.

Her father was Mayor of Sydney for seven terms. Her father's only defeat is directly responsible for her becoming not only Kentville's first woman mayor, but also along with it the honour of being the first woman chief magistrate in Eastern Canada, it is believed.

Incidentally, the same year she came to Kentville, W. E. Porter, her future father-in-law, was defeated for the Kentville mayoralty by 12 votes.

A tireless worker in the community, Mrs. Porter is credited with a fine record of service, particularly during the war years. She is the head of several organizations but politically has remained strictly an independent.

After working at the polls all of election day, Mrs. Porter, without waiting for the final returns, took over her duties as instructor of the cooking class at the Kentville Evening Technical Class.

On returning to her home she was greeted by scores of congratulatory telegrams and phone calls. The first telegram was from Mayor Ira B. Lohnes, of Windsor.

The collector supreme

Dr. Mary Helen Creighton was a prominent Canadian folklorist. She collected over 4,000 traditional songs, stories, and beliefs in a distinguished career that spanned several decades, and she published many books and articles on Nova Scotia folk songs and folklore. She received numerous honorary degrees for her work and was made a Member of the Order of Canada in 1976.

Born on Portland Street in Dartmouth on September 5, 1899, she developed an early interest in folklore and the supernatural. She had a sister who suffered from a mental disability.

Between 1914 and 1916, she attended Halifax Ladies College and earned a junior diploma in music at McGill University in 1915. In 1918, she joined the Royal Flying Corps in Toronto and by 1920, she had returned to Nova Scotia as a paramedic with the Red Cross Caravan. She was Dean of Women at the University of Kings College between 1939 and 1941.

In 1928, Creighton returned to Nova Scotia in search of literary material, and met with Dr. Henry Munro, the Superintendent of Education for the Province of Nova Scotia. Munro showed her a copy of *Sea Songs and Ballads from Nova Scotia* by W. Roy MacKenzie and suggested Creighton attempt to find more songs.

She began to travel around Nova Scotia, collecting songs, tales and customs of Gaelic, English, German, Mi'kmaq, African and Acadian origin. Frequently, she had to walk or sail to remote regions to satisfy her interest, all the while pushing a metre-long melodeon in a wheelbarrow.

Among Creighton's many contributions was the discovery of the traditional *Nova Scotia Song*, widely called *Farewell to Nova Scotia*, which has become widely a sort of provincial anthem.

Between 1942 and 1946, Creighton received three Rockefeller Foundation fellowships to collect songs in Nova Scotia. The second of these fellowships was used to collect songs with equipment loaned by the Library of Congress. Creighton also made recordings for the Canadian Museum of Civilization from 1947-1967.

She made excursions outside of Nova Scotia, notably to New Brunswick from 1954 to 1960 (*Folksongs from Southern New Brunswick* contains material from that period). However, she preferred not to collect in the places of fellow researchers such as Louise Manny.

Her home, Evergreen House, is a part of the Dartmouth Heritage Museum and is open to the public.

As she collected songs, Creighton also became interested in the ghost stories and superstitions in Nova Scotia and the Maritimes. She presented these stories first in the themed collection of ghost stories *Bluenose Ghosts* published in 1957 and later in an additional book *Bluenose Magic* in 1968.

The Nova Scotia Archives says Creighton's professional interests ranged broadly and deeply across Maritime folklore and history, and included extensive work within the Gaelic, Acadian, Mi'kmaq, English, German and African-Nova Scotian traditions.

"The archival record accumulated from these investigations is rich in information and material about folk songs and ancient ballads, folk tales, dances, games, cures, proverbs, children's folklore — and, of course, the subject area for which Dr. Creighton is perhaps best known, namely the world of the supernatural — ghosts, superstitions, witchcraft and buried treasure."

Creighton died at the age of 90 on December 12, 1989, in Dartmouth.

In addition to the many accolades she received throughout her lifetime, the Canadian Song-writers Hall of Fame awarded her the Frank Davies Legacy Award in 2011 and she was named a National Historic Person in 2018.

5 FAST FACTS

1. Fort Edward, located in Windsor, was built by Major Charles Lawrence in 1750 to protect the route from Halifax to the Annapolis Valley. The blockhouse is the oldest in Canada. It, along with the earthworks, is all that remains of Fort Edward. Acadian families were detained here after the 1755 deportation. The fort was an important base during the Seven Years' War, the American Revolution and the War of 1812.

2. On October 26, 1979, Ken Fraser caught the biggest Bluefin tuna ever recorded by the International Game Fish Association. It weighed 1,496 pounds. Fraser landed the world record Bluefin tuna while fishing with Capt. Eric Samson aboard Lady and Misty out of Port Hood. Fraser needed just 45 minutes to bring the largest tuna ever caught close enough to gaff after it ate a trolled mackerel.

3. Canadian marathon runner, Johnny Miles was born in England on October 30, 1905. As a child he moved with his family to Florence, a coal town located near Sydney Mines on Cape Breton Island. He worked in the coalmines of Cape Breton at the age of 11 and he died at the age of 97 on June 15, 2003. He was winner of the 1926 and 1929 Boston Marathons, and also represented Canada in the 1928 and 1932 Summer Olympics. Since 1975 the Johnny Miles Marathon has been held in New Glasgow in his honour. An annual 5K race is also held in his honour in Sydney Mines. Sydney Mines also displays his image on a sign at the entrance of the town and a statue of Miles is displayed on Main Street.

4. Aileen Aletha Meagher, born November 26, 1910, in Halifax, was a Canadian athlete who competed in the 1936 Summer Olympics, sharing bronze in the 4×100 metres event. She was also a respected painter. She died on August 2, 1987.

5. Halifax-born gymnast Ellie Black became the most decorated Canadian gymnast at 2019 Pan Am Games, winning a total of 10 medals in two Games. Five time medalist including AA Gold and was named flag-bearer Canada at the closing ceremony.

Battiste makes election history

Jaime Battiste made history on October 21, 2019, when he became the first Mi'kmaq politician to represent Nova Scotia in the House of Commons. The 40-year-old legal expert and Indigenous activist was elected as a Liberal in Cape Breton in the riding of Sydney-Victoria.

Battiste was born in Sydney and grew up on Cape Breton's Chapel Island 5 reserve, now known as the Potlotek First Nation. He graduated from Dalhousie University's law school in 2004 and served as chairman of the Assembly of First Nations Youth Council and a regional chief with the Assembly of First Nations.

His parents, Marie Battiste and James (Sakej) Henderson, are both professors at the University of Saskatchewan: Battiste specializes in Aboriginal learning, de-colonization, violence prevention and historical studies of Indigenous education; Henderson is an international human rights lawyer and one of the drafters of the United Nations Declaration on the Rights of Indigenous Peoples.

Jaime Battiste is also known for his work with the Mi'kmaq education authority, which has helped boost the graduation rate among Mi'kmaq high school students from 30 per cent 20 years ago to 90 per cent in 2016-2017 — the highest on-reserve graduation rate in the country.

Battiste, who is well known in Nova Scotia for his work on improving education for Mi'kmaq youth, said following his election that he hopes his electoral breakthrough will serve as an example for Indigenous youth.

"When I was growing up on a reserve, there was a greater chance that I would have died a violent death or committed suicide than get a nomination to run for a federal party," he said in an interview following his election.

A story carved in stone

John Albert Wilson was a Canadian sculptor of some note who produced public art for commissions throughout North America. He was a professor in the School of Architecture at Harvard University for 32 years.

Wilson is most famous for his American Civil War Monuments — the Confederate Student Memorial (Silent Sam) on the campus of the University of North Carolina, Chapel Hill, and the Washington Grays Monument (Pennsylvania Volunteer) in Philadelphia.

He was born in 1877 near New Glasgow in a small community named Potter's Brook. He was the son of John and Annie (Cameron) Wilson. His grandfather was a stonemason who emigrated from Beauly, Scotland.

Wilson attended New Glasgow High School and in 1891 at the age of 15 he created his first sculpture of a lion out of freestone.

In 1896, at age 19, he went to Boston to study art. During the day he attended the Cowles Art School of the Museum of Fine Arts, Boston, where he studied drawing and painting under Bella Pratt.

He worked in the evenings as an usher in a theatre, and he worked on the weekends as a professional boxer at the Boston Athletic Club. While at the Fine Arts school, Wilson displayed his work "The Crawling Panther" (also known as the "Stalking Panther") at the Boston Art Club in 1905.

He received attention from the *Boston Glove* and *Boston Herald* newspapers for this work. The latter wrote that it was a "powerful work by a very young man."

He graduated from the School of the Museum of Fine Arts in 1905 and beginning in 1906, Wilson taught classes for the Copley Society of Art in Boston. He joined the board of directors in 1913 and taught there for 32 years until 1945. In 1927, he was named Director of Classes. One of his students at the Society was John Hovannes (1900-1973).

In 1917, Wilson started to teach at Harvard University when the scholarly Abbott Lawrence Lowell was president. He was appointed Instructor in Modelling, School of Architecture, Harvard University. He served at Harvard for 32 years, retiring in 1949. During his tenure at the Copley Society and Harvard, Wilson also taught in various other places.

Wilson taught for five years at the Worcester Art Museum (1917–22), where he would complete the Hector Monument (1923) with his student Evangeline Eells Wheeler. He taught one year at the School of the Museum of Fine Arts (1921–22), three years at Children's Walker School and three years Bradford College. He also taught at his own studio in Chestnut Hill.

In 1913, he had built his home and his "Waban Studio" at 101 Waban Hill Rd, Chestnut Hill, where he lived for 36 years. After 50 years away from Nova Scotia, Wilson retired and returned in 1949 to New Glasgow. He lived there for five years at East River, Potter's Bridges.

Wilson died on December 8, 1954, at Aberdeen Regional Hospital, New Glasgow. A plaque in his honor hangs in the hospital's cafeteria. He is buried in the Riverside Cemetery in New Glasgow.

This American hero has Nova Scotian roots

Joseph Benjamin Noil was a United States Navy sailor and a recipient of America's highest military decoration — the Medal of Honor.

Few might know that this American hero was actually born in Liverpool, Nova Scotia, in 1841.

When Noil first enlisted in the Navy the records say he was from New York but when he re-enlisted for a three-year hitch on December 29, 1874, he was described as 34 years old, born in Nova Scotia and a "Negro." His civilian occupation was as a caulker, and his physical stature was described as being five feet, six inches tall.

On December 26, 1872, while serving on USS *Powhatan* at Northfok, Virginia, he saved a drowning shipmate, Boatswain J.C. Walton. For his conduct on this occasion, he was awarded the Medal of Honor.

On May 25, 1881, Noil, who by that time had been promoted to the rating of Captain of the Hold and was in service on the USS *Wyoming* (1859), was admitted to the Naval Hospital in Norfolk, suffering from "paralysis" or PTSD.

About a week later, he was transferred to Saint Elizabeth's Hospital in Washington, D.C., where he died on March 21, 1882. He was buried in the hospital graveyard under the name of "Joseph B. Noel."

His grave was rediscovered in 2011 by the Medal of Honor Historical Society of the United States, a group whose mission is to identify and photograph the "lost" resting places of Medal of Honor recipients.

A new headstone noting that Noil is a Medal of Honor recipient was dedicated in April 2016, in a ceremony attended by representatives from the Canadian Embassy in Washington and by Noil's great-great-great granddaughter.

Noil's Medal of Honor citation reads:

> "Rank and organization: Seaman, U.S. Navy. Born: 1841, Nova Scotia.
> Accredited to: New York.
> Serving on board the U.S.S. Powhatan at Norfolk, 26 December 1872,
> Noil saved Boatswain J. C. Walton from drowning."

Noil was married to Sarah Jane Gambier from New York City and they had two daughters — Florence Gambier Noil and Sarah E. Noil.

His granddaughter, Cora Hunter Parks, was an actress, dancer, and vaudeville artist who appeared in a number of Broadway shows. As a member of the Rhythmettes, she sang *Optimistic Voices* in the 1939 classic movie *The Wizard of Oz* and on Broadway in 1939. Again with the Rythmettes, with Louis Armstrong, Moms Mabley, Oscar Polk and others, she sang and danced in the show *Swingin' the Dream*.

What's a Civil War hero doing in a Bridgewater cemetery?

The story of how Capt. Lee Nutting, a veteran of the American Civil War, came to be buried at the historic Brookside Cemetery in Bridgewater is an interesting one.

According to historian Peter Oickle, Capt. Nutting was born in Orange County, New York, on October 14, 1837. He enlisted as a private in Company H of the 61st New York Infantry in October of 1861, after the outbreak of the Civil War.

By 1863, Nutting had been promoted to captain and he fought in several notable battles, including Second Bull Run, Antietam and Fredericksburg. Capt. Nutting was wounded on May 8, 1864, at the Battle of Todd's Tavern in Virginia.

Miraculously, it is said he survived the battle when a small Bible that he kept in the left breast pocket of his jacket deflected the potentially deadly shot.

Following is an account of his actions as described in the medal's citation: "In May 1863, after assuming command of the Union Army, General Grant launched his offensive against Confederate General Robert E. Lee, marching towards Richmond, Virginia. By May 5, most of Grant's army had crossed the Rapidan River, where for three days they engaged the Confederate forces in the opening battles of the Wilderness Campaign. On May 8, following the three-day initial Wilderness battle, Captain Lee Nutting led his regiment against rebel forces at Todds Tavern, Virginia, in the continuing series of battles leading to Richmond. As the head of his men, he continued to valiantly lead against a murderous fire, until he fell severely wounded."

Had it not been for that Bible, his wounds would surely have been fatal and although Capt. Nutting survived, he was sufficiently wounded to receive a discharge and a pension from the military. On August 21, 1893, Capt. Nutting was awarded the Congressional Medal of Honor for leading his regiment in a charge at a critical moment.

Capt. Nutting's oldest surviving daughter, Grace, was married to a man named Phillip H. Moore, who owned and operated Rossignol hunting camp and eventually opened White Point Beach Lodge. His involvement with a company named the MicMac Mines, brought him to Bridgewater

Subsequently, Capt. Nutting and his wife, Arrietta, came to Bridgewater to be with their daughter. Both Arrietta and Lee Nutting spent their summers in Bridgewater for the remainder of their lives.

Mrs. Nutting was killed in 1907 in an accident at Weagle's Hill near the MicMac Mines located in the Hebbville area. When two wagons collided, Mrs. Nutting died when the one in which she was seated overturned and she was mortally wounded.

Brookside Cemetery in Bridgewater is the unlikely final resting place for American Civil War hero, Capt. Lee Nutting.

She and her daughter and granddaughters were in a carriage going down the hill. The horse broke loose and the driver felt he could get it under control. At the bottom, however, the carriage struck a slow moving ox cart and the carriage was upset, spilling the passengers. Mrs. Nutting died a few hours later.

According to Oickle, Capt. Nutting died the following year July 11, 1908, on the front lawn of what was then Clark's Hotel in Bridgewater. He was 71 years old.

The Maritime Civil War Living History Association estimates that as many as 9,500 Maritimers served in the Union forces during the Civil War. Oickle says as far he knows there are only three Congressional Medal honourees buried in Nova Scotia — two in Halifax and Capt. Nutting in Bridgewater.

His name was synonymous with true crime stories

Anyone reading newspapers in Canada between the early 1970s and the mid-2000s will recognize the name Max Haines.

He was a widely syndicated true crime columnist and author and he was born in Antigonish in 1931.

Haines attended Morrison High School in Antigonish. He began researching murders from around the world, past and present, as a hobby.

His *Crime Flashback* column made its debut in the *Toronto Sun* in 1972 with a column about Lizzie Borden. Over the next 35 years, he researched over 2,000 crimes. His *Crime Flashback* column was syndicated across Canada and in several Latin and South American countries; readership was over three million per week.

He lived in Toronto with his wife Marilyn. He retired in 2006.

In addition to his popularity as a columnist, Haines also wrote 27 true crime books as well as a memoir, *The Spitting Champion of the World,* about growing up in Nova Scotia.

In 2005, he was awarded the Derrick Murdoch Award, one of the Arthur Ellis awards, by the Crime Writers of Canada.

Haines died from progressive supranuclear palsy (PSP) on September 30, 2017, aged 86.

The tallest man on record

The world's tallest genetically normal giant may have been born in the Hebrides of Scotland in 1825, but he moved to St. Anns, Cape Breton, when he was a child.

Angus MacAskill was of normal size at birth but by the time he was in his twenties, he was 2.36 metres (7.55 feet) tall and weighed more than 190 kg (418 pounds). MacAskill's hands measured 20 by 30 centimetres (8 by 12 inches).

While not in the circus, he did tour for a few years with a sideshow in which he demonstrated astonishing feats of strength. He eventually returned to Cape Breton in 1853 and ran a business.

MacAskill died on August 8, 1863, in Englishtown, Cape Breton, at 38 years of age and was buried in Englishtown Cemetery.

The 1981 *Guinness Book of World Records* says he is the tallest non-pathological giant in recorded history (7 feet 9 inches, or 2.36 metres) and had the largest chest measurements of any non-obese man (80 inches, or 200 centimetres).

The tallest Nova Scotian ever!

The tallest person ever born in Nova Scotia was Anna Swan. She was born on August 6, 1846, in Mill Brook, New Annan, near Tatamagouche in Colchester County and grew to the astounding height of seven feet, eleven inches.

Swan spent most of her life on stages around the world as P. T. Barnum billed her as the world's tallest person at a height of eight feet, one inch. In England she was presented to Queen Victoria and when sailing back to New York she met another giant, Capt. Martin VanBuren Bates of Kentucky who was only one inch shorter than she was.

When they were married in London, Queen Victoria presented Swan with a gold watch. When they left the circus circuit, Swan and Capt. Bates moved to a custom-built house in Seville, Ohio.

They had two children, both of which weighed over 20 pounds at birth, and both died in their infancy.

Swan died suddenly and unexpectedly in her sleep at her home on August 5, 1888, one day before her 42nd birthday.

Knocking down the colour walls

William Andrew White II was a Nova Scotian who was commissioned as the first black officer in the British army. He served in the Second World War as a chaplain and was the only black chaplain in the British Army during the war.

White was born on June 16, 1874, to former slaves in King and Queen County, Virginia. His family moved to the city of Baltimore, Maryland, where he attended public school.

After his Canadian schoolteacher impressed him with descriptions of the province, where freed American slaves had been resettled after the Revolutionary War, White moved to Nova Scotia in 1900.

He had imagined this land as his key to freedom. He became the second black man accepted by Acadia University, and in 1903 became its first black graduate. White graduated with an arts degree in theology, and was ordained a Baptist minister. He worked the next two years as a traveling missionary for the African Baptist churches of Nova Scotia.

Once he settled in Nova Scotia, White met and married Izie Dora White (no relation) of Mill Village in Queens County. She was a descendant of Black Loyalists. They raised a family of 13 children.

One of their daughters, Portia White, became a world-famous singer. Their son Bill White Jr., became the first black Canadian to run for federal political office in Canada when he stood as a candidate for the Co-operative Commonwealth Federation in the 1949 federal election. Son Jack was a noted Canadian labour union activist and the second black candidate to run for office in the Legislative Assembly of Ontario.

In 1916, White enlisted in the No. 2 Construction Battalion, an all-black segregated unit serving in the First World War. He was the only black chaplain in the British Army and was a commissioned officer serving with the rank of Honorary Captain.

Following the war, White returned to Halifax and was called to Cornwallis Street Baptist Church. He served as rector for more than 17 years. During the early 1930s, his services were broadcast over the radio every month, and they were heard throughout the Maritimes.

In 1936, White was awarded an honorary doctorate from Acadia University, the first black person to be honoured with a Doctorate of Divinity from Acadia. He was also the first black Canadian to be given an honorary doctorate.

He died of cancer on September 9, 1936, in Halifax.

White and Izie Dora's grandchildren include Senator Donald Oliver, politician and activist Sheila White, and folk musician Chris White. The novelist and playwright George Elliott Clarke is a great-grandson.

Their great-nephew, actor and filmmaker Anthony Sherwood, produced a documentary film entitled, *Honour Before Glory*. This was based on the diary of William White while he served in France during the Great War.

The donut king

Ronald (Ron) Joyce was co-founder of the Tim Hortons donut chain as Tim Horton's partner and first franchisee in 1964. After the death of Tim Horton, Joyce was instrumental in establishing the Tim Horton Children's Camps and the Tim Horton Children's Foundation.

Born on October 19, 1930, and raised in Tatamagouche, Joyce moved to Hamilton, Ontario, at age 16. He worked a number of odd jobs until eventually enlisting in the Royal Canadian Navy in 1951, where he was trained as a wireless operator. In 1956, he joined the Hamilton Police Service and served as a police officer until 1965.

Joyce decided to get involved in the newly emerging food-service industry and in 1963, purchased a Dairy Queen franchise in Hamilton. He wanted to open a second Dairy Queen, but the city declined his license. Instead, Joyce decided to open a coffee shop when he saw a "For Sale" sign posted in a storefront.

Joyce entered a franchise partnership with Tim Horton in 1967. After Horton's death in an auto accident in 1974, Joyce purchased Horton's share for about $1 million, and assumed control of the full Tim Hortons franchise. He hired a management team and began to franchise the company throughout the late 1970s until the 1990s.

During the early 1990s, Danny Murphy, a franchise owner of both Tim Hortons coffee shops and Wendy's fast food restaurants in Prince Edward Island wanted to combine both franchises under one roof in a new development in Montague. Murphy asked Joyce and Wendy's founder, Dave Thomas, to be present for the opening.

In 1995, Wendy's and Tim Hortons merged and Joyce became the combined company's largest shareholder. Joyce eventually sold his Wendy's stock and retired from management, but even in retirement continued to be active in his holding company, Jetport Inc, which has significant real estate, aviation, and commercial interests.

One of the most popular items Tim Hortons are timbits.

He received an appointment to the Order of Canada on October 21, 1992, and in April 1999, Ron Joyce was inducted into the Canadian Business Hall of Fame.

In November 2005, Joyce was the 2005 Humanitarian Award Recipient by the Canadian Red Cross, Nova Scotia Region, for his work with the Tim Horton Children's Foundation and for his continued support of education and health organizations across the world.

On November 11, 2007, the Bombardier Global 5000 business jet in which Joyce was travelling crashed short of the runway at his Fox Harb'r Resort's airport. He suffered two fractured vertebrae as a result.

Joyce died at his home in Burlington on January 31, 2019, at the age of 88.

The Great Sam Gloade remembered for his bravery

Decorated for his bravery in battles like Vimy Ridge and Passchendaele, Sergeant Sam Gloade (often spelled Glode) is remembered for saving the lives of many. The Mi'kmaq soldier was an infantryman and then a tunneller with the 6th Field Company and Battalion.

Gloade was a decorated Mi'kmaq soldier born and grew up in Milton, Queens County, on April 20, 1878. He served in the First World War and was awarded the Distinguished Conduct Medal, the British War Medal and the Victory Medal.

He trained first with the 64th Battalion, CEF, an infantry reinforcement holding unit in England. He then joined the 1st Canadian Tunnelling Company, Canadian Engineers.

After taking part in the Battle of Messines in Flanders, Belgium, from June 7 to 14, 1917, Gloade reported:

"Late that afternoon the German artillery on Messines Ridge began to shell our trench and kept it up for a long time. They scared us bad, I tell you. We were all green hands, and we would leave our rifles and run along the trench away from shell burst. Then another shell would burst near us and we would run down the trench again. Some fellows got hit and they hollered and there was a lot of blood."

Gloade was known as an excellent utility man. He dug trenches under Vimy Ridge, patched roadways near Amiens and defused mines after the war. On one occasion he was in charge of 20 soldiers who got trapped underground. He is credited with single-handedly digging for hours before he was able to burrow a hole to the surface.

He worked from the La Clytte Camp (close to Ypres in Belgium) for more than a year. Gloade was also in the Battle of Passchendaele and Battle of Amiens (1918).

After the armistice was signed, Gloade continued his military service, searching for mine and demolition charges, and personally removed 450.

His son Louis was a member of the Nova Scotia Highlanders and was wounded by a piece of shrapnel.

Years later in an interview with Kelly Linehan on CTV Atlantic, Gloade's great-great-grandson Jeff Purdy, read a note handwritten by his great-great grandfather: "I stayed out most of the night, watching the flares go up over No Man's Land like fireworks, and hearing the cannons and bursts of rifle and machine-gun fire."

The note details the sights and sounds of Gloade's first night at war, but the majority of his service was spent underground.

Before the war, Gloade was a hunting and fishing guide, often working with his son Louis, who eventually followed him to the battlefield.

As the story goes, he was cutting wood somewhere with a friend, and they just decided to go off to war because as he was quoted as saying, "it was the right thing to do."

While Gloade's one room house may be gone, the legacy he left behind is still very much alive in his hometown community.

Gloade died on October 25, 1957, and is buried in the St. Gregory's Roman Catholic Church Cemetery, Milton, the same community in which he was born. He was buried with his three medals.

According to Veteran's Affairs, First Nations were originally discouraged from enlisting and some were turned away. Once at war, their military roles were among the most dangerous — like snipers and reconnaissance scouts.

Others like Glode served in support units, including tunnelling companies. According to Veteran's Affairs, half of the eligible Maliseet and Mi'kmaq men from New Brunswick and Nova Scotia enlisted in the First World War.

Across Canada, 4,000 (or one in three) able-bodied First Nations men signed up, but 300 never came home. The total number of Indigenous volunteers in unknown.

Who was Sam Slick?

We've all heard of Sam Slick. He's a legend, a part of Nova Scotian culture, but the truth is, Sam Slick was not a real person.

In fact, he was a fictional character created by pioneering author Thomas Chandler Haliburton.

Born on December 17, 1796, in Windsor, Haliburton was a politician, judge and author. He made an important political contribution to the state of Nova Scotia before its entry into the Confederation of Canada. But more than that, he was the first international best-selling author of fiction from what is now Canada.

In 1856, Haliburtan emigrated to England, where he served as a Conservative Member of Parliament. He had two sons and five daughters but none of them had children. He was the father of the British civil servant Lord Haliburton and of the anthropologist Robert Grant Haliburtan.

Despite all of his political accomplishments, Haliburtan is best remembered as a writer and creator of the literary character, Sam Slick.

In the mid-1830s, Haliburton wrote satiric sketches for the Nova Scotia publication, *Novascotian*. The works were eventually collected into a book titled *The Clockmaker*. After moving to Great Britain, Haliburtan continued writing Sam Slick books.

Some of the modern expressions that we continue to use today came from these books, such as it's raining cats and dogs; honesty is the best policy; the early bird catches the worm; an ounce of prevention is worth a pound of cure; and jack of all trades and master of none.

Haliburtan died in Islesworth, England, at the age of 68 on August 27, 1865, but left behind a powerful legacy that continues to impact today's culture and landscape.

The community of Haliburton, Nova Scotia, was named after him. In Ontario, Haliburton County is named after Haliburton in recognition of his work as the first chair of the Canadian Land and Emigration Company.

In 1884, faculty and students at his *alma mater* founded a literary society in honour of the College's most celebrated man of letters. The Haliburton Society is still active at the University of King's College in Halifax. It is the longest-standing collegial literary society throughout the Commonwealth of Nations and North America.

The mention "hurly on the long pond on the ice," which appears in the second volume of *The Attaché, or Sam Slick in England*, a work of fiction published in 1844, has been interpreted by some as a reference to an ice hockey-like game he may have played during his years at King's College. It is the basis of Windsor's disputed claim to being the town that fathered hockey.

A memorial to Haliburton and his first wife was erected in Christ Church, Windsor, in 1902 by four of their children. The former Haliburton home in Windsor is preserved as a museum.

The mysterious Samuel Ball

Samuel Ball was a former landowner on Oak Island, the small island located off the coast of Nova Scotia's south shore and the home of one of the world's most famous, longest running treasure hunt. In fact, Ball could be a crucial key to solving the mystery of the legendary treasure rumoured to be buried there.

The enigmatic Ball was a former American slave born in South Carolina in 1765 to a very poor black family. Samuel was born into a life of misery, a life of no hope for the future but a hard day's work and a poor ration of food. Samuel's family were in fact, slaves for the rich landlords of the infamous southern plantations.

Following the end of the American Revolution, the free man relocated to Canada. He left the US at the end of the war in 1784 and came to Nova Scotia. Ball went on to own property on Oak Island and reportedly went into farming. At the time of his death in 1846, Samuel Ball was said to be one of the richest men in Nova Scotia.

Historical records show that Ball spent two years in Shelburne and 23 more years in Chester. He would then have to be living on Oak Island no earlier than 1808 or 1809, 10 years or so after the discovery of the famous Money Pit, believed to be a repository for treasure.

At the time of his death, Ball owned over 100 acres both on Oak Island as well as on another nearby, smaller island. His wealth has led many to believe that in addition to farming, Ball had actually discovered riches on Oak Island.

Of particular interest to treasure hunters is the island's Lot 25, once owned by Ball and where his modest homestead was located. There, a number of artefacts and historical objects have been found.

The question remains for those trying to solve the mystery of Oak Island— did the objects that have been discovered belong to Ball? Or perhaps to soldier and privateer James Anderson, an American who defected to the British side and later settled in Canada? Anderson sold Lot 26 to Ball in 1788.

Samuel Ball was not named as one of the original participants in the search for treasure on Oak Island in the earliest documented account from J.B. McCully of the Truro Company in the Liverpool Transcript (published October 1862). McCully states that the Money Pit was found by Daniel McGinnis who later enlisted the help of his friends Anthony Vaughn and John Smith to aid in a dig.

In a book, *History of the County of Lunenburg,* first published in 1870 and written by Mather Byles DesBrisay (1828-1900), a Canadian lawyer, judge, politician, and historian in Bridgewater, Samuel Ball is named as one of the three men enlisted by Daniel McGinnis to aid in the digging of the Oak Island Money Pit.

In later editions of the *History of the County of Lunenberg* (second edition, revised edition published in 1895) Samuel Ball's name is replaced with that of Anthony Vaughn. To date, there has been no explanation as to why this revision occurred.

Was this an error on the part of Judge Mathers Byles DesBrisay or did he have another source with a differing account of what actually occurred in the earliest days of the Oak Island Money Pit?

Oak Island has seen a more pastoral history; men and the women who accompanied them broke the soil not to look for buried loot, but to grow crops, raise livestock, fish and eke out an existence in the boreal forests and headlands of Eastern Canada.

Many black men were offered all sorts of promises by the British forces during the American Revolution and none were so promising than the chance for some land and to be free.

Adopting the name of his former master, Ball made his way to New York serving with General Henry Clinton and then spent some time with Major Ward in the Jerseys where he served until the end of the war on January 14, 1784, with the signing of the Treaty of Paris. It was also reported that he served some time with Lord Cornwallis after the war.

From here, historical records show that Ball made his way to Shelburne, Nova Scotia, and lived there for two years. Not being at all happy with his treatment in Shelburne, he then pulled up stakes and moved to Chester where it is reported he lived for 23 years. He bought a piece of land on Oak Island and then was granted four acres more at lot number 32.

As time went on, he eventually owned around 100 acres of land, and an island called Hook Island along with his farm on Oak Island consisting of around 36 acres. In 1795, Samuel Ball found love in Halifax and married a young woman, Mary, who worked as a domestic for Treasurer Wallace. They had three children, Andrew (1798), Samuel (1801) and Mary (1805) all born in Chester.

Among his many friends, he could count on one of the treasure hunters, Anthony Vaughan, who was named as executor of his will. On Lot 25 on Oak Island, Samuel and his small family built a house, broke the land into ploughed acreage, raised crops and maintained cattle.

The foundation of his home can still be seen on Oak Island to today. Somewhere along the way, his wife Mary died, but history does not record her passing or reason for the absence from the family. In his will of 1846 he speaks of his wife, Catherine.

When he died at home on December 14, 1846, at the age of 81 years, those who knew Samuel Ball could say that he was a "good man." He left behind a legacy of assistance to others and made provision in his will for them.

He had at least one grandson, and was so proud of his adopted surname that in his will he declared that, "None shall possess same (land) unless they take the name Ball." He was also thought to be Lunenburg County's only black Loyalist.

From his fields, he no doubt watched the frantic digging of the men from the Onslow Company of 1804 but he did not live to see another treasure hunt.

A lifetime in service of others

Sara Corning, was a nurse and humanitarian, was born on March 16, 1872, in Chegoggin, a small community near Yarmouth. She was the daughter Captain Samuel and Delilah (Churchill) Corning.

She trained as a nurse in New Hampshire and joined the U.S. Red Cross during the First World War and subsequently signed on with the Near East Relief, a US charitable foundation established to assist the displaced populations of the Balkans, Asia Minor and the Middle East.

In 1919, Corning arrived in a small Turkish village at the foot of Mount Ararat to take charge of an orphanage. In 1922, Corning travelled to Constantinople, where the Near East Relief was headquartered. She was then sent to Yerevan to be in charge of an orphanage.

Years of civil strife and ethnic turmoil — in which the Turks had driven the Armenians from their homeland — had left hundreds of thousands without homes and starving. Nearly a million had died since 1915 as the Turks took revenge on the Armenians for allegedly helping the Russians during the First World War.

At the end of 1922, Corning was sent to Smyrna while the Turkish army was capturing the city. Corning gathered the orphaned children and led them through the city to safety aboard an American ship, where they were then taken to Constantinople. She later established an orphanage for the children on the Greek island of Syros.

Guiding small groups of children, most under 12 years old, and almost all female, through the turmoil and the slaughter in the burning city, Corning delivered them to the harbour, where American sailors rowed them out to waiting destroyers. No record remains of the time required to evacuate the orphans, but when the operation was complete, more than 5,000 children had been rescued.

In June 1923, King George II of Greece presented her with the Order of the Knights of St. Xavier for her courage and bravery.

Corning spent 11 years of service in Armenia, Turkey and Greece between 1919 and 1930. She later retired and moved back to her childhood home in Cheggogin and died in Yarmouth on May 5, 1969, at age 97.

The epitaph on her headstone: "She lived to serve others."

In 2004, Karekin II, the current Catholicos of all Armenians, the supreme head of the American Apostolic Church, gave a Message of Blessing, which contained a tribute to Corning. She is the namesake to the Sara Corning Centre for Genocide Education in Toronto.

This statue is seen as a continued fitting way to honour the Yarmouth heroine. Sara Corning had returned to Chegoggin, Yarmouth County, in her retirement, where she lived until her death in 1969 at the age of 97.

Corning was also posthumously awarded the Outstanding Canadian Award by the Armenian Community Centre of Toronto in the fall of 2017.

In a ceremony on September 14, 2019, attended by the Hon. Arthur J. LeBlanc, Lieutenant Governor of Nova Scotia, and by Anahit Harutyunyan, Ambassador of Armenia to Canada, the Sara Corning Society unveiled a statue of Corning behind the Yarmouth County Museum and Archives complex on the former site of the Zion United Baptist Church, which Corning attended in her lifetime.

The statue will be a permanent fixture outside the Museum.

The Sara Corning Society in Nova Scotia has worked diligently to ensure Corning's life and humanitarian work is remembered and honoured. A street — Sara Corning Way — was named after her in Yarmouth.

Nova Scotia's man of science

Simon Newcomb was one of the most famous American scientists from the 18th century, but the truth is, he was a Canadian. Not only that, he was born in Nova Scotia.

Newcomb was born in the town of Wallace, Nova Scotia, on March 12, 1835. His parents were Emily Prince, the daughter of a New Brunswick magistrate, and itinerant schoolteacher John Burton Newcomb.

John moved around teaching in different parts of Canada, particularly in different villages in Nova Scotia and Prince Edward Island. Emily was a daughter of Thomas Prince and Miriam Steeves, making Simon a great-great-grandson Heinrich Stief, and a not-too-distant cousin of William Henry Steeves, a Father of Canadian Confederation.

Newcomb seems to have had little conventional schooling other than from his father and from a short apprenticeship to Dr. Foshay, a charlatan herbalist, in New Brunswick in 1851. Nevertheless, his father provided him with an excellent foundation for his future studies.

Despite this lack of a formal education, he went on to become an American astronomer, applied mathematician and autodidactic polymath. He was a professor of mathematics in the United States Navy and Johns Hopkins University. He made important contributions to timekeeping as well as other fields of applied mathematics such as economics and statistics, in addition to writing a science fiction novel (*His Wisdom the Defender* published 1900.)

Newcomb's apprenticeship with Dr. Foshay occurred when he was 16 years old. They entered an agreement that Newcomb would serve a five-year apprenticeship during which time Foshay would train him in using herbs to treat illnesses.

For two years he was an apprentice but became increasingly unhappy and disillusioned with his apprenticeship and about Foshay's unscientific approach, realizing that the man was a fraud. He made the decision to walk out on Foshay and break their agreement.

In 1854, he walked 190 kilometres to the port of Calais in Maine where he met the captain of a ship who agreed to take him to Salem, Massachusetts, so that he could join his father who had moved earlier to the United States, and the two journeyed together to Maryland.

After arriving in Maryland, Newcomb taught for two years from 1854 to 1856; His first position was in a country school in Maryland then he taught for a year at a school not far south in Sudlersville in Queen Anne's County, Maryland. In his spare time he studied a variety of subjects such as political economy and religion, but his deepest studies were made in mathematics and astronomy.

In particular, he read Newton's *Principia*. In 1856, he took up a position as a private tutor close to Washington and he often travelled to that city to study mathematics in the libraries there. Newcomb studied mathematics and physics privately and supported himself by teaching before becoming a human computer (a functionary in charge of calculations) at the Nautical Almanac Office in Cambridge, Massachusetts, in 1857. At around the same time, he enrolled at the Lawrence Scientific School of Harvard University, graduating with a BSc in 1858.

In the prelude to the American Civil War, many US Navy staff of Confederate sympathies left the service. In 1861, Newcomb took advantage of one of the ensuing vacancies to become professor of mathematics and astronomer at the United States Naval Observatory, Washington D.C.

Newcomb set to work on the measurement of the position of the planets as an aid to navigation, becoming increasingly interested in theories of planetary motion.

He was offered the post of director of the Harvard College Observatory in 1875 but declined, having by now settled that his interests lay in mathematics rather than observation.

In 1877, Newcomb became director of the Nautical Almanac Office where he embarked on a program of recalculation of all the major astronomical constants. Despite fulfilling a further demanding role as professor of mathematics and astronomy at John Hopkins University from 1884, he conceived a plan with A.M.W. Downing to resolve much international confusion on the subject.

By the time he attended a standardisation conference in Paris, France, in May 1896, the international consensus was that all ephemerides should be based on Newcomb's calculations — *Newcomb's Tables of the Sun*. A further conference as late as 1950 confirmed Newcomb's constants as the international standard.

Newcomb married Mary Caroline Hassler on August 4, 1863. The couple had three daughters, as well as one son who did not survive infancy.

Newcomb died on July 11, 1909, in Washington, DC, of bladder cancer and was buried with military honours in Arlington National Cemetery with President Howard Taft in attendance. He was 74 years of age.

Newcomb was the first president of the American Society of Psychical Research. Although sceptical of extrasensory perception and alleged paranormal phenomena, he believed the subject was worthy of investigation.

By 1889, his investigations were negative and his skepticism increased. Biographer Albert E. Moyer has noted that Newcomb "convinced and hoped to convince others that, on methodological grounds, psychical research was a scientific dead end."

Included in Newcomb's legacy:

- Asteroid 855 Newcombia is named after him.
- The crater Newcomb on the Moon is named after him, as is Newcomb crater on Mars.
- The Royal Astronomical Society of Canada has a writing award named after him.
- The Time Service Building at the US Naval Observatory is named The Simon Newcomb Laboratory.
- The U.S. Navy minesweeper *Simon Newcomb* (YMS 263) was launched in 1942, served in the Pacific Theater during the Second World War, and was decommissioned in 1949.
- Mt. Newcomb (13,418 ft/4,090 m) appears on USGS topographic maps at coordinates 36.5399° N, 118.2934° W in the Sierra Nevada mountains.

Sophia's tragic tale

Many people find cemeteries frightening but others have discovered cemeteries are not only are fascinating places, they also have a wealth of interesting stories to tell.

One such tale involves the tragic saga of Sophia McLachlan, a Lunenburg lass who died suddenly on September 19, 1879, at the tender age of 14 and is buried in Hillcrest Cemetery.

According to cemetery staff, McLachlan's grave is visited by more people each year than any other on the grounds, and a pair of plagues erected by the Bluenose G.R.S. Society have been placed next to the plot to relate the details of her calamity.

It seems that young Sophia was employed by a Mrs. Trask as an apprentice dressmaker at a business that was located at what is now 242 Lincoln Street when the "princely" sum of $10 went missing.

Sophia McLachlan died at the tender age of 14 and is buried in Hillcrest Cemetery located in Lunenburg.

Accused of stealing the money by her employer, Sophia pleaded her innocence but soon became ill and could "often be observed lying on her sister's grave."

"Sophia's grief was added by her mother's acceptance of Mrs. Trask's story," the plaques relate, adding that her condition worsened, confining her to her room at what is now 169 Pelham Street.

"At the insisting of a friend, a doctor was called, but he could not prevent her death … amid much speculation by members of the community's a coroner's jury was summoned to hold an inquiry into Sophia's death. The ultimate decision for the cause of her death was 'paralysis of the heart brought on by extreme agitation and peculiar circumstances.'"

Just before she passed, Sophia wrote a note to Mrs. Trask maintaining her innocence.

"I am near gone. My hand trembles so that I can scarcely write," she is alleged to have penned. "There will be many a long hour that you think of this if you have a heart at all."

She went on to write that she did not take the money and that "it is a fearful thing to lie.

"Tell _____ [sic] to read for my sake XX Chap of Exodus 16 verse. Also Matthew Chaps V, VI and VII. I am not afraid to fear death. I know a secret but I ain't going to say anything about it. I can't write any more. From your friend Sophia McLaughlin."

The Bible verses Sophia quotes include, "Thou shalt not bear false witness against thy neighbour,"

"Blessed are they which are prosecuted for righteousness sake for theirs is the kingdom of Heaven,"

"Blessed are ye when men shall revile you and shall say all manner of evil against you falsely, for my sake," and "Rejoice and be exceeding glad: For great is your reward in Heaven: for so persecuted they the prophets which were before you."

Ironically, after Sophia's passing, Mrs. Trask's son admitted to stealing the money and mother and son soon moved from Lunenburg, "and no record of their place of residing exists."

"Those who knew Sophia remembered her as a pretty girl who will not be forgotten," the plaque concludes.

Bravery, valour and gallantry

The Victoria Cross is the highest award of the United Kingdom honours system.

It is awarded for gallantry "in the face of the enemy" to members of the British Armed Forces. It may be awarded posthumously. It was previously awarded to Commonwealth countries, most of which have established their own honours systems and no longer recommend British honours.

Established in 1856, the Victoria Cross has been awarded to service personnel for extraordinary valour and devotion to duty while facing a hostile force. It may be awarded to a person of any military rank in any service and to civilians under military command although no civilian has received the award since 1879.

Since Queen Victoria presented the first awards in 1857, two thirds of all awards have been personally presented by the British monarch and these investitures are usually held at Buckingham Palace. Canadians are no longer eligible for the Victoria Cross, that medal having been superseded by the Canadian Victoria Cross in 1993. It is of equal honour, but has yet to be awarded.

The Victoria Cross has been presented to 96 Canadians, or people closely associated with Canada, between its creation for acts performed during the Crimean War and 1993 when the Canadian Victoria Cross was instituted. No Canadian has received either honour since 1945.

The first Canadian to be awarded the Victoria Cross was Alexander Roberts Dunn for his actions at the Battle of Balaclava during the Crimean War in 1854. William Hall from Nova Scotia was the first black recipient of the Victoria Cross. The last living Canadian recipient of the British Victoria Cross, "Smokey" Smith died in August 2005.

Five Canadians with ties to Nova Scotia have received the Victoria Cross. They are, in alphabetical order:

Lieutenant Colonel Philip Eric Bent, who was born on January 3, 1891, in Halifax. He was educated at the Royal High School, Edinburg and Ashby Grammar School, Ashby de la Zouch.

He joined the training ship HMS Conway in 1907 and served two years as a cadet before going to sea. He was taking his Merchant Navy officer's ticket when the war broke out in 1914. He was commissioned in the Leicestershire Regiment of the British Army in November 1914.

He was awarded the Distinguished Service Order in the 1917 Birthday Honours. He was 26 years old, and a Temporary Lieutenant Colonel in the 9th Battalion, the Leicestershire Regiment, when he performed the deed for which he was awarded the VC on 1 October 1, 1917, east of Polygon, Wood, Zonnebeke, Belgium.

According to *The London Gazette,* No. 30471, January 11, 1918, Lt. Col. Bent personally collected a platoon that was in reserve, and together with men from other companies and various regimental details, he organized and led them forward to the counter-attack, after issuing orders to other officers as to the further defence of the line. The counter-attack was successful and the enemy were checked.

"The coolness and magnificent example shown to all ranks by Lt.-Col. Bent resulted in the securing of a portion of the line, which was of essential importance for subsequent operations," the account in the Gazette says. "This very gallant officer was killed whilst leading a charge which he inspired with the call of 'Come on the Tigers.'"

Bent has no known grave and is commemorated on the memorial wall at Tyne Cot Cemetery in Belgium. In 2015, a new road in Ashby de la Zouch was named Philip Bent Road and is located approximately 0.6 miles west of the town centre off Moira Road.

Bent's sword is displayed in All Saints Cathedral in Halifax. His Victoria Cross is held by his old school, Ashby School, but is on loan to the Royal Leicestershire Regimental Museum.

John Bernard Croak was a soldier in the Canadian Expeditionary Force and a posthumous recipient of the Victoria Cross, which he earned for events that occurred during the Battle of Amiens in August 1918.

Croak was born in Little River, Newfoundland, on May 18, 1892, but the family moved to Glace Bay when he was two years old. He attended school there and at the age of 14, began work as a coal miner.

In 1915, Croak enlisted in the Canadian Army and volunteered for service abroad with the Canadian Expeditionary Force. Posted to the 55th Battalion as a private, he embarked for Europe in November 1915. He soon transferred to the 13th Battalion, which was serving on the Western Front as part of 3rd Brigade, 1st Canadian Division.

Through 1917 and the early part of 1918, Croak participated in several engagements as part of 13th Battalion, including the Battles of Vimy Ridge, Hill 70 and Passchendaele.

On August 8, 1918, the opening day of the Battle of Amiens, and the beginning of the Hundred Days Offensive, the 3rd Brigade, accompanied by a battalion of tanks, was at the forefront of the 1st Division's advance. The 13th Battalion became held up by machine gun posts in the vicinity of Hangard Wood.

Croak attacked a machine gun post and took several prisoners whom he escorted to his company headquarters. Ignoring instructions to seek medical treatment for a wound to his arm, he carried out an attack on another machine gun post nearby. He was wounded again, this time fatally, and died that same day, August 8, 1918. He was recognized for his actions with the Victoria Cross.

Croak is buried at Hangard Wood British Cemetery, which is located 12 miles southwest of Alberta. His VC, the first to be awarded to a soldier born in Newfoundland, was presented to his mother at Government House in Halifax by MacCallum Grant, the Lieutenant Governor of Nova Scotia, on November 23, 1918.

In Glace Bay where Croak grew up, a school and a Royal Canadian Legion are named in his honour. There is also a park named for him as well. It is located on the site of his former workplace, the Dominion No. 2 Colliery. In 1992, the park was the scene of the unveiling of a memorial plaque to Croak, made of Cape Breton rock.

In 1972, Croak's medals, which included the British War Medal and the Victory Medal in addition to the VC, were gifted by his nephew to the Army Museum at the Citadel in Halifax. The medals are now displayed at the Canadian War Museum.

William Edward Hall, who was born at Horton on April 28, 1827, received the Victoria Cross for his actions in the Siege of Lucknow during the Indian Rebellion. He was the first black person, the first Nova Scotian and the third Canadian to receive the medal.

Hall was the son of Jacob and Lucy Hall, who had escaped American slave owners in Maryland during the War of 1812 and were brought to freedom in Nova Scotia by the British Royal Navy as part of the Black Refugee movement.

The Halls first lived in Summerville, Hants County, where Jacob worked in a shipyard operated by Abraham Cunard, until they bought a farm across the Avon River at Horton Bluff. Hall first worked in shipyards at nearby Hantsport, before going to sea at the age of 17. He sailed first on merchant ships based out of the Minas Basin including the barque *Kent* of Kentville.

Hall briefly served in the United States Navy from 1847 to 1849, during the Mexican-American War. He served for a time aboard USS *Ohio*. Hall volunteered for the Royal Navy in February 1852, serving at first aboard HMS *Rodney*. Hall fought in the Crimean War, serving ashore in a Naval Brigade from *Rodney* at the battles of Inkerman and Sevastopol in 1854.

After a brief tour on HMS *Victory*, he transferred to the screw frigate HMS *Shannon*, where he became captain of the foretop.

When the Indian Mutiny broke out in May 1857, *Shannon* was among the fleet escorting a troop detachment to China. Upon arrival at Singapore, news of the situation in India reached the fleet, however the fleet completed its mission, arriving at Hong Kong. There, *Shannon* was ordered to Calcutta (since renamed Kolkata).

A brigade from *Shannon*, comprising 450 men, was constituted under Captain William Peel. The ship was towed over 600 miles (970 kilometres) up the Ganges River to Allahabad. Then the force fought across country to Campbell's headquarters at Cawnpore and were in time to take part in the Siege of Lucknow.

At Lucknow, India, naval guns were brought up close to the Shah Nujeff mosque, one of the key locations in the siege. One of the gun crews was a man short and Hall volunteered to fill the position.

The gun crews kept up a steady fire in an attempt to breach and clear the walls, while a hail of musket balls and grenades from the mutineers inside the mosque caused heavy casualties. After having little effect on the walls, two guns were ordered closer. Of the crews, only

Able Seaman Hall and Lieutenant Thomas James Young, the battery's commander, were able to continue fighting, all the rest having been killed or wounded. Between them they loaded and served the last gun, which was fired at less than 20 yards (18 metres) from the wall until it was breached.

According to the joint citation for Hall's medal, Lieutenant (now Commander) Young, late Gunnery Officer of HMS *Shannon*, and William Hall, Captain of the Foretop, of that Vessel, were recommended by the late Captain Peel for the Victoria Cross, for their gallant conduct at a 24-Pounder Gun, brought up to the angle of the Shah Nujjiff, at Lucknow, on 16 November 1857.

Hall remained with the Royal Navy for the rest of his career. He joined the crew of HMS *Donegal* in 1859. On October 28, 1859, he was presented with the Victoria Cross by Rear Admiral Charles Talbot while *Donegal* was anchored at Queenstown Harbour Hall.

He rose to the rating of Petty Officer First Class in HMS *Royal Adelaide* by the time he retired in 1876. He returned to his home village in Horton Bluff where he ran a small farm until his death on August 27, 1904, at the age of 77.

He was originally buried in an unmarked grave without military honours. He was reinterred in 1954 at the Hantsport Baptist Church Cemetery in Hantsport, where his grave is marked by a monument. The Royal Canadian Legion (now closed) in Hantsport was named "The Lucknow Branch" in honour of his Victoria Cross action.

Hall's original Victoria Cross was repatriated from Britain in 1967 by the government of Nova Scotia and is on permanent display at the Maritime Museum of the Atlantic in Halifax.

He is also featured in exhibits at the Halifax Citadel and at the Black Cultural Centre for Nova Scotia. Canada Post commemorated William Hall on a stamp, first issued on February 1, 2010, in Hantsport, and officially launched at the Black Cultural Centre on February 2, 2010.

Hall was designated a National Historic Person by the Canadian Historic Sites and Monuments Board at Hantsport on October 8, 2010, and a new plaque was unveiled in his honour.

In November 2010, a connector road in Hantsport was named the William Hall V.C. Memorial Highway. A sign, bearing Hall's likeness, was erected on the road from Highway 101 to Trunk 1 near Hantsport.

It was announced on June 26, 2015, that the fourth ship in the Royal Canadian Navy's *Harry DeWolf* class would be named for William Hall. The ship will be constructed at Halifax Shipyards in Halifax.

John Chipman Kerr was born on January 11, 1887, in Fox River, Nova Scotia, and eventually relocated to British Columbia to find work.

In 1912, after working as a lumberjack in the Kootenay district, he bought a homestead in Spirit River, Alberta, where he and his brother farmed until war broke out. Immediately they set out for Edmonton, leaving only a single note tacked to the door of their humble shed that read, "War is Hell, but what is homesteading?"

Kerr was 29 years old and a private in the 49th (Edmonton) Battalion, Canadian Expeditionary Force, when the following deed took place for which he was awarded the Victoria Cross:

On September 16, 1916, at Courelette, France, during a bombing attack, Private Kerr was acting as bayonet man and noting that bombs were running short, he ran along the parados under heavy fire until he was in close contact with the enemy when he opened fire at point-blank range, inflicting heavy losses. The enemy, thinking that they were surrounded, surrendered: 62 prisoners were taken and 250 yards of enemy trench captured. Earlier, Private Kerr's fingers had been blown off, but he did not have his wound dressed until he and two other men had escorted the prisoners back under fire and reported for duty.

Kerr returned to farm in Alberta after the war, but also worked in the oil patch and as a forest ranger in Alberta. He died on February 19, 1963, in Port Moody and was buried in Mountain View Cemetery, Vancouver.

His Victoria Cross is displayed at the Canadian War Museum in Ottawa. Mount Kerr in the Victoria Cross Ranges in Jasper National Park, Alberta, was named in his honour in 1951 and Chip Kerr Park in Port Moody, British Columbia, was dedicated in 2006.

He was a great uncle of Greg Kerr, who served as Member of Parliament for West Nova from 2008 to 2015.

James Peter "Pete" Robertson was born October 26, 1883, in Albion Mines (now called Stellarton), Pictou County.

Robertson lived most of his life in Medicine Hat, Alberta, with his mother. He enlisted in the Canadian Expeditionary Force in June 1915, and became a private in the 27th (City of Winnipeg) Battalion, Canadian Expeditionary Force.

According to *The London Gazette*, no. 30471, January 11, 1918, Roberston was 34 years old, during the Second Battle of Passchendaele when he performed the following deed for which he was awarded the Victoria Cross:

When his platoon was held up by uncut wire and a machine gun causing many casualties, Pte. Robertson dashed to an opening on the flank, rushed the machine gun and, after a desperate struggle with the crew, killed four and then turned the gun on the remainder, who, overcome by the fierceness of his onslaught, were running towards their own lines. His gallant work enabled the platoon to advance. He inflicted many more casualties among the enemy, and then carrying the captured machine gun, he led his platoon to the final objective. He there selected an excellent position and got the gun into action, firing on the retreating enemy who by this time were quite demoralised by the fire brought to bear on them.

During the consolidation Pte. Robertson's most determined use of the machine gun kept down the fire of the enemy snipers; his courage and his coolness cheered his comrades and inspired them to the finest efforts.

Later, when two of our snipers were badly wounded in front of our trench, he went out and carried one of them in under very severe fire. He was killed just as he returned with the second man.

Robertson died November 6, 1917, at Passchendaele salient in Belgium. He is buried in Tyne Cot Cemetery, Passchendaele.

A tale of true grit and lasting legacy

It is difficult to imagine a better example of determination and selfless dedication than what we see in the life of Walter Callow.

Information on the Nova Scotia Museum website explains that when the First World War came along, the Parrsboro-born young man enlisted in the Royal Flying Corps' Canadian (RFC) training program. He was born in 1896.

The RFC was a British unit formed to give its side a military presence in the air. While training in Ontario, Callow crashed in a test flight in 1918. He survived, but incurred a serious back injury and a heart condition.

Callow returned to Nova Scotia, where he operated a lumber business in Advocate. In 1931, however, his earlier injuries made him bed-ridden. That same year, his wife and mother both died, leaving him alone to look after his young child.

He turned to selling real estate to make a living but his health deteriorated. By 1937, he became (for the rest of his life) a full-time resident of the Camp Hill Hospital in Halifax. Two years later he was blind and a quadriplegic.

Hard to believe, yet that is not the end of Callow's story.

After the Second World War began in 1939, Callow decided to establish a service for soldiers who were overseas. He instituted the Callow Cigarette Fund and with staff he supervised, sending cigarettes to soldiers over-seas.

After the war, with revenue from the cigarette fund, he came up with a fresh idea. He wanted to develop a specially-designed accessibility bus for disabled veterans and anyone else who used a wheelchair. As he envisioned it, the vehicle would take those in need out to the countryside, to sporting events or other activities.

Callow had two custom-made buses built in Pubnico, then turned to major automobile manufacturers to build his wheelchair coaches. Walter Callow Wheelchair Buses still exist today, and still do exactly what their creator wanted.

The only time that Walter rode on the bus was when his body was returned to Advocate for burial, after a funeral in Halifax that featured full military honours. He died in 1958.

The Walter Harris Callow Foundation was established to honour the legacy of Walter Callow, a humanitarian and veteran of the First World War, who invented the first wheelchair bus in Canada to serve the needs of veterans confined in Camp Hill Hospital in Halifax.

For more than 70 years, Callow Wheelchair Buses provided service to veterans and others with mobility challenges. Today, the Foundation continues to support veterans, military, RCMP and their families by directing proceeds of the Foundation to their highest priority needs.

The father of street illumination

Walter D'Arcy Ryan was born in Kentville on April 17, 1870, and educated in Canada for a military career but instead emigrated to the United States around 1890.

He was an influential early lighting engineer who worked for General Electric in Lynn, Massachusetts, as director of its Illuminating Engineering Laboratory, the world's first institution for research into lighting.

The laboratory was formally established around 1908 in Schenectady, New York, with Ryan at its head. He and his team developed and patented much of the technology for lighting applications, including the Ryan-Lite reflector-equipped headlamp.

He was a pioneer in skyscraper illumination, designed the Scintillator coloured searchlights display, and was responsible for the lighting of the Panama-Pacific International Exposition in San Francisco and the Century of Progress Exposition in Chicago, in addition to the first complete illumination of Niagara Falls. He combined illumination into both an art and a science.

In particular, under his direction, the Illuminating Engineering Laboratory developed the ornamental street lighting scheme called the White Way after Broadway, and General Electric promoted it to towns and cities. The first installation was on Broadway Avenue in Los Angeles in 1905.

Ryan also made use of searchlights for non-architectural display in the Scintillator, sometimes called the Ryan Scintillator. This consisted of searchlights equipped with color filters and refracted through steam. The beams of light were also made to form different shapes, including a peacock's tail and a sunrise.

The Scintillator was on display at the Hudson-Fulton Celebration, with shows twice nightly at Riverside Drive and 155th Street. Forty huge searchlights of varying colour shot enormous beams high in the air, radiating in fan-like effect and changing from the most intense white to the softer greens and yellows; now again shifting bodily from east to west and back again with frightful speed.

The steam was supplied by a 200-horsepower boiler, and black powder and smoke bombs were also used.

In 1915, Ryan was the lighting designer for the San Francisco Panama-Pacific International Exposition. This marked the first widespread use of floodlighting at a fair, and also the first use of high-pressure gas mantle lamps and of high-wattage tungsten filament lamps.

Previous expositions had used outline lighting with strings of incandescent bulbs and more recently, arc lamps. Ryan restricted these to the "Joy Zone" (the midway) and also used screens, filters, and reflecting to manipulate the floodlights.

Almost 20 years later, in 1933, Ryan was also the lighting designer for Chicago's Century of Progress Exposition, which again was notable for its lighting innovation.

To match the *art modern* architecture, Ryan used the new electric gaseous discharge lamps, especially neon (over 75,000 feet of neon tubing in addition to more than 15,000 incandescent lamps). The largest electric incandescent filament lamp in the world, 50 kilowatts, was on display.

For its second year, in 1934, the illumination was increased by about half, and the Ford Building had a Pillar of Light created by 24 searchlights projecting a mile into the sky. The closing program for the exposition on October 31, 1934, was titled "The Festival of Illumination: The Apotheosis of Man-Made Light."

Again, the fair was influential: the expositions at Dallas and Cleveland the following year both emulated both the architecture and the lighting of the Chicago fair.

In June 1932, Ryan became a consulting engineer for General Electric and died on March 14, 1934, in Schenectady, New York, after a heart attack.

From Amherst to Nobel Prize winner

Willard Sterling Boyle, a Canadian physicist, was born in Amherst on August 19, 1924. He was the son of a medical doctor and moved to Quebec with his father and mother, Bernice, when he was less than two.

He was home schooled by his mother until age 14 when he attended Montreal's Lower Canada College to complete his secondary education.

Boyle was a pioneer in the field of laser technology and co-inventor of the charge-couple device. As director of Space Science and Exploratory Studies at Bellcomm he helped select lunar landing sites and provided support for the Apollo space program.

On October 6, 2009, it was announced that Boyle would share the 2009 Nobel Prize in Physics for "the invention of an imaging semiconductor circuit — the CCD sensor, which has become an electronic eye in almost all areas of photography."

He was appointed a Companion of the Order of Canada — the award's highest level — on June 30, 2010. Boyle died on May 7, 2011.

Innovator and businessman

In 1908, Winfred Theodore Ritcey started the Acadia Gas Engines Company on the banks of the LaHave River in Bridgewater, which soon became the largest manufacturer of marine engines in Canada.

According to an article published by the DesBrisay Museum, the company was known the world over for its two-cycle gas engines. With the company's rapid expansion, Acadia Gas Engines began exporting internationally, making them the largest manufacturer of marine engines in Canada.

In 1918, it was reported that 8,000 Acadia engines were already in use and 2,400 were being produced each year.

Winfred T. "W.T." Ritcey was born August 17, 1878, in Riverport, the only son of Daniel H. and

Anna V. (Strum) Ritcey. The family moved to Colorado when he was only nine. Educated in Boston, Massachusetts, as a young man Ritcey worked in New England with his father in the lumber and building business, and he studied accounting.

In 1903, he relocated to Newfoundland and built a mill. It was destroyed by fire, so in 1907, he moved to Alberta. In 1908, he returned home to Nova Scotia, bringing with him his wife, Bessie Blake from Maine, who he married in 1906. In 1914, Ritcey had a large home built at the corner of Park and King Streets in Bridgewater for his wife and three daughters, located across the street from his rapidly expanding marine engine business.

Ritcey set out to provide mechanization at a reasonable cost for many inshore fishermen in Nova Scotia with about 1,200 agents and dealers across Canada. Preferring to be on the shop floor with his workers, he was always thinking of new ideas.

In 1918, the company employed nearly 100 men on average. Ritcey had a natural bent for engineering and a solid academic background in accounting. In 1918, he secured the dealership for Chevrolet automobiles and became the agent for the Maritimes Smith Form-A-Truck equipment.

Ritcey was President and Managing Director of Acadia Gas Engines Company for over 35 years until his death in 1946 at the age of 68.

He also played a prominent role in his community, serving as Bridgewater's seventh mayor in 1919, and was president of the board of trade, Bridgewater Curling Club, and Lunenburg County Fish and Game Protection Association. In religion, he was a member of the Grace United Church.

In his spare time, Ritcey was a champion tuna fisherman and enjoyed hunting and motor boating.

Eventually the Acadia Gas Engines plant declined and was sold. In the 1980s, the waterfront buildings were demolished, and in 1998, the area was designated as a town park called "Shipyard's Landing."

Making hockey history

Art Dorrington, born March 13, 1930, in Truro, earned his place in sports history as the first hockey player to sign a professional contract in the National Hockey League (NHL) when he joined the New York Rangers organizations in 1950.

Despite putting up impressive statistics in the minor leagues playing centre for the Atlantic City Seagulls of the Eastern Hockey League, Dorrington was never able to make it to the major league ranks.

After retiring from hockey, Dorrington become a sheriff's officer with the Atlantic County Sheriff's Office.

In the late 1990s, he created the Art Dorrington Ice Hockey Foundation, a program that teaches hockey to children from low-income families in Atlantic City.

He died on December 29, 2017, at the age of 87.

Remembering a fallen hero

Sgt. Derek Burkholder goes down in provincial history as the first RCMP officer shot in the line of duty in Nova Scotia.

Sgt. Burkholder was 49 years of age when he was shot and killed on June 14, 1996, while attempting to defuse a reported domestic dispute. The 30-year RCMP veteran was shot without warning in the rural community of Maders Cove, near Lunenburg.

Sgt. Burkholder, who was known to be honest and straightforward, was born in Brampton, Ontario, and raised in New Brunswick. He served in several detachments throughout Nova Scotia during his RCMP career before being stationed in Lunenburg County.

He was great community supporter and belonged to the Lions' Club and worked for the Big Brothers and Big Sisters. He was known to be an avid curler and loved to play golf.

Sgt. Burkholder's death goes down as the first murder of a Mountie in Nova Scotia. He is buried in Brookside Cemetery in Bridgewater.

A rock legend with Nova Scotian roots

Bruce Palmer, born September 9, 1946, was a Canadian musician best known as the bassist in the Canadian-American folk rock band Buffalo Springfield inducted into the Rock and Roll of Fame in 1997.

But would it surprise you to know that he was from Nova Scotia? He was in fact born on the province's South Shore in Liverpool but relocated to Toronto in the early 1960s in pursuit of a musical career. Today, he is part of rock music history.

Buffalo Springfield was active from 1966 to 1968. Its most prominent members were Stephen Stills, Neil Young and Richie Furay. The group released three albums and several singles, including *For What It's Worth*.

The band combined elements of folk and country music with British invasion and psychedelic-rock influences. The band, along with others like The Byrds, was part of the early development of folk-rock.

With a name taken from the manufacturer's nameplate from a steamroller, Buffalo Springfield formed in Los Angeles in 1966 with Stills (guitar, keyboards, vocals), Dewey Martin (drums, vocals), Palmer (bass), Furay (guitar, vocals), and Young (guitar, harmonica, piano, vocals).

The band signed to Atlantic Records in 1966 and released their debut single *Nowadays Clancy Can't Even Sing*. It became a hit in Los Angeles. The following January, the group released the protest song *For What It's Worth*, for which they are now best known. Their second album, *Buffalo Springfield Again*, marked their progression to psychedelia and hard rock.

After various drug-related arrests and line-up changes, the group broke up in 1968.

Before helping to form Buffalo Springfield, however, Palmer followed a winding road to meet his destiny. In Toronto, he started playing with Robbie Lane & The Disciples, then graduated to a local, otherwise all-black group by Billy Clarkson.

Next came British invasion-inspired Jack London & the Sparrows, which after Palmer left, evolved into Steppenwolf. In early 1965, he left to join The Mynah Birds, where he first met Neil Young who was playing lead guitar in the band.

The Mynah Birds, fronted by future funk legend Rick James, had a bright future. The group was signed to the prestigious Motown Records to do some demo recordings before it was discovered that James was actually in Toronto to avoid serving in Vietnam with the United States Navy, from which he had gone AWOL.

The group was forced to disband, and Young and Palmer drove Young's hearse to Los Angeles in the hope of meeting with Stephen Stills, a journey folk musician with whom Young had played briefly in Canada two years earlier.

Young and Palmer ran into Stills while stuck in traffic in Los Angeles, Stills having recognized Young's distinctive hearse. It was not long before the trio, along with fellow Canadian Martin and Furayon formed Buffalo Springfield and the rest is rock 'n' roll history.

Palmer was arrested on numerous occasions for drug possession. These legal problems, compounded by his predilection to sit at home reading mystical texts, led to his being shunned by most of the group.

Another arrest led to his deportation from the United States In 1967. Palmer was replaced in the band by a rotating group of bassists and shortly thereafter, Young left the group due to tensions with Stills. During his time back in Toronto between January and May 1967, Palmer gigged briefly with a local band called The Heavenly Government.

In late May, Palmer returned to the United States disguised as a businessman, and rejoined the band (Young eventually returned as well.) However, the group had lost trust in their original bassist and continued to rely on session players despite Palmer's return.

Meanwhile, Palmer continued to rack up a lengthy arrest records, which included yet another drug possession bust and driving without a license. In January 1968, Palmer was removed from the band and officially replaced with Jim Messina. Then, after embarking on a tour opening for the Beach Boys, Buffalo Springfield disbanded on May 5, 1968, after a final hometown concert at the Long Beach Sports Arena.

Palmer resurfaced in the summer of 1969 for two weeks as the bassist for Crosby, Stills, Nash & Young but was soon replaced by Motown prodigy Greg Reeves. Back in Toronto, Palmer gigged briefly with Luke & The Apostles in 1970.

In 1971, Palmer released his lone solo record, *The Cycle I Complete*. The album was a commercial disaster, and Palmer seemingly retired from music, but in 1977, he joined former Kensington Market singer/guitarist Keith McKie and lead guitarist Stan Endersby in the Toronto group, Village, for some local gigs.

In 1982-1983, Palmer resurfaced as the bassist in Neil Young's Trans Band, playing a mixture of Young classics and electronica-infused material to audiences throughout America and Europe, as seen in the documentary *Neil Young in Berlin*, filmed in 1982.

Palmer was inducted with his Buffalo Springfield bandmates in the Rock and Roll Hall of Fame in 1977.

Palmer died of heart attack on October 1, 2004, in Belleville, Ontario at the age of 58.

5 FAST FACTS

1. The first public library in Nova Scotia formed in Yarmouth in January 1822 and it was then known as the Yarmouth Book Society.

2. Gold was first discovered in Nova Scotia in 1858 at Mooseland on the Tangier River, inland from the Eastern Shore of Halifax County. A British army officer, Captain Champagn L'Estrange of the Royal Artillery, made the discovery while out for a day of moose hunting with a Mi'kmaw guide named Joe Paul.

3. The Astor Theatre in Liverpool is the oldest performing arts venue in Nova Scotia. Built in 1902 as part of the historic town hall, the theatre was known as the Liverpool Opera House. Its stage hosted touring and local shows until 1917 when silent films were introduced. Gradually, the film presentation gained in frequency and popularity. In 1930, talking pictures were shown for the first time. At the same time, the name was changed to the Astor Theatre after a theatre in New York.

4. The Astor Theatre is the oldest operating movie theatre in Canada. Until 2014 when it converted to a digital video and audio system, it used 35 millimetre film reels.

5. During the early days of settlement, the province's Annapolis Basin region served as the cradle for both French and English language theatre of Canada. Théatre de Neptune was the first European theatre production in North America. English theatre in Canada also started at Annapolis Royal. The tradition at Fort Anne was to produce a play in honour of the Prince of Wales's birthday. George Farquhar's "The Recruiting Officer" was produced on January 20, 1733, by the officers of the garrison to mark the Prince's birthday.

Open for Business

Bluenose Ski Factory slides into history

From shipyard-fashioned wood to modern fibreglass, Canada has an intriguing history of ski manufacturing history that spans more than a century and half and Nova Scotia was right in the middle of the activity.

By the 1920s and 1930s there was a flourishing ski-manufacturing scene across the eastern half of the country, with companies such as Propeller Wood Working of Montreal, Ketchum & Company of Ottawa, Allcock, Laight & Westwood of Toronto, the Super Diagonals Company of Canada, and Bluenose Ski Factory that got its start in Liverpool.

The late historian Robert Long records that William Millard was the founder of the Liverpool Woodworking Company. Millard also owned the Carriage Factory.

Millard's son, Clifford, built rocking horses called Shoo Fly Rockers, and sold them to Eaton's. You can see them for sale in the early Eaton's catalogues. Clifford was also the founder of the Bluenose Ski Factory, turning out hundreds of pairs of skis. He sold his business in 1929 to The Canada Ski Company in Annapolis.

Bob Soden wrote in an article titled *Made In Canada* that appeared on the Canadian Ski Museum website, "With an abundance of natural resources in their forests and demand afloat off their coasts, the Maritime Provinces naturally became centers of shipping production. Their sleek schooners caught fish on the Grand Banks, captured unwary ships as privateers during revolutionary years, and in peacetime won international sailing races."

These wood-shaping skills transferred easily to carriage production and in the 1920s, to skis. At one point during the decade, there were five ski manufacturers in Nova Scotia.

The most prominent was the Liverpool Woodworking Company, which manufactured the well-known "Bluenose" ski, crafted in "hickory, white ash, birch, maple and pine."

By 1929, the rights to the Bluenose ski had been purchased by the Canada Ski Company, which moved production to Annapolis Royal.

In 1938, the Harvey E. Dodds Company acquired the manufacturing equipment of Canada Ski and moved the fabrication to Montreal. Also known as "The Ski People," Dodds promoted a line of skis named Chalet Skis during the 1930s and 1940s, and in 1934 introduced the Chalet Binding.

This circa 1940 photo shows the original Gow's hardware store located at 668 King Street, Bridgewater. There was eventually a larger Gow store across the street. This image is the location on the waterside of King Street.

Home of the handyperson

Gow's Home Hardware in Bridgewater has the distinction of being Canada's oldest hardware store.

According to the company history, Gow's Home Hardware dates back to 1848, making it the oldest known hardware store in the country. It was run by the Gow family from 1929 until a longtime employee Amanda Fancy bought the business in 2012.

Gow's Home Hardware has moved three times so far in its 171 years in business. In May 2019, it moved to its new 58,000 square foot location on High Street in Bridgewater.

The Chickenburger is reputed to be the oldest drive in diner in Canada.

Chickenburger is the oldest diner in Canada

Located in Bedford, The Chickenburger is not only a roadside landmark it is also reputed to be the oldest drive-in diner in Canada.

Information found on the Chickenburger's official website says "The Chick" was opened in 1940 and is reputed to be the oldest drive in restaurant in Canada. Today, the historical landmark remains a community icon as a destination for families and friends alike.

"Throw a tune on the jukebox while you enjoy great food in the nostalgic '50s setting. This iconic '50s inspired diner provides a snapshot into the past, with both indoor and outdoor seating," the website says.

"For almost 80 years, The Chickenburger has maintained a reputation of excellence by providing high quality fresh food and superb customer service. The same chicken recipe crafted in 1940 is still used to ensure customers keep coming back for the same great taste."

Salter Innes founded the Bedford Sunnyside canteen along the Bedford Highway in 1930. He hired Bernice Simpson to work the counter. She later married his son Jack, and they bought property across the road to start their own restaurant.

It was originally established in 1939 as the Shadyside take-out counter by Jack and Bernice who was known as "The Chickenburger Lady." It became Chickenburger after Bedford Shadyside burned down and was rebuilt in 1940.

In 1952, due to road realignment, the restaurant was moved further back on the lot. It developed into a full-fledged restaurant, and still maintains its 1950s styling. In 1986, the dining area was expanded, using material from Sunnyside.

Nova Scotian businessman Mickey MacDonald bought the restaurant from the Innes family in 2007 and he sold the restaurant to the Micco Group of Companies, its current owner.

The Fo'c'sle Tavern has been the centre of social activity in Chester since 1764.

The oldest pub in Nova Scotia

Affectionately known as *Chester's Living Room*, The Fo'c'sle is an inviting restaurant and bar that welcomes year-round and summer "locals" as well as those just passing through. Depending on where you sit, you are in a former grocery store, stable, inn or tavern dating back to 1764.

Until 2015, The Fo'c'sle Tavern in Chester had the distinction of being known as the oldest rural pub in Nova Scotia, while the Seahorse Tavern in Halifax was known to be the oldest pub in the province. However, since the Seahorse moved from its former location and required a new license, that made The Fo'c'sle the oldest drinking establishment in the province.

This record is simple to verify as all pubs and taverns in Nova Scotia were prohibited by law to sell alcohol during the Prohibition years so modern records date back to 1946-47, which is when The Fo'c'sle received its liquor licence.

The Fo'c'sle has been in operation since 1764 in one form or another — not only as a tavern, but throughout the years, parts of the building were used as a grocery store, an inn and even stables.

In fact, in the section of the pub where a pool table is currently located, it is possible to still see the original wood that was the framework for the stables, a feature that adds a certain character to the historic building.

The Frenchys story

What started in the late 1990s as one small outlet in rural Nova Scotia selling used clothing, has grown into a major Maritime retail chain almost 50 years later.

According to the company's official website, the first Guy's Frenchys opened its doors in Digby in 1972.

"Used clothing was a relatively unique concept in 1972 but the idea caught on fast with consumers," the site says. Industrial wipers were also a key part of the initial business. "That enterprise as well as an exporting business carries on today under the Acadian Wipers division."

From a small, one-store beginning, Guy's Frenchys has grown to encompass many stores throughout Nova Scotia and New Brunswick processing thousands of pounds of clothing each and every day.

"The many advantages offered by Guy's Frenchys has made it a favourite destination for individuals and families. Friendly service, quality clothing, clean stores, and a constantly changing selection are all factors that make Guy's Frenchys a great shopping experience."

The locations in Nova Scotia include Berwick, Bridgewater, Coldbrook, Digby, Liverpool, Sackville, Saint Bernard, Shelburne, Truro, Wilmont and Yarmouth.

There are also five locations in New Brunswick.

The first Guy's Frenchys opened its doors in Digby in 1972.

The King of Pain Relief

"Good for man or beast, taken internally or externally, Minard's Liniment — the King of Pain Relief."

That was the early promotion of a miracle cure that was invented by Levi Minard in the 1860s but continues be used to this day, a medicine that can trace its roots all the way back through time to Queens County.

Levi Minard was born in Milton, Queens County, in 1816, to John Minard (1877-1817) and Mehitabel "Hetty" Draper (1778-1849). Levi was the youngest of nine children.

His father and his great-great-grandfather, John Mullis, drowned on May 31, 1817, off the coast near Coffin's Island in Liverpool Harbour while barging supplies from the nearby village of Port Medway to Liverpool.

The tragedy left his mother, Hetty, a widow at 37 but she remarried in 1820 to Abner Harlow, Sr. (1772-1850).

Five Minard brothers, including Levi, continued to live in the Milton area and all became leading citizens of the day. According to the late Queens County historian Harley Walker, Levi even became the Sunday School principal and church clerk at the Milton Church Christ in the 1850s.

Interesting enough, some descendants of the original Minard family continue to reside in and around the same area of Milton.

According to the book, *Freeman Families of Nova Scotia*, Levi married Grace Watt of England (1817-1874) and they made their home in Milton while he continued to pursue his desire to be a physician.

It is said that at an early age, Levi showed an interest in everything pertaining to medicine, and that he had a natural talent for helping the ill.

"He made ointments and liniments in his home and later moved to larger quarters in a part of the old Methodist church in Milton," reads a passage in the book. "He studied medicine in his spare time."

As a result of his interests in medicine and experiments, Levi created Minard's Liniment in the 1860s to relieve muscle pain and stiffness, back pain and arthritis pain among others. Walker claimed that the liniment was first made in Levi's barn in Milton (then called Potanic). Later, he made the medicine in an abandoned Methodist Church in Milton.

Originally popular in the Maritime Provinces and in Newfoundland where it was recognized as a source of comfort for fishermen exposed to the cold and humidity of the ocean, Minard's Liniment also became a coveted product in Quebec and Ontario.

Eventually, the growing of the liniment's popularity earned Levi recognition as the "King of Pain Relief" because of the immediate relief it provides. It also cemented Levi's life-long aspirations of wanting to become a doctor.

In 1869 at the age of 52, Levi received a degree from the Eclectic Medical Institute in Cincinnati, Ohio. With is medical degree in hand, he then relocated his family to Hants County, where he established his first medical practice in Burlington and Summerville.

Once he became settled, Levi continued to manufacture his white liniment, which became one of the well-known home remedies of the day. Sold under the trademark Kind of Pain Relief, Walker said it boasted being the greatest internal and external remedy for man and beast. It was taken internally mixed with sugar, while externally it was rubbed on aching muscles on inhaled to relieve blocked sinuses, just like smelling salts.

Following the death of is first wife, Grace, in Woodville on March 28, 1874, Levi moved to Brooklyn, Hants County, where he married Mary Nelson (1820-1904) from Avondale.

Mary's brother, William Nelson (1805-1883) became Levi's helper and they manufactured his liniment. Later, Levi sold

Minard's Liniment — the King of Pain Relief can trace its roots to Milton, Queens County.

his secret formula with rights to manufacture it to her brother's son, William Johnson Nelson (1845-1912), who eventually moved the distribution plant to Boston, although some historians say he moved the operation to Bridgewater.

Dr. Levi Minard died in 1884 at the age of 68 and was buried beside his first wife at West Gore Cemetery. Levi never realized any great wealth form his liniment as he left an estate of less than $1500 when he died, and his widow's estate was equally small.

His second wife, Mary, died in 1905 and was buried beside her first husband.

The story of Minard's Liniment lived on even after the doctor's death.

Eventually, William Johnson sold the recipe for Minard's Liniment to Captain Angus Cann and C.C. Richards of Yarmouth. In turn, they formed Minard's Liniment Company, which bottled the product for most of the next 100 years, becoming the household staple for pain relief.

In time, the company was bought by the Beechum Company and moved to Weston, Ontario. The Minard's Liniment brand was acquired by Stella Pharmaceutical in 1998 and continues to be used today.

Frieze and Roy has been serving the community of Maitland since 1839 — that's 28 years before Confederation, making it the oldest general store in the country.

A matter of convenience

It might surprise you to know that a quaint little village located on Nova Scotia's Cobequid Bay is home to Canada's oldest general store.

You read that right — the oldest general store in the country.

Frieze and Roy has been serving the community of Maitland since 1839 — that's 28 years before Confederation, making the general store older than the country it calls home.

The store's co-owner Troy Robertson is quoted in a CTV news article as saying, "There's been just millions and millions of people that have walked through here."

The 181-year-old store was the centre of shipping, shipbuilding and trading on the Bay of Fundy and Shubenacadie Canal during the 1800s and 1900s.

Historic buildings often have their fair share of stories, including ghost stories, and Frieze and Roy is no different.

Employees like Jennifer Wiles is quoted in the CTV article as say they have had experiences in the building that they can't explain.

"A friend of mine who works here, Linda, she was doing breakfast and then all of a sudden I heard, 'Jennifer!' and I'm like, 'One moment Linda!' And then I heard my name again, louder," recalled Wiles.

However, it wasn't Linda. In fact, Wiles told CTV she couldn't find anyone else in the store at the time.

There have been a slew of ghostly encounters over the years, and with millions of people passing through the doors, Robertson said they may never know who haunts Frieze and Roy.

What he does know is that the store has had a significant impact on the community and the people it serves.

"It's the heart of the community, it's where people come in," Robertson said. "They meet each other, they talk about things happening in the community. It all gets shared here."

5 FAST FACTS

1. Wallace "Wheeler" MacDonald of Mulgrave was one of the Keystone Kops in the first-ever comedy feature film, *Tillie's Punctured Romance*, starring Charlie Chaplin. He also directed some Three Stooges films and had a minor role in *Gold Diggers* in 1933, starring another Nova Scotian actor, Ruby Keeler of Dartmouth.

2. William Knapp Buckley was born in 1890 in Wallace, Nova Scotia, and is in fact, the creator of Buckley's medicine known for its slogan, "It tastes awful. And it works." In 1914, William travelled to Ontario, where he attended the Ontario College of Pharmacy. He graduated a year later. During the global Spanish flu pandemic in 1919, he worked for a pharmacy until he was able to open his own drugstore in Toronto.

To help people struggling to survive the pandemic, William created a cough syrup made from ammonium carbonate, menthol, pine-needle oil and Irish moss extract. Even with the bitter taste, people were desperate for something that might remedy their symptoms. Within the first year, he sold over 2000 bottles. Because of such high demand, he created a space for manufacturing, naming his business W.K. Buckley Ltd.

Buckley's cough syrup is still one of the best medicines for the common cough and cold. William passed away in 1978. His son, Frank, who had joined the family business as a salesman, became the company president.

3. Myra Freeman is a philanthropist, teacher, and the 29th and first female Lieutenant Governor of Nova Scotia. She was born in Saint John, New Brunswick, and graduated from Dalhousie University with a Bachelor of Arts and a Bachelor of Education. In 1971, she started teaching with the Halifax Regional School Board until her appointment. Governor General Adrienne Clarkson appointed her Lieutenant Governor on the advice of Jean Chrétien. She served until September 7, 2006.

4. Mayann Francis, born February 18, 1946, in Sydney was the 31st Lieutenant Governor of Nova Scotia. She was appointed on June 20, 2006, by Governor General Michaëlle Jean on the advice of Prime Minister Stephen Harper. She assumed office on September 7, 2006. Francis is the first African Nova Scotian and the second woman to serve as Lieutenant Governor of Nova Scotia.

5. Between 1930 and 1945, almost 60,000 men from Nova Scotia enlisted in the Canadian Armed Forces and 2, 525 died in battle.

A tasty tale

The traditional donair has origins in Greece but the Halifax donair, complete with its trademark sweet sauce, was introduced in Halifax in the early 1970s, according to legend. King of Donair founder, John Kamoulakos, claims he developed the Maritime donair — a variation on the traditional Middle Eastern doner kebab — and first served up the now-popular meal at his restaurant on Quinpool Road in 1973.

Maritime donairs are characterized by their distinctive sauce, a sweeter version of a traditional garlic sauce, made from evaporated milk, sugar, garlic or garlic powder and white vinegar. Tradition garlic sauce is usually made with yogurt or mayonnaise instead of evaporated milk and vinegar, and lemon juice rather than sugar.

However, neither the meat nor the sauce were patented, leaving the donair's true origins up for debate.

The legendary Halifax donair consists of thin slices of spiced beef laid on a warm Lebanese pita, topped with diced onion and tomato, and finally, drizzled with the sweet, garlicky sauce.

Donair flavours are becoming so popular that there are now donair pizzas, donair subs donair sandwiches, donair eggs Benny, donair soup, donair poutine, donair tacos, donair egg rolls, donair lasagna, donair hotdogs, donair gelato, donair beer, and even donair doughnuts and donair cheesecake.

Halifax Regional Municipality declared donairs the official food of the city in December 2015.

The Halifax donair, complete with its trademark sweet sauce, was, as the legend goes, first created in Halifax in the early 1970s.

Glossary of Names

A

Name	Pages
Angwin, Dr. Maria	175, 176
Adams, Wayne	110,153
Alline, Henry	28
Arab, Edward Francis	135
Arnold, William	106
Arundel, Russell	17
Atwell, Yvonne	110

B

Name	Pages
Baker, George Herman	117, 118
Ball, Samuel	192, 193,194
Barss, Joseph Jr.	163, 164
Barss, Joseph Sr.	163
Battiste, Jamie	182
Belcher, Jonathan	35
Bent, Philip Eric	199, 200
Benton, Catherine	171, 172
Best, Carrie M.	171
Best, James Calbert	171
Binney, Stephen	163
Bishop, Scott	170
Black, Ellie pp.	181
Boutilier, Edward Thomas	60, 61
Bower, Marshall	86
Boyd, George	110
Boyle, Willard Sterling	206
Brocklesby, William	150, 151
Brown, William	106
Buckley, William Knapp	219
Burkholder, Derek	208

C

Name	Pages
Callow, Walter	204
Cartcel, Peter	53
Chapin, Harry	80
Chiasson, Paul	149, 150
Clarke, George Elliot	110, 188
Cleveland, George Alan	167
Cook, James	129
Corning, Sara	194, 195
Corson, Henry and Julia	42
Cox, Esther	160, 161
Creighton, Mary Helen	19, 78, 180, 181
Croak, John Bernard	200, 201

D

Name	Pages
Daniel, Charles	38
Davison, Edward (E.D) Doran	176, 177
de Costa, Mathieu	109
de Razilly, Isaac	36, 105
Dimock, Joseph	28
dit La Verdue, Pierre Melanson	40
Dixon, George	109
Dorrington, Art	207
Douglass, Bethiah	112, 128

E

Name	Pages
Earhart, Amelia	88, 89, 90
Ellis, Henry	35

F

Name	Pages
Farmer, Everett	51, 55, 56
Fenerty, Charles	172, 173
Fielding, George	54
Fish, Frances Lillian	166, 167
Fletcher, Dr. Richard	134
Flint, David and Wallace	42
Fortune, Rose	109, 111
Francis, Mayann	219
Fraser, Ken	88, 181
Freeman, Myra	219

G

Name	Pages
George, David	120
Gerhardt, Hans	152, 153
Gloade, Sam	190, 191
Glooscap	131, 132
Goodsides, Abraham	53
Gorham, Jabez	95
Gorham, James	95
Gorham, John	35
Grey, Zane	62, 88

H

Name	Pages
Harnish, Guildford	26
Haines, Max	186
Haliburton, Thomas Chandler	94, 191, 192
Hall, William Edward	201

Hartling, Gordon 60
Hawkins, Dr. Arthur 104
Hearn, Cyril 73
Howe, Joseph 51, 115, 116

I

Innes, Salter 213

J

Jackson, David 41
Jerome 141, 142, 143
Johnson, Frederick 138
Johnston, James Robinson 109
Jordan, Bernadette 169
Jordan, Edward 'Black Irishman' 164, 165, 166
Jordan the Pirate 147
Joyce, Ronald (Ron) 189, 190

K

Kamoulakos, John 220
Keith, Alexander "Sandy," Jr. 61, 96, 98
Kenney, George Churchill 168
Kerr, John Chipman 202, 203
Keyte, Lou 62
Kidd, William "Captain" 140, 147
Koretz , Leopold "Leo" 62, 63

L

Lawrence, William D. 67,
Lewis, Daurene 111, 130
Lindsay, Annie 155
Lightfoot, Alfred Ross 49
Low, Ned 147
Lutz, Aubrey 53, 54

M

MacAskill, Angus 187
MacDonald, Wallace "Wheeler" 219
Mack, Samuel 99, 100
MacNeil, Freeman 54, 55
Marconi, Guglielmo 129
Marshall, Donald Jr. 57
"Marvin" the Mastodon 100
Matisoo, Julie 126, 127, 128
McDonald, Arthur Bruce 168
McGinnis, Daniel 140, 193
McLachlan, Sophia 198

McNab, Jack 144
Meagher, Aileen Aletha 181
Miles, Johnny 181
Millard, William 211
Miller, Arthur Frederick 29
Minard, Levi 216
Morris, Charles 35
Muise, Darren 54, 55
Muise, Xavier 41
Murray, Bessie 85

N

McNutt, Alexander 29
Newcomb, Simon 196, 197
Noil, Joseph Benjamin 183, 184
Nutting, Capt. Lee 184, 185

O

Oliver, Rev. W.P 110

P

Palmer, Bruce 208, 209, 210
Pattillo, Thomas Robert 106, 107
Payzant, Louis 135
Payzant, Marie Anne 135, 136
Perkins, Colonel Simeon 99, 126, 127, 150, 157
Phillips, Erasmus 27
Phils, Isaac 110
Porter, Gladys Muriel 179
Prescott, Jonathan 137, 138, 139
Price, George Lawrence 177, 178
Pudsey, Rosalie 53

Q

R

Riley, William (Bill) 169, 170
Ritcey, Winfred Theodore 206, 207
Robbins, Phoebe 83
Robertson, James Peter "Pete" 203
Robertson, Troy 218
Roosevelt, Franklin Delano 81
Roberts, Bartholomew "Black Bart" 149
Ross, John 123
Ross, Robert 112

Ross, William   46
Roult, John   86
Ruth, George Herman "Babe" 74
Ryan, Walter D'Arcy   205, 206

S

Schmidt, Dennis Richard 174
Sherbrooke, John Coape 30
Shermuller, Johann Gotlieb   144
Shubenacadie Sam   16
Sigogne, Jean-Mandé   39
Slick, Sam   191
Smith, Michael   60
Squires, Jimmy   60
Stafford, Billy   59
Stafford, Jane (Hurshman   59, 60
Swan, Anna   187

T

U

Uniacke, Richard John   47

V

Vacon, Peter and Louis   74

W

Walters, Angus J.   75
Wentworth, John 21
White, William Andrew II 188
White, William Andrew (Bill) III   188
Williams, Captain James 121
Wilson, John Albert   182, 183
Wood, Derek   54, 55

X

Xavier, Francois   41

Y

Young, Hannah   82
Young, William and Lila 57, 58

Z
Zwicker, Ana Catherina   116

Index of Images

Unless otherwise stipulated, all photos in this book were either taken by the author or are from the author's private collection.

Kellen Oickle: 10

Kim Robicaud: 15

Wildlife Park.ca: 16

Tourism Nova Scotia: 18

Peter Arsenault: 22, 23, 33, 36, 40, 41, 45, 77, 106, 114, 122, 213

Dennis Jarvis (accessed from the American Forts Network Facebook page): 29

Queens County Museum: 43, 74, 87, 88, 107, 163

Nova Scotia Archives: 46, 90, 91

Steven MacNeil: 50

Library and Archives Canada: 64

Fisheries Museum of Atlantic: 76

John Townsend: 87

Robert Hirtle: 115

Angela Ahmad: 123

Darryll Walsh: 144

Ted Pritchard: 156

Bernadette Jordan: 169

Wikipedia: 184, 211

Peter Gow: 212

Frieze and Roy (Facebook): 218

Thank you!

The author gratefully acknowledges the support and assistance of all those who provided photos and illustrations for use in this book. Thank you as well to editor Arvel Gray for her sharp eye, designer Denis Cunningham for his creativity and publisher John MacIntyre for believing in this project.